The Transnational Family

D1431277

Cross-Cultural Perspectives on Women

General Editors: Shirley Ardener and Jackie Waldren, for The Centre for Cross-Cultural Research on Women, University of Oxford

ISSN: 1068-8536

Recent titles include:

The Transnational Family

New European Frontiers and Global Networks

Edited by
*Deborah Bryceson and
Ulla Vuorela*

Oxford • New York

First published in 2002 by
Berg
Editorial offices:
150 Cowley Road, Oxford OX4 1JJ, UK
838 Broadway, Third Floor, New York NY 10003-4812, USA

© Deborah Bryceson and Ulla Vuorela 2002

All rights reserved.
No part of this publication may be reproduced in any form or by any means
without the written permission of Berg.

Berg is the imprint of Oxford International Publishers Ltd.

Library of Congress Cataloging-in-Publication Data

The transnational family : new European frontiers and global networks / edited
by Deborah Bryceson and Ulla Vuorela.
     p. cm. – (Cross-cultural perspectives on women, ISSN 1068-8536)
Includes bibliographical references and index.
  ISBN 1-85973-676-9 – ISBN 1-85973-681-5 (pbk.)
  1. Family–Cross-cultural studies. 2. Transnationalism. 3. Family–Europe.
4. Immigrants–Europe. 5. Refugees–Europe. I. Bryceson, Deborah Fahy.
II. Vuorela, Ulla. III. Series.
  HQ519 .T73 2002
  306.85–dc21

                        2002011074

British Library Cataloguing-in-Publication Data

A catalogue record for this book is available from the British Library.

ISBN 1 85973 676 9 (Cloth)
       1 85973 681 5 (Paper)

Typeset by JS Typesetting Ltd, Wellingborough, Northants.
Printed in the United Kingdom by Biddles Ltd, Guildford and King's Lynn.

Contents

Contributors

Nadje Al-Ali is a lecturer in social anthropology at the Institute of Arab and Islamic Studies. She has studied in the US, Egypt and the UK where she received her PhD at the School of Oriental and African Studies. Her research interests revolve around gender issues and political cultures in the Middle East, Muslim migrants and refugees, transnationalism and feminist theory. Her publications include *Secularism, Gender and the State in the Middle East: The Egyptian Women's Movement*, Cambridge University Press, 2000 and *New Approaches to Migration? Transnationalism and Home,* London and New York, Routledge, 2001, which she edited together with Khalid Koser. Nadje Al-Ali is a committed political activist involved in Women in Black as well as a founding member of Act Together: Women Against Sanctions on Iraq.

Rohit Barot studied at Gujarat University in India, at Makerere University in Kampala, Uganda, and the University of California, Berkeley. His PhD is from the School of Oriental and African Studies at London University. He has researched the Swaminarayan movement and migration and group formation among Bristol Indians. His publications include *Religion and Ethnicity: Minorities and Social Change in the Metropolis* (1993), *The Racism Problematic: Contemporary Sociological Debates on Race and Ethnicity* (1996) and *Ethnicity, Gender and Social Change* (1999). His most recent article in *Ethnic and Racial Studies* (July 2001) examines the concept of racialization. His teaching focuses on diaspora, racism and the formation of South Asian communities in the UK.

Reynald Blion is the scientific director of the Migration, Pluri-cultural and Development programme at Institut Panos Paris. Before joining Panos in 1998 he worked for a French non-governmental organization (NGO), managing several development co-operation programmes. Previously, as a socio-economist, he worked for Institut de Recherche pour le Developpement (IRD) (a scientific research center specializing in development) on a research programme on West African immigration networks. He has published several articles for scientific reviews such as *Studi Emigrazione*

(Italy), *Mondes en Développement* (Belgium) and *Migrations Sociétés* (France). Recently, he was scientific editor of, and contributor to several articles of the book '*D'un Voyage à l'autre – des Voix de l'Immigration pour un Développement Pluriel*', Paris, Panos/Karthala, Juillet 2001. He has participated in several conferences and symposiums around the world (US, South Africa, Netherlands, Senegal) on migration and development issues.

Deborah Fahy Bryceson is a senior research fellow at the African Studies Centre, Leiden and has a multi-disciplinary background in geography, economic history and sociology. She studied for her first and second degrees at the University of Dar es Salaam before doing her PhD at Oxford. Her work has spanned a number of areas, notably mobility and transport, urbanization, employment patterns, and gender. Her recent books include: *Women Wielding the Hoe* (Berg Publishers), *Farewell to Farms: De-agrarianisation and Employment in Africa* (Ashgate, edited with Vali Jamal), *Disappearing Peasantries* (Intermediate Technology Publications, edited with Cris Kay and Jos Mooij) and *Alcohol in Africa: Mixing Business, Pleasure and Politics* (Heinemann).

Umut Erel studied anthropology at Hamburg University, Germany and has an MA in gender and ethnic studies from Greenwich University, UK. Currently she is a PhD student at the Cultural Studies Department, Nottingham Trent University in the UK and works at Münster University, Germany on a research project focusing on migrant domestic workers in Germany. Her research interests are on the intersectionality of gender, ethnicity and class, gender and migration, hybridity and citizenship in Britain and in Germany. She is co-editing with Mirjana Morokvasic and Koko Shinozaki *On the Move! Gender and Migration: Crossing Borders and Shifting Boundaries* (Opladen, Leske & Budrich).

Misa Izuhara is Research Fellow in the School for Policy Studies at the University of Bristol, UK. After completing her Master's Degree in planning at the University of British Columbia, Canada in 1995, she undertook her PhD at the University of Bristol. Her research interests include ageing and gender issues in welfare state, housing, urban and social change. She is the author of *Family Change and Housing in Post-war Japanese Society* (Ashgate 2000) and the editor of the forthcoming *Comparing Social Policies: Exploring New Paradigms in Britain and Japan* (The Policy Press). She is currently working on a project on the 'generational contract' between care and inheritance in Japan and Britain, funded by the UK Economic and Social Research Council.

Abdoulaye Kane studied sociology and political science at the University of Saint-Louis in Senegal between 1990 and 1995. He entered the University of Amsterdam in 1996 where he completed his PhD on informal financial institutions across borders at the Amsterdam's School for Social Science Research. His main research areas are Senegal and France where he has carried out fieldwork on rotating savings and credit associations, burial societies, village mutual funds and other social networks among Senegalese migrants. His current interest is international migration, transnational communities, local development, popular financial arrangements, micro credit institutions and poverty.

Daniela Merolla has specialized in anthropology and in the intercultural study of literature. She graduated from the University La Sapienza in Rome and now works at the University of Leiden. Her field of research is North Africa (Berber minorities, Algeria, Morocco) and north African immigrant communities in Europe. She has published extensively and taught courses in anthropological and literary approaches to gender, ethnicity and narrative in Africa at the University of Leiden, the Institut National des Langues et Civilisations Orientales, Paris, the University of Rome and the Istituto Orientale, Naples. She contributed to the collective work *Hommes et Femmes de Kabylie* edited by S. Chaker, Ina-Yas/Edisud, Aix-en-Provence/Alger, 2000 and is currently co-editing the book *Migrant Europes* with Sandra Ponzanesi.

Monika Salzbrunn has studied sociology, anthropology, French and psychology at the Universities of Cologne, Bielefeld and the Ecole des Hautes Etudes en Sciences Sociales, Paris. Her PhD dissertation was on the transnational politics of West African Muslim migrants in France and Germany. She has done fieldwork in Europe, Senegal and New Zealand. She is currently teaching at the University Paris X Nanterre and researching religion, minorities in mirror and female Islam at the Institut d'Etudes de l'Islam et des Societes du Monde Musulman (EHESS), Paris.

Hiroshi Shibata is a Professor in the Department of Psychology, Health and Sports Science at Obirin University, Japan. He graduated from Hokkaido University Medical School in 1965, and trained as a resident doctor in Tokyo University Medical School (1966–72). His research interests include geriatrics and gerontology specialised in the longitudinal interdisciplinary study of aging. His recent book is: *Longitudinal Interdisciplinary Study on Aging*, coedited with T. Suzuki and Y. Shimonaka. Serdi, Paris, 1997.

Mahamet Timera is a researcher at the École des Hautes Études en Sciences Sociales in Paris. His work focuses on transnationalism and Sahelian communities in France. Recently he has worked with Catherine Quiminal on a survey of Sahelian youth in France.

Rijk van Dijk is an anthropologist working at the African Studies Centre, Leiden. He has done extensive research and published on the rise of Pentecostal movements in urban areas of Malawi and Ghana. He is the author of *Young Malawian Puritans* (Utrecht, ISOR Press, 1993) and has co-edited with Richard Fardon and Wim van Binsbergen *Modernity on a Shoestring* (London, SOAS/Leiden, ASC 1999) and with Mirjam de Bruijn and Dick Foeken *Mobile Africa* (Leiden, Brill 2001). His current research focuses on the transnational dimensions of Ghanaian Pente-costalism and particularly on its relation with the migration of Ghanaians to the Netherlands (The Hague) and to Botswana (Gaborone).

Ulla Vuorela is a professor of social anthropology at the University of Tampere in Finland. She has worked with issues related to gender and development with particular reference to Tanzania. She is the first holder of the five-year Minna Canth Professorship dedicated to women's studies. She is currently directing two large research projects sponsored by the Academy of Finland: 'Beyond marginalisation and exclusion' which deals with transnationalism, ethnic relations and difference in the Finnish context and 'The rich, the poor and the resourceful: aspects of gender in a post-colonial, post-development context' focusing on welfare contracts in the private sphere in Pakistan, Tanzania and Japan.

Acknowledgements

This collection of papers emanates from a conference on migrant families in Europe held at the African Studies Centre, Leiden, in November 1999. The conference was funded by the European Union with the express purpose of giving young scholars from European universities the opportunity to meet and discuss recent research findings. From amongst the many valuable contributions, the editors selected those papers that problematized transnational networking and family formation. These case studies document the creativity of people in devising ways and means of sustaining the idea of familyhood amidst family members' worldwide dispersal. We wish to thank all the conference participants, the European Union funders, and Cathy Lloyd and Lucy Butterwick at Queen Elizabeth House (QEH), University of Oxford, for their role in facilitating the event. We are also very grateful to Shirley Ardener and Jackie Waldren at the Cross Cultural Centre for Research on Women at QEH for their encouragement to publish this collection of articles. We would like to especially thank Ann Reeves whose copyediting work has been a vital component in the production of this book, as well as Claire Taylor for her indexing work. We gratefully acknowledge all the infrastructural back-up provided by the African Studies Centre.

Part I

Introduction

1

Transnational Families in the Twenty-first Century

Deborah Fahy Bryceson and
Ulla Vuorela

By their very nature, transnational families constitute an elusive phenomenon – spatially dispersed and seemingly capable of unending social mutation. Their ability to reconstitute and redefine themselves over time contingent on spatial practicality and emotional and material needs challenges even the most multi-disciplinary social scientist's analytical efforts. 'Transnational families' are defined here as families that live some or most of the time separated from each other, yet hold together and create something that can be seen as a feeling of collective welfare and unity, namely 'familyhood', even across national borders.

This collection explores the many facets of transnational families with individuals or branches resident in Europe[1] currently or in the recent past. Cognitively, these families can be approached through several different burgeoning literatures with none individually capable of encompassing their social complexity as argued in the next section. In this introduction, the manner in which transnational families constitute themselves and their identification with and linkages to nation states and wider community and global networks are considered. The concepts of 'frontiering' and 'relativizing' are introduced to explore intra and inter-familial relations and their interface with the wider society. The next chapter considers the historical background to the European transnational family formation. This contextualizes the case-study chapters that follow.

Apprehending Transnationalism and Transnational Families

Transnational families straddle divisions in social science literature as well as national borders. During the 1990s, transnationalism was discussed primarily with regard to the movement of commodities and capital. Controversy surrounding the World Trade Organization has centred on the regulatory framework within which goods and capital circulate internationally. The impassioned debate about border-crossing regulations intersects with issues arising from transnational families' multiple national residences, identities and loyalties. Globalization studies, on the other hand, have focused on the communications and transport of people through space with little regard for their effect on the family membership of individuals. Migration and diaspora studies have a long track record in documenting people's movements across national boundaries, primarily traced in terms of ethnic streams moving from a clearly specified country of origin to a specified destination country. To the extent that they have traced the influence of locational change on individuals at different stages of their families' life cycles, they provide useful insights.

The recent emergence of what may be called transnational family studies lodges itself across this epistemological terrain, and has so far drawn strong disciplinary sustenance from post-modern anthropology. Transnationalism has been mostly studied as a set of cultural changes and the emergence of new cultural forms depicted as hybrids (Appadurai 1996, Escobar 1995).

However, the discourse on transnational families would be impoverished if it was restricted to hybridity, a theme currently applicable to relatively sedentary as well as highly mobile people in this age of global consumerism. Migration and diaspora studies provide valuable insights into transnational families *vis-à-vis* national borders as well as the positions of individuals and minorities within states. Concepts of diasporic space and transnational processes capture parts of transnational family stories. They emphasize boundaries and space, whereas aspects of agency and everyday practice that are even more central to understanding the mobility, future orientation and the dynamics of networking within transnational families and transnational ways of life are left far hazier.

Historically, the globalizing tendencies of colonialism and trends in the international division of labour, labour policies, trade relations and the formation of power blocs have contributed to the shuffling about, splitting and sometimes disintegration of families. Mass movements of people have been examined in the diaspora literature. Cohen (1997) has classified different types of diasporas in modern history, notably the 'victim diasporas' of mass movement of Africans connected with the slave trade and Armenians connected with religious persecution; the 'imperial diasporas' of South Asians to service British imperial labour needs; and the 'trade diasporas' of the Chinese and Lebanese (see Barot, Chapter

10). One essential characteristic of all diasporas, particularly the Jewish one, has been their nurturing idea of an original home to which they may one day return. Cohen stresses the external push factors and the occupational niches that these diasporas come to occupy in the destination countries. In line with migration studies generally, he adopts a macro-perspective, where the actors are amalgamated populations or communities. The inner logic of the family and their extended networks are largely overlooked in this approach.

Similarly, Brah (1998) advocates the notion of diasporic space devoid of family formation considerations. Diasporic space refers to the intersection of contemporary conditions of transmigrant people, capital, commodities and culture, a realm where economic, cultural and political implications of crossing or even transgressing different borders is experienced; where contemporary forms of transcultural identities are constituted; and where belonging and otherness are appropriated and contested. Brah sees current diasporic space as different from previous historical diasporas as it foregrounds the 'entanglement of the genealogies of dispersal' with those of staying put. Here, the politics of location, of being situated and positioned, derive from the simultaneity of diasporization and rootedness. The concept decentres the subject position of the 'native', 'immigrant', 'migrant', and the 'in/outsider', in such a way that the diasporian is as much a native as the native now becomes a diasporian. Brah retains the discussion at the level of wide segments of population and cultural processes that ensue when people who move encounter those who stay put. In a way, this is a discussion of cultural encounters and their consequences. Hence the making of 'indigenous cultures' such as that of the English emerges from transnational influences notably the effect of British colonialism (Brah 1998, McClintock 1995, Strathern 1992). The very notion of 'Englishness' can be seen as a new ensemble, created by the accretion of cultural contributions from British-based Afro-Caribbeans, Asians, Irish, and so forth. Each contribution has its own specificity, but it is an ever-changing specificity that adds to as well as imbues elements of the other. In the words of Brah (1998: 209):

> Englishness has been formed in the crucible of the internal colonial encounter with Ireland, Scotland and Wales; imperial rivalries with other European countries; and imperial conquests abroad. In the post-war period this Englishness is continually reconstituted via a multitude of border crossings in and through other diasporic formations. These border crossings are territorial, political, economic, cultural and psychological.

Cohen and Brah primarily discuss cultural processes at the level of larger communities and their interaction with nation states, whereas the focus of this collection is the construction of families themselves under diasporic conditions, the ways in which certain families have dispersed and the ways they enact their sense of being part of the same family. Through history, we approach these processes from within the confines of individual families and the inner logic of family networks. The case studies in the chapters that follow demonstrate how families both constrain and enhance individual members' goals and how members make use and benefit from their reliance on family networks.

Delocating Transnational Families

Transnational studies have increasingly suggested that the identification of an individual, an ethnic group or a nation with a fixed locality and a state is not self-evident. Going beyond a view of migration as bipolar moves of people and mapping transnational space *vis-à-vis* the accelerated and densified movement of people, current literature stresses how one's sense of place and associated social identity is changing as a result of the relative ease of movement and communication. Multi-locational identities bridge geographical space, but most of the literature problematizes this process and international mobility at the level of individuals or ethnic communities as exemplified by Braidotti's (1994) 'nomadism', Appadurai's (1996) 'deterritorialization' or Brah's (1998) 'diasporic space'.

This book stresses the impact that transnationalism has on people's family lives and lifestyles. The perception of belonging to one or another state and the attendant problems of either integration or assimilation of the 'immigrant', would straightjacket the analysis of transnational families who may have entirely different ideas about networking and connecting. Similarly, seeing the migrant in the framework of nostalgia and an orientation towards the past, as is the case in diaspora studies, provides only a partial picture. By focusing on transnational ways of living, this book highlights individuals' negotiations between movement and staying put, between different levels of loyalties and their orientation to past, present and future.

The making of space within which people move can be seen within the context of various globalizing trends and the kind of spaces that each of them have created. Family diasporas produce myriad forms and situated histories, however. They tell stories of locational volatility and changing social identifications and nationalities. Any attempt at 'locating' transnational families would be self-defeating. Their attitudes to place are highly varied, ambiguous, and subject to change. Transnational families are primarily relational in nature. They are constituted by relational ties that aim at welfare and mutual support and provide a source of identity. Their fundamental *raison d'être* is mutual welfare, which can be severely tested. Transnational families have had to face the atrocities of genocide, wars, forced migration and intolerant immigration laws. Family members may become forcibly separated from each other. Like other families, transnational families have to mediate inequality amongst their members. Within transnational families, differences in access to mobility, resources, various types of capital and lifestyles emerge in striking ways.

This phenomenon of families living far apart is not new. Fictional writing supplied stories of such families earlier and more voluminously than the social science literature. In fact, transnational families can be seen as a result of a whole range of ways of life whereby people come to be on the move, whether by their own design to take advantage of opportunities or prompted by compelling circumstance such as famine, other traumatic events or economic necessity. It can be argued that, in this way, they have sometimes followed a logic that can be comparable to that of transnational corporations seeking comparative advantage by crossing national borders. In the discourse on globalization, transnational corporations serve as prime examples of transnational moving and globalizing trends. By centre-staging transnational families, we are examining the processes of globalization from below, specifically from the point of view of individuals whose lives are largely inscribed by membership of transnationally mobile families.

Transnational families, or what are sometimes referred to as multi-local or multi-sited families, or families living in spatial separation, are certainly not creations of recent globalizing trends but have played an integral part in European colonial and settler histories. However, it is only with the creation of the 'informational society' and transnational restructurings of capitalist production and international trade that they are increasingly becoming a pronounced part of everyday European ways of life.

Worldwide, there are many families leading transnational lives, who are generally not seen as migrants, such as people working in the higher echelons of transnational companies, or those working in 'foreign service' of various kinds, such as the UN and development cooperation organizations, the EU bureaucracy and a whole array of mobile professions. The word 'migrant' tends to carry class connotations and is applied more readily to people that are considered economically or politically deprived and seek betterment of their circumstances. Transnational families at the higher end of the income scale, who tend to move for financial or status reasons, are seen as somehow different, bestowing their presence and skills on the receiving nation as opposed to other migrants who are imposing or even inflicting their needs on the receiving country. Transnational elites are perceived as 'mobile' rather than 'migrant'. As cosmopolitans – people who have entered international careers – transnational elites seem to move more by choice and be in a better position to negotiate their connections, their nationalities, and benefits associated with their choice of a national residence. The symbolic capital of education and language enable them to move freely, offering relatively easier access to border crossing and citizenship. However, the issues of connecting, mixing and networking are very much the same between the mass of international migrants and transnational elites.

The case studies that follow point to the need for periodizing and contextualizing any discussion of transnational family forms. However much transnational families may be seen as individual creations or as outcomes of events that 'just happened', history is needed to situate them in a wider context. Our emphasis is on how families shape and are shaped by movement, separation, and reunion and the boundaries and vistas they establish for themselves.

The study of families as transnational phenomena requires the processes of globalization to be considered from the level of everyday life and the perspective of civil society. It is useful to separate the levels of the family, the civil society and the state for analytical reasons, as Yuval-Davis (1997) does, but the various levels also need to be seen in the way in which they articulate and affect on one another.

The global map has become vividly criss-crossed with multi-centred processes, each with its own logic. At the level of the family, one might be tempted to think that there is no pattern according to which individual family networks carve out space for themselves. There is even no need to construct closed categories for such networks. Yet, in a historical sense, patterns and processes have emerged. If one thinks of colonialism as a globalizing trend, its labour and educational policies contributed to both family formation and class formation. In both, socially divisive impacts are evident. Moreover, the following case studies not only testify to the varied spaces moulded by European colonial powers, but also new transnational spaces associated with the dynamics of post-war Europe and the 'era of development'.

Global trends, as discussed in Chapter 2, are similarly providing the impetus for transnational family formation. Today's transnational families are characterized by a more elastic relationship to their place of origin, ethnicity or national belonging. There is a different sense of belonging both with reference to the past and to the future. This raises questions about the relationship between transnational families and the nation state.

Demythologizing Nation-states and Transnational Families

Are transnational families in contradiction with national feelings and loyalties? This question increasingly surfaces in international literature both from the perspective of those concerned with national cohesion as well as those focusing on issues related to modern family welfare. On one hand, transnational families are seen as subversive threats to the coherence of nation states and, on the other hand, the dispersal of families associated with international conflicts, labour markets and other global phenomena is seen as a corrosive force on family units and the welfare of individual family members who are often denied the security of enduring conventional caring relationships.

In anthropology there has been a long tradition that sees the family and the nation state as parallel structures. In fact, the study of kinship was largely prompted by the assumption that social relations within the nation state reflect familial structures and relations. Coward (1983) argues that the notion of the nuclear male-headed household can to some extent be traced to endeavours to shape both the family/household and the nation in parallel images nurturing each other. She suggests that the plethora of studies in anthropology/sociology dealing with parental or patriarchal authority as models for authority structures within the state can be seen as derivative of these concerns and part of a long tradition of European patriarchal thinking. Family units encompassing mothers, and children under the authority and protection of the father were seen to expand and proliferate as children married and formed new family offshoots that remained under his authority. Each son generated families in the image of the original one, connected by common descent, who lived under the authority of their common progenitor. In the nineteenth century, this theory offered an explanation for the development of wider groupings and society itself, and finally the making of a nation of tribes united by blood.

Maine (1861) had challenged the notion that society simply represented an enlargement of the biologically based primary family by suggesting that the primary family was not based on the natural rights of the first progenitor, but on cohesion emanating from the patriarch's power and authority, *patria Potestas*. Maine considered that the authority of the patriarch and the ties of the family were arbitrary and the family could readily include slaves and those it adopted as well as excluding women who were related to it by blood. Maine, who was interested in demonstrating the arbitrary basis of kinship, argued that the family was not a biological unit *per se*, but a unit generating a fiction of biological unity, or in other words, a social construction. Maine's notion of the patriarchal family as a property-holding unit and system of government gained more attention than his views on the family as a social construction. But the latter has gained resonance today.

Similarly, Anderson (1985) argues that despite people's propensity to 'naturalize' their national belonging and the issue of citizenship, these are not natural, given facts, but imagined. The case studies in this volume draw attention to the parallel imaginings of the family. Families, ethnicities and nations can be seen as imagined communities. One may be born into a family and a nation, but the sense of membership can be a matter of choice and negotiation. One can alter one's nationality and citizenship just as one can alter one's family and its membership in everyday practice. The inclusion of dispersed members within the family is confirmed and renewed through various exchanges and points of contact.

Families are imagined communities. When the family is taken as a parallel and central metaphor for the nation, it remains unproblematized, assumed to be a natural community. Nations and families can be seen historically as both imagined and real. The inner logic of how families are imagined does vary. Anthropology has documented a myriad of various family forms around the globe. Within Europe, there are family structures within which equality and the hierarchy of succession vary in fundamental ways (Todd 1990). Moreover, even if we think that we do not choose our relatives, we in fact do, considering the family members with whom one actually interacts in everyday life.

Imagining a family means giving it a definition that may conflict with the nation state's definition of legitimate immigrant families. There is a large discourse on the ways in which immigration policies construct different notions of family. Mohanty (1991), for example, has indicated how British nationality and immigration laws continuously define and construct 'legitimate' citizenship in racialized and gender-biased ways. The 1968 Commonwealth Immigrants Act had a pervasive influence on black and immigrant women in Britain. As workers, women were forced to leave their families behind. As wives they were assumed to live wherever their husbands resided and be dependent on them. As mothers, particularly single mothers, they had difficulty bringing their children to the UK to join them. Changing immigration legislation continually redefines the nation state by redefining the status of its inhabitants and their familial relations.

Thus, the state and the individual are mutually selective. The state can and does choose or reject applications for citizenship, just as individuals abandon, seek or combine different citizenships. Choice is a two-way street but the exercise of choice is not balanced between the state and the individual, and the power to choose is highly differentiated between individuals. The class distinction between 'migrants' and 'cosmopolitan transnationals' comes to bear. Migrants are left waiting and wondering about their residence and citizenship applications, whereas highly educated and skill- endowed cosmopolitan transnationals are actively sought and offered residential privileges or fast-track citizenship.

When examining the transnational family *vis-à-vis* European states, political anchorage is generally lodged at the level of individual agency. Individuals take risks seeking residential rights and/or citizenship, and if successful, they may be forging easier conditions of entry for other family members. However, there are a number of political forces currently erecting new barriers and undoing older ones. In the process, Fortress Europe has emerged whereby the division between those who move at ease and those who stay put has tended to deepen (Bauman 1998).

Frontiering Families

Despite ample debates in the field of transnational studies, there is little agreement on the concepts to be used. They range from 'transnational spaces' to 'transnational communities', 'transmigration', 'transnational ways of living', 'diasporic spaces', and so forth. Variation relates to the disciplinary backgrounds of authors, and is reflected in the collection of articles in this volume. We have not meddled with the vocabulary of individual authors, but advance two concepts in this chapter that attempt to capture the processes that are central to transnational family making and community networking.

We suggest the term 'frontiering', to denote the ways and means transnational family members use to create familial space and network ties in terrain where affinal connections are relatively sparse. The term seems more appropriate than the term 'negotiation', which is used in literature about identity formation. Frontiering denotes the encounter between people, and hints at various ways of encountering that may be more or less amiable, creative and fulfilling or conflict-ridden. Associating frontiering with confrontation is relevant at times, whereas frontiering may also be used to denote the act of defining identities, differences, and agreements about the appropriation of space or roles. Frontiering proceeds as movement towards implicit understanding about the interface and encounter, where boundaries are drawn between acceptable and unacceptable.

The word 'frontier' has European imperial origins: the Latin, *frons frontis*, referred to Roman 'civilization's' advance into 'barbarian' territory. Frontiering in its original usage has connotations of conquest, whereby the mobile subject is defined as 'civilized' and those encountered are the 'barbarian others'. Interestingly the words 'frontier' and 'affinity' have similar Latin roots, *finis* and *frontis*, both alluding to crossing borders.

Likewise fontiering has been used to describe the central motivational concept in European expansion in North America during the nineteenth century. The idea of conquest is inherent also here with a messianic undertone: the American frontier was where Western civilisation 'conquered' Indian savagery (Limerick, Milner and Rankin 1991). The frontier marked the westward expansion of populations of primarily European origin at the expense of North American Indians.

In our usage of the term, the connotations of conquest and dispossession are expurgated. We define frontiering as agency at the interface between two (or more) contrasting ways of life. Rather than European societies' hegemonic conquest of 'others', the tables are turned. Frontiering in Europe in the late twentieth and early twenty-first century is about the reversal of mass migration flows and their orientation *to* rather than *away* from Europe and the significance of transnational families and multiculturalism in Europe during an age of spatial mobility and historical upheaval. European societies come to terms with other cultures *within* European borders.

As already stressed, transnational families are not new to Europe. European trade, colonization and out-migration have created circumstances for their proliferation through the centuries. However, these transnational families tended to have their epicentres in Europe or be propelled by economic and political forces originating in Europe (see Barot, Chapter 10). Now, Western European countries have strong gravitational pull for settlement but migration and family construction is not responding to outward-bound European political or economic initiatives deliberately encouraging migration. Quite the contrary, the relative prosperity of Europe in a grossly uneven world economy is the main pulling force or, as has recently been the case with the political disintegration of Yugoslavia, Europe is the stage upon which war disrupts and scatters families (Al-Ali, Chapter 4).

Frontiering in this context relates to the criss-cross and clash of cultural values that is ongoing within transnational families and in the larger society. In many cases, this cultural experimentation amounts to confrontation between genders, generations and individuals within the family. Merolla (Chapter 5) cites gender behaviour as an indicator of difference between cultural worlds. Intergenerational lifestyle conflict common to families everywhere may be more marked in transnational families where cultural and generational divides combine to produce yawning age gaps between family members. Given the availability of contrasting, sometimes even conflictual cultural patterns that can be used to try to validate claims to a moral high ground, intra-familial struggles can be extremely fractious and seemingly unresolvable, and can result in bodily harm to family members (Barot, Chapter 10). Why are transnational families through their mobility willing to expose themselves to these destabilizing risks? Van Dijk (Chapter 9) cites the case of Ghanaians in the Netherlands whose membership of Pentecostal Churches provides them with a delocalized protective moral circle within which the dilemmas of reconciling traditional Ghanaian kin obligations with more Western-style transnational family relations are deflected.

By deploying the term frontiering we challenge its historically entrenched Eurocentricity. Frontier societies are inherently open ended. The image of the Western frontier championed by American history textbooks is that of pioneers in search of prosperity and democratic freedom. The American frontier and the European out-migration that it absorbed were, to a large extent, an outcome of the lack of economic opportunity and political constraints as they existed in nineteenth-century deagrarianizing Europe.

At present, the overwhelming motivation for transnational family movement and residence in alien, potentially destabilizing cultural contexts is the belief that family security, economic welfare, social opportunity and/or political freedom will be more fully realized elsewhere. It is for this reason, that transnational families can be said to be forging new cultural, economic and social frontiers to benefit their own families in the first instance, but ultimately contributing to a richer societal culture, economy and polity of their host countries in Europe as well.

The next two sections will consider the nature of individuals' frontiering within the transnational family unit and through their social networking. Frontiering will be discussed in terms of 'familial relativizing', a term that will be elaborated in the following section. Thereafter, frontiering with respect to local and global networking will be examined.

Relativizing within Transnational Families

Another term that we suggest is 'relativizing', used here to refer to the variety of ways individuals establish, maintain or curtail relational ties with specific family members. It is intended to stress the sense of relativity, of being related, that occurs in transnational family relations that are created by active pursuit or passive negligence of familial blood ties and the possible inclusion of non-blood ties as family members. When families are split and dispersed across long distances, the need to keep family ties alive and renewed comes to the fore. Relativizing refers to modes of materializing the family as an imagined community with shared feelings and mutual obligations. Given the physical distances that separate them, many family members are not subject to daily or frequent face-to-face interaction with each other. Individuals 'relativize' family membership against a background of declining contact time or spatial proximity associated with transnational mobility. Relativizing involves the selective formation of familial emotional and material attachments on the basis of temporal, spatial and need-related considerations.

Spatial Dynamics

Personal familial attachment preferences and practicalities are heavily influenced by the geographical location of family members. On the one hand, within the residential home, certain family members are physically absent thereby reducing the range and depth of *in situ* emotional and material need fulfilment. On the other, the expanded locational spread of family members affords greater spatial scope for need fulfilment. Blion (Chapter 12) cites the magnitude of remittances migrants send home. Salzbrunn and Kane's case studies (Chapters 11 and 13) show how Senegalese migrants in France send remittances to their families for day-to-day basic needs. Erel (Chapter 6) describes the multiplicity of childcare arrangements for Turkish children, growing up in the absence of their migrant mothers, involving grandparents, aunts, siblings or other extended relations. During the Bosnian war, Bosnian migrants in the Netherlands and the UK attended to their Bosnian-based families' needs and sometimes facilitated their migration out of distressing war-torn circumstances (Al-Ali, Chapter 4). Japanese migrant women in the UK wrestle with the responsibilities they feel for providing old-age care for their elderly parents (Izuhara and Shibata, Chapter 8). Similarly, Ghanaian migrants in the Netherlands face heavy moral obligations to send remittances to extended family relations back home in Ghana even though they may be barely managing to survive financially in their new work environment

(Van Dijk, Chapter 9). Bosnian migrants sometimes have to choose between maximizing nuclear family welfare in the host country or being more outward directed in trying to help extended family members back home (Al-Ali).

In addition to individuals working out the nature of their relationships to other family members, relativizing entails the construction and continual revision of one's role and family identity throughout the individual's life cycle. This may take place in relative isolation from family pressure and the need to conform to conventional familial roles. Thus, there may be non-fulfilment, surrogacy or redefinition of the conventional nuclear family roles of father, mother, son, daughter, sibling, as well as more extended roles of aunts, uncles, cousins, and so forth. Erel (Chapter 6) describes how older siblings sometimes take on maternal roles with younger siblings in the absence of their Turkish mother, who is either away in a foreign land or working long shifts in low-paid jobs.

At one level people everywhere work consciously and unconsciously at making their families succeed as social units of emotional interdependence and shared affections. In addition families to greater or lesser degrees pool or at least exchange economic resources of various kinds for their mutual benefit. Not unlike other families, transnational family members constitute themselves as viable social units in this way. However, given their often unpredictable, sporadic physical encounters with each other, they have to construct their notion of a family and its emotional and economic utility more deliberately, rather than taking it for granted through continuous day-to-day interaction. A family in the absence of regular physical proximity requires conscious rationalization. Erel (Chapter 6) describes a Turkish woman's childhood memories of the sticks of gum enclosed in letters from her migrant mother, which took on umbilical significance for the small child. A transnational family member may be more interactive with and reliant on neighbours close at hand than with distant family members. Hence, there is a need to explain, in the face of the material facts of one's daily life and relative lack of contact with familial relations, why and how some of these distant relatives nonetheless are family.

Individual members of transnational families centre their family stories and sense of belonging differently from the vantage points of their own histories of growing up and moving through various life-cycle stages. In this way, a transnational family may differ in composition and structure depending on each family member's conception of it. This imagining process makes for fluid family relationships. If and when circumstances, like family gatherings or other forms of informational exchange, create the opportunity for juxtaposing these stories, the collective rendering of the family may be heavily influenced by the strength of individual personalities. This contrasts with conservative families in which male patriarchs customarily enforce behavioural rules and familial roles on an ascriptive basis. Family members' individual decision making is circumscribed by community-enforced marriage practices and other rites of passage handed down from generation to generation, as outlined by Barot (Chapter 10) with respect to the transnational Swaminarayan religious movement. Barot refers to the intra-familial tensions as well as intra-community splintering that arises in this highly structured social organization. Al-Ali (Chapter 4) shows how family visits in the aftermath of the Bosnian war and family division may engender painful memories and call into question issues related to family solidarity that some prefer to avoid by curtailing their visits to Bosnia.

Both fluid and unyielding conceptions of the family can exist in the minds of different family members within a single transnational family. The relative strength of contending views depends on several factors including family members' geographical proximity, community opinion and state laws. For example, Timera and Salzbrunn (Chapters 7 and 11) refer to the struggles of French-born female youth who are at odds with their Sahelian immigrant parents over the choice of marriage partner and circumcision. These girls do not share their parents' village-based values about family and the role of women. Their parents worry about what their family back in the Sahel and the Sahelian immigrant community in France will think of their daughters' non-conformist behaviour, whereas the daughters, with a different, more French-influenced notion of family membership, find such concerns unreasonable and unfair. Similarly young women within the Swaminarayan movement have been known to rebel.

Conservative forces within the family may try to recreate power relations in a family's new location along the model of their homeland, the physical absence of key family members, notably the male patriarch, can preclude the effectiveness of these attempts. Erel (Chapter 6) notes that some Turkish women left behind in Turkey by their migrant husbands, or alternatively migrants themselves working in Germany, enjoyed considerable decision-making power that was thereafter often retracted by family reunion or their return to Turkey. Various conventional relationships between husband and wife, parent and child or amongst siblings can be subjected to substantial revision through transnational familial relativising. Al-Ali's interviews (Chapter 4) with Bosnian men suggest that some shed patriarchal attitudes and begin to appreciate greater involvement in day-to-day family relationships and domestic labour.

Temporal Dimension

One's emotional and material needs are strongly linked to stages of the individual life cycle, although individuals vary in the intensity with which they experience and express these needs. Interaction with other family members directed at realizing one's own need fulfilment and contributing to the need fulfilment of other family members must be seen over time and in relation to the spatial distribution of transnational family members.

Decisions to migrate are often based on reaching a particular threshold, such as completing one's schooling and/or coming of age in terms of being expected to find work and become self-supporting. Being engaged with schooling on the other hand, or with childbearing and rearing, or caring for elderly parents, may be reasons for not moving. Thus, being already educated, unmarried, and aged 18 to 35 is considered the prime time for travelling or moving to a new locality. Yet, examples abound in this volume and elsewhere indicating that spatial mobility is not restricted to any one age group or gender.

Whether moving is an individual or group decision can be heavily influenced by the family life cycle. Family-choreographed movements are unlikely unless the nuclear family consists of children whose parents locate the family on the basis of childcare and schooling considerations. Erel demonstrates the importance of children's schooling in deciding family movements. Movement for some families, particularly those of the elite, may be linked with career planning. They seek opportunities to maximize income and family welfare at particular locations and at particular times in their family life cycle. By contrast, most migrant families are not able to pick and choose in this way, and their movement arises more from force of circumstance, as in the case of refugees fleeing war, or economic circumstances. In Ghana, where the economy has been depressed for more than two decades, extended families have relied on the emigration of their offspring for material survival. Van Dijk (Chapter 9) shows how extended family relations have been underpinned by ancestral worship and communally shared rituals associated with the rites of passage of birth, death and marriage. Membership in Pentecostal Churches in the Netherlands provides Ghanaian migrants with a different set of rites of passage from that of Ghanaian family structures with the onerous obligations of their internal gift economy and provides them with a sense of community networking.

Once an individual or group of family members has relocated, the question arises of whether and how ties will be retained between sending and receiving branches of the family. The age and gender of absent members can strongly influence the nature and degree of contact that is pursued by both sides. When elderly parents of the family are the ones left behind in the home area, there is greater compulsion to keep in contact (see Al-Ali, Izuhara and Shibata) and parental death may mark the cessation of frequent family exchanges. In Japan, this is accentuated by the stem family structure, which does not encourage strong ties between adult siblings who establish their own largely autonomous nuclear families. Several authors stress that points of contact weaken substantially in the transition from the first to second generation of immigrant populations. Second generation immigrants often face language barriers and a general lack of knowledge about their families' home areas and their cultural complexities (Izuhara and Shibata, Kane, and Salzbrunn). The two Dutch-Moroccan stories reviewed by Merolla reveal the second generation Moroccans' 'illusive origins' and the cultural distance they feel from their parents' homeland.

Practical Realities

Material assets and income level strongly influence decisions related to family spatial separation as well as the maintenance of family members' contact with one another. As Bryceson documents in Chapter 2, international migration both historically and now depends on being able to mobilize cash for travel and accommodation costs. Once the migrant locates away from the core family the cost of international telephone calls, faxes, emails and airfares may serve as barriers to communications within low-income transnational families. On the other hand, they may feel greater insecurity and more compulsion to retain links with distant family members than higher income families. They may be exposed to a more pronounced cultural divide in their adopted country and have more need for a fallback in case they lose their livelihood or residential rights. In view of cheaper airfares and telephone calls, they find the means to keep in close contact despite their tighter financial circumstances.

For those who can afford it, family visits are often cast as holidays, scheduled around the school recess. Al-Ali (Chapter 4) observes that many migrants look forward to those times as not only getting back to their roots and the warm, familiar bosom of family and friends, but also a pleasurable interlude when they can escape the harsh northern European climate and cold impersonal relationships. These pleasurable associations, however, are weighted against the pragmatic need to be vigilant against losing one's residence rights or prospects for citizenship in the host country by making home visits. For Moroccans returning to their homeland, the younger generation may be propelled mostly by the promise of a sun-filled holiday whereas the older generation go with social and economic investments in mind. Building a house or arranging the marriage of one's daughter to a family within the original home community cements continued ties with the homeland (Merolla, Chapter 5).

Family traditions and individual needs are weighed against the sheer physical practicalities of transnational families' temporal and spatial logistics. In sum, transnational families are not simply blood ties nor are they fixed entities. They are highly relative.

Frontier Networking: Families and Communities Mapping New Social Spaces

It is important to differentiate analytically between the institutions of the state, civil society and the family, so as to avoid a Western-biased reading of social organization (Yuval-Davis 1997). Transnational families have multiple community identities related to all the places where their members are resident or have been resident in the past. There is thus a complex locational spread, with some nodes more important than others given the number and depth of contacts found in that location.

A transnational family's community identification is inextricably linked to its extra-familial networks. We will refer to these as 'frontier networks' directed at supportive interaction. The functions they serve are too diverse to list. Essentially they provide vital mutual support for the realization of family and individual welfare. Moreover, they may service livelihood and business associational needs or be a link to home areas for altruistic or status-seeking aims.

Given the dispersed and internally diverse nature of transnational families and their internal gender and generational differences, their networks are likely to be disjointed and non-overlapping. When mapped, the networks form a patchwork of heavily and lightly traversed nodal areas that constitute the family's community linkages. Such linkages can be divided into four main categories on the basis of location/organizational criteria, namely those focused on: first, the original home area; second, the current residential neighbourhood/work area; third, the transnational realm of residential and cultural choice; and fourth, transnational realm of moral institutional identification. The transnational family networks documented in this book span all of these categories.

Original Home Area Networking

As stressed earlier in this chapter, not all transnational families strongly identify with or yearn for their original home area. Nonetheless, many families, especially those who have migrated relatively recently or form part of large ethnically based mass settlement, tend to espouse strong attachments to their home area.

Salzbrunn and Kane (Chapters 11 and 13) document how Senegalese migrants to France retain personal and community linkages with their villages in Senegal. Kane describes how these associations develop for mutual support, and even offer unemployment benefits to members. As distance from the home area increased, associational ties widened in scope. In view of a lack of critical mass of extended family members living abroad, early Senegalese migrants to France restructured their associational ties by broadening them from extended family to village-wide recruitment of network members. Within the association, however, fracture lines have appeared along age strata and have been accentuated by changing migration laws that have curtailed numbers of incoming migrants. Informally, youth develop strong relationships with others on the basis of involvement in sports or cultural pursuits, whereas older men relate in terms of religious or locational proximity of their wards. Links to their home villages have altered generationally, as younger French-born Senegalese without the same emotional feelings or practical 'home area' concerns of their parents refashion the organizational networks.

Al-Ali (Chapter 4) discusses Bosnian youth whose lack of Bosnian language capabilities estranges them from the desire for frequent contact with their parents' home areas. Turkish and North African migrants, who have settled in Europe over the past 30 years, now have family members whose contacts with the original sending areas are minimal, and who have adopted or indeed rejected more immediate cultural associational ties within ethnic neighbourhoods within Europe. Nonetheless, in the Swamin-arayan movement, individuals are often removed from their 'home areas' by generations of international movement, yet great value is placed on making pilgrimages to the original sites of the founding sects, which reinforces appreciation of their economic trek through time around the world (Barot, Chapter 10).

Blion (Chapter 12) introduces the interesting case of home area networking mediated by European-based immigrant and ethnic minority organizations (IEMOs). Ideally, such IEMOs could align with European NGOs to channel aid back to their home areas, even though they may rival each other for funding. Blion argues that institutional cooperation between them is of mutual benefit to aid recipients, the migrant associations and European donors because of its facilitation of the otherwise cumbersome aid-targeting process. Salzbrunn cites the example of Senegal's national elections in 2000 in which migrants resident in France exerted considerable influence through telephone contact with their rural families in Senegal – a clear demonstration of the power of original home area networking.

Neighbourhood Networking

Processes of localizing may involve various degrees of proximity and connecting with others in one's immediate home and work environment. Migrants consciously and unconsciously choose the extent to which they interact socially with people in the host society and the extent to which they engage in activities with fellow immigrants. They can mix and match their involvement with respect to different realms of activity. Local networks can be vital to everyday life by providing information about housing, employment, and basic needs provisioning. They are generally structured by mutual obligations embedded in complex systems of loyalty. Salzbrunn (Chapter 11) argues that interaction of network members in transnational space contributes to the making of local hybrid forms of culture.

Apart from religion, ethnicity has often provided the glue for community construction. However, there are also obvious material reasons for the emergence of ethnic neighbourhoods. In Europe, they are often related to housing policies and prices. Low-income immigrants seek areas of low-cost or government-subsidised social housing. Slowly, with the residential settlement of increasing numbers and the development of restaurants and services geared to ethnically defined tastes, European cities' ethnic neighbourhoods are taking shape. However, amidst these material forces, the formation of ethnic neighbourhoods represents social convenience, especially the ease of interacting with people who speak the same language.

There are, however, some transnational families who consciously try to avoid people of similar cultural background to themselves when settling in a new place. This is common amongst the elites who may feel they have more in common with people of similar income levels and who may be comfortable speaking several languages. They welcome living abroad as an opportunity to mix with people of other nationalities and may deliberately avoid networking with their fellow countrymen for fear of becoming ghettoized expatriates.

In fact, many of the case studies in this book, rather than confirming the importance of home area and immediate ethnic community networking, demonstrate 'reverse cultural alienation'. We define this as the tendency to alienate oneself from one's original cultural background, as opposed to the more common form of cultural alienation in which newcomers feel estranged and out of harmony with their new adopted surroundings as non-naturalized foreigners. Izuhara and Shibata (Chapter 8) show how many Japanese migrant women living in Britain with their English husbands had little recourse to networking with other Japanese back in Japan or in Britain. They fully imbibed British culture in their daily lives and raised their children to be almost entirely British. Their home area and local Japanese networking was kindled only when they entered middle age and began anticipating old-age care. Similarly, Merolla's (Chapter 5) textual reading of the fictional short stories about the trials and tribulations of young Dutch-Moroccan men indicates that these men are relatively removed from 'home area' and 'local community' networks enforcing Moroccan cultural norms.

Transnationals' Contingent Space Networking

This brings us to the third network category, what might best be called the 'transnational realm of like-minds'. As transnational families grow in number they can become a social force in and of themselves, especially in large cities where they are likely to be concentrated. People in this category are open to creating new links wherever they move. This may mean becoming engaged in the making of the local, such as involvement in activist movements of a local, national or transnational nature, for example a peace movement or consumer cooperative. This is manifested in Vuorela's case study (Chapter 3) of a family that became involved in Tanzania's nationalist movement. The family's progression of residences and its expansive geographical dispersal imparted a sense of locational and cultural choice that was pragmatically transnational.

There may also be a desire to 'modernize' and do away with identifications that link a person to life in the home country. The debate about allochotonous/autochtonous divisions of young Moroccan authors who wish to be considered on their own merit as individual writers rather than as a group of Moroccan authors is a case in point. The fictional Dutch-Moroccan characters that Merolla (Chapter 5) reviews may be less spatially mobile, but they exercised cultural choice and in so doing have a 'critical distance from the cultural traditions of both sending and receiving lands'.

Both cases exemplify locational and cultural relativity. Rather than 'acculturating', and wholeheartedly adopting a new national culture or conforming to an existing national or ethnic sub culture, their transnational migration experience can impart a sense of relativity that they hold in common with others subjectively like them. Furthermore their openness to new cultural and societal aspirations downplays an idealization of the past and the notion of returning one day to one's homeland.

The offspring of many Moroccan and Turkish migrant families have family relations in more than one European country. The transnational family settlement has fanned out over Germany, Switzerland, the Netherlands, France, Spain, Belgium and to a lesser extent Scandinavia. Unwittingly, their parents' migration history makes it possible for them to effortlessly form transnational networks of the mind and of practical substance. They are in a position to be perhaps the most 'European' of any group within the EU.

However, it should be stressed that the term 'networking' applied to inter-relationships amongst transnationals may be misleading. They may simply share an appreciation of not belonging to any one place, and edging towards global citizenship.

Moral Universe Networking

In contrast to the loose common bonds of those sharing a feeling of cultural relativity, some transnational families have innovatively combined cultural and moral elements of home and current locations to create a *modus operandi* for common economic and social endeavours. Such transnational families generally have an occupational orientation or a long migration history that inclines them to conscious networking. Over time, many of them have consensually established institutional means for networking, frequently through delocalized religious ties as highlighted in the chapters by Barot and Van Dijk. Furthermore, these transnational families may combine the amassing of economic or symbolic capital to strengthen their positions and enhance their network capabilities still further.

Bourdieu (1998) sees the family as one of the key sites of the accumulation of capital in its different forms including that of symbolic capital and its transmission between generations. Property inheritance is a pivotal means for family bonding as well as possible family dissension and it is an arena that is bound to be influenced by new residential settings where laws as well as cultural attitudes differ from a migrant's place of origin. Group acceptance of religious or other consensual moral sanctions is a way of precluding potentially destabilizing dissension.

Barot's study (Chapter 10) of British Asians in the Swaminarayan Movement best illustrates the amassing of economic and symbolic capital within transnational families who share religious beliefs and clear business and welfare objectives. Arising within the context of British colonialism's impact on India and Hindu anti-caste sentiments, the movement's religious community and business networks have evolved over a century and a half and now span four continents. Their effectiveness has been facilitated by adherence to common moral principles and endogamous marriage practices. Given the economic success and the family welfare they have generated, the community networks achieve a virtuous cycle of mutuality and goal fulfilment that helps to instil continued group compliance. Nonetheless, the community networks face internal tensions along the fracture lines of gender, generation and income differentiation. The obligation to donate 10 per cent of one's income to the Swaminarayan movement and collective temple building help to dispel the tension generated by differential wealth holdings within the community. Gender and generational dissension, reflecting the absorption of British values by youth that their parents disapprove of, remains highly problematic.

The Dutch Ghanaian pentecostalists that Van Dijk (Chapter 9) considers do not have such a long tradition of collective religious and welfare-seeking endeavour but make up for this with the intensity of pentecostal sanctions imposed on them and the fervour of their newly adopted beliefs. They represent a translocal community that is relatively structured around the intersection of kinship and religious community membership. Their frontiering community is a site of power struggles between traditional local elders and transnational authority figures who are gaining dominance in the name of modernity.

Salzbrunn (Chapter 11) contrasts these conscious networking efforts and the contradictory forces of Islamic institutional politicization and personal depoliticization of Islamic practice. She demonstrates how French West African Muslims use their religious affiliations as one resource amongst others to effect their desired economic and political goals. Rather than representing a collective imperative, moral and cultural aspects of Islam are individually appropriated and applied to individually defined objectives giving rise to various hybrid amalgams of everyday beliefs and practices.

Relativizing in Many Worlds

One of the main themes of this book is the fluidity of intra- and inter-family relations in the face of far more fixed cultural norms and national laws. All of the chapters testify to the importance of agency whereby individual migrants, their families and communities chart their way through new transnational spaces. An examination of the history of transnational living reveals the varied conditions and diversity of life-styles, stratified by class, race and gender, and above all individual variation reflective of cultural experimentation.

In the context of Europe, one must ask how important place is now. Many transnational communities structure their communities around concerns related to their home areas but some individual transnationals espouse no origins, no permanent geographical attachments, and no final destinations. Others actively seek to establish operative ties with places as far flung as their network contacts will take them. Access to many cultures helps amass symbolic capital (Bourdieu 1998). In this bewildering flux, European countries and cultures are subject to fundamental transformative processes. The following short summaries of each chapter highlight the experimentation process at multiple levels of the family, community and nation state.

Vuorela's study of a globally dispersed transnational family suggests that geographical dispersal can be an asset rather than a divisive factor in family coherence. In effect, familyhood becomes a transnational way of life. In her case study, family members' residential separation from one another results from individual choices about careers and spouses with movements both constrained and facilitated by British colonialism and subsequent service in international bureaucracies. Transnational mobility, although impinging on family life, was nonetheless an enabling environment for an upwardly mobile life path. Their attainment of educational qualifications in Anglo-American cultural space provided the necessary symbolic capital for family members' mobility between continents. Over the years, the family established a *modus operandi* that took residential movement for granted. The family's elite status was secured through this movement.

Quite different circumstances prevail in Al-Ali's case study of middle-class Bosnian families who moved to Britain and the Netherlands. Here we see a more belaboured transition that entails families learning new languages and struggling with unwelcoming labour markets. Under stress, gender roles are transformed and Bosnian women migrants sometimes found themselves assuming the role of family provisioner, much to the chagrin of their husbands.

Merolla's exploration of the burgeoning Dutch-Moroccan literature demonstrates the extent to which relativization is taking place in this migrant community. Inverting the ethnic and gender stereotypes, the story plots revolve around the vexed theme of betrothal and marriage in a transnational context. Rather than thrusting the main characters into choosing between Dutch or Moroccan culture, they are instead charting their own unique ways in surrealistic landscapes of cultural upheaval. The stories point to the impossibility of returning to a past, be it a location or a culture.

Part III focuses on life-cycle influences, raising a number of issues related to how migration affects relativization between distant family members at vulnerable stages of the life cycle. These encompass the coping strategies and social attitudes arising from the separation of mothers from young children, the tensions of adolescents and young adults growing up in tightly-knit migrant communities where familial pressures to conform are strong, and the worries and guilt of transnational family members facing questions of old-age care.

The immediate nuclear family is, in Erel's case study of Turkish migrants in Germany, a mini-United Nations requiring language translators. The diversity of languages and local political involvement across various nation states does not preclude a sense of familyhood. Frequent correspondence, memory recall, visits and the exchange of gifts and symbols gives German Turkish families a sense of unity that bridges distance. Erel focuses on the nature of mothering *in absentia*, questioning dominant representations of migration as a male-dominated phenomenon and motherhood as a necessarily *in situ* relationship between mother and child. Her work challenges the view that the daily enactment of the biological mother-child dyad is requisite for a child's welfare. Mothering cannot be seen outside its specific context or in isolation from other familial and caring relationships. This study poignantly demonstrates that whereas the experience of physical separation of family members, particularly separation of a mother from her children, can be painful, it can also be mitigated in various ways that turn out to be enriching in the end. Furthermore, the actual practice of migrant families can undermine theories that rely on the assumption that the family is a linguistically and culturally uniform entity.

Timera's chapter graphically demonstrates the mixing of culturally discordant values within transnational families. His examination of French Sahelian families reveals the diametrically opposed perceptions of parents in relation to their sons and daughters. Daughters, seeking to redefine their role and status in the family, are considered troublesome in contrast to seemingly dutiful sons who fulfil their parents' expectations. However, in the eyes of the French state and civil society, perceptions are reversed and often sensationalized. Boys are rabble-rousing troublemakers who refuse to conform to French laws and societal conventions, dropping out of school and facing unpromising working lives. Girls more seriously pursuing their studies are, by comparison, model French citizens. This study illustrates the contradictory positions family members may adopt as they relativize their family relationships in a new setting.

Izuhara and Shibata's case study of middle-class Japanese women migrants documents perhaps more than any other chapter the sway of life-cycle considerations on relativization. Theirs is a study of individual Japanese women marrying British men and subsuming themselves into British culture for decades largely cut off from Japanese culture or ties to relations in Japan. Nonetheless, old-age provisioning, either that of their parents or their own, causes them to rethink their positions. In late middle age, their sensitivity to Japanese familial responsibilities and relationships is reawakened. However for many, geographical and cultural distance and the passage of time is too great and the continuous inter-generational chain of old-age support in Japanese family culture is short-circuited by their transnational existence

Part IV examines transnational families' community networking, specifically the role of religious organizations in offering extensive deloc-alized associational ties, sometimes as an alternative to highly localized family and community ties of the original home area. Religious affiliation can be central to contestation over authority within family life, not only in moral terms but also in terms of gendering intra-familial authority and economic behaviour.

Van Dijk's chapter demonstrates how Dutch Ghanaians look to the Pentecostal Church in the Netherlands for the deconstruction of Ghanaian traditions in favour of international mobility. The Pentecostal Church strongly identifies and indeed propagates modern notions of individualism and the nuclear family. In this way traditional matrilineal social organiz-ation is displaced by more Western-style conjugality mediated by Pente-costalist beliefs.

Barot's chapter examines a different religious tradition, that of East African Asians in the Swaminarayan movement of Britain, who trace their community networks back to outward-directed merchants in the British colonial context of nineteenth-century Gujarat, India. Motivated by both religious and commercial goals, adherents of the Swaminarayan move-ment have successfully mobilized symbolic and financial capital for the attainment of family economic welfare and business success. There are strong familial pressures on youth to conform to the older generation's economic trajectory and marriage partner preferences, but there is some flexibility in the system, and the transition of the younger generation into lucrative professional careers, as opposed to more traditional business careers, assuages parental opinion.

Part V examines religious, political and economic forms of networking, especially those that stretch across the north-south divide of rich and poor countries. Salzbrunn writes of the creation of transnational social spaces as a kind of new migration. Embedded in these spaces, different types of networks facilitate the exchange of various kinds of resources. Focusing on the 'reprivatization of religion' with respect to Sahelian Muslim immigrants in France, she shows how migrants are restricting religion to the individual sphere allowing for the combination of secular and modern, and the freedom to adapt to French cultural influences. In this way the religious grip on everyday behaviour is relaxed and lifestyle activities and mannerisms that were not considered appropriate in a strictly Islamic frame of reference become an acceptable part of everyday life for many Sahelian Muslims in France. Through transnational networks linking France with Senegal, this approach to life has started to have an effect on national Senegalese politics.

Blion (Chapter 11) highlights recent discussions in the arena of non-governmental organizations about development aid and the role of migrants in advancing aid transfers. There has been considerable publicity about this but it is generally recognized that migrants' remittances to their home countries are substantial in magnitude and represent vital injections of cash and in-kind payments. Beyond this, migrant associations as conduits for Western aid efforts can be effective, not only in cutting out various middle men but in being capable of identifying forms of aid and their optimal destinations.

Kane's study (Chapter 13) bears out several of the above points. Senegalese River migrant associations have an impressive track record in provisioning goods and services to village communities in West Africa. However, he questions whether this will be carried on by the next generation who have far weaker ties to those village communities, and whether Western donor intervention by its very nature has an ambiguous influence on the success of these transfers.

Conclusion

From a Western perspective, there has been a tendency to make the family synonymous with the household; the management and sharing of everyday life in a common dwelling. This conflation, largely due to the positioning of households as targets of social policies, would woefully fail to capture the composition and structure of transnational families. Transnational families' sense of place is continually being reformulated through their locational dispersal.

When historical conditions or traumatic events cause people to disperse, can we start talking of transnationalism as a way of life, a frontiering lifestyle? What factors contribute to the making of transnational family identities? How do transnational family members relate to one another throughout their life cycles? How are geographical distances bridged within the transnational family? How do transnational families build community and more extended national and international networks? As transnational families cohere within and between various nation states, how do nation states and transnational families accommodate each other? Are transnational families simultaneously dependent on the existence of nation-states and incongruent with nation-states' underlying principles? The following chapters wrestle with these questions.

References

Anderson, B. (1985), *Imagined Communities*, London, Verso.

Appadurai, A. (1996), *Modernity at Large: Cultural Dimensions of Globalization*, Minneapolis, University of Minnesota Press.

Bauman, Z. (1998), *Globalization: The Human Consequences*, Cambridge, Polity Press.

Bourdieu, P. (1998), *Practical Reason: On the Theory of Action*, Cambridge, Polity Press.

Brah, A. (1998), *Cartographies of Diaspora: Contesting Identities*, London, Routledge.

Braidotti, R. *Nomadic Subjects: Embodiment and Sexual Difference in Contemporary Feminist Theory*, New York, Columbia University Press, 1994

Cohen, R. (1997), *Global Diasporas: An Introduction*, Seattle, University of Washington Press.

Coward, R. (1983), *Patriarchal Precedents: Sexuality and Social Relations*, London, Routledge & Kegan.

Escobar, A. (1995), *Encountering Development: The Making and Unmaking of the Third World*, Princeton, Princeton University Press.

Limerick, P.N., Milner, C.A. and Rankin, C.E. (eds) (1991), *Trails: Toward a New Western History*, Lawrence, Kansas.

Maine, H.S. (1861/1906), *Ancient Law*, London, John Murray.

McClintock, A. (1995), *Imperial Leather: Race, Gender and Sexuality in the Colonial Contest*, New York and London, Routledge.

Mohanty, C.T. (1991), 'Cartographies of Struggle: Third World Women and the Politics of Feminism' in C.T. Mohanty, A. Russo and L. Torres (eds) *Third World Women and the Politics of Feminism*, Bloomington, Indiana University Press.

Strathern, M. (1992), *After Nature: English Kinship in the Late Twentieth Century*, Cambridge, Cambridge University Press.

Todd, E. (1990), *Invention de l'Europe*, Paris, Editions du Seuil.

Yuval-Davis, N. (1997), *Gender and Nation*, London, Sage.

Notes

1. In this chapter and throughout the book, the term 'Europe' is used as shorthand to refer primarily to Western European countries, specifically the countries of the EU and those countries that are not technically members of the EU but whose boundaries are surrounded by Union members, notably Norway and Switzerland.

2

Europe's Transnational Families and Migration: Past and Present

Deborah Bryceson

The age of European nation states emerged from centuries of regional conflicts of loyalty and bloodshed. The European nation offered and, of course, enforced a streamlined locational and cultural identity amongst its citizenry. Transnationalism, the espousal of different locational loyalties and cultures, was potentially subversive, yet European trade and colonial conquest have provided a major impetus to transnationalism over the past four centuries. Transnational family formation in Europe, and indeed worldwide, is tied to economic and political trends in Europe's history. This chapter provides a broad sketch of how transnational families have cohered in and beyond Europe through time. Today's transnational families in Europe are compared with families involved in mass migration from Europe to the Americas in the latter half of the nineteenth century. Similarities as well as striking contrasts emerge.

The first two sections centre on past and present migration patterns in Europe and their impact on the formation of transnational families and networks. The third section cites two case studies of transnational family mobility from the Netherlands in the nineteenth century and to the Netherlands in the twentieth century to illustrate converging and diverging tendencies, before concluding with a brief consideration of Europe's mixed legacy of fostering as well as denying and sometimes destroying transnational families through time.

Migration and Transnational Family Formation in European History

Since the establishment of nation states, the spatial mobility of mass populations has been closely associated with political border controls and occupational restructuring. Western Europe has witnessed periods of relatively high mobility as well as long periods of relative immobility of its national populations. Four mobility regimes are distinguished here: first, the relative immobility of pre-industrial Europe; second the long-distance mass movement of outbound Europeans from 1840–1910; third, the checks on European mass movement from 1910–1950, and fourth, the reactivation of mass mobility and its reorientation towards rather than away from Europe from 1950 onwards. Migration and transnational family formation during all four periods will be outlined in this section.

Pre-industrial Europe before the 1840s

In the agrarian societies of medieval and early modern Europe, the spatial mobility of the vast majority of families was restricted. Inheritance practices tied sons, particularly oldest sons, to homesteads that were passed down from generation to generation. Exogamous marriage practices ordained limited mobility on the part of young women, who usually married men in the region surrounding their natal homestead (Laslett 1965, Mitterauer and Sieder 1982). European serfdom rooted farmers in the agrarian landscape of a specific locality. As feudal power waned and towns and nation states took shape, occupational mobility spurred rural-urban migration rather than international migration.

Transnational families post-date the formation of European nation states by definition. Europe's first transnational families were primarily drawn from the nobility and extremely wealthy merchant classes. Intermarriage across national boundaries was the norm for Western Europe's royal families. Rigidly hierarchical class systems ordained that individuals at the pinnacle of the social pyramid had to find marriage partners of equivalent social standing to ensure the continuation of 'blue blood'. This frequently entailed matchmaking over long distances. Dynastic marriages were a vital tool for forging strategic geographical alliances and consolidating the political power of Europe's royal families. Along with great battles, they formed the very essence of the region's political history. Reading between the lines, many of these transnational marriages posed great trials for the individuals involved. Language barriers, cultural alienation and homesickness were common. Children born from these unions sometimes found themselves within two competing rather than blended cultures, as courtly power politics weaved an intricate web around them. However, far from being a mass phenomenon, these early transnational families, privileged and often socially problematic, were highly restricted in number.

At the opposite end of the class spectrum, at the instigation of European trading interests between the sixteenth and the eighteenth centuries, an estimated 11 to 13 million slaves were transported to the Americas (Hopkins 1973). The vast majority of the people seized and transported into slavery were between the ages of 15 and 30, two-thirds of them being men. Needless to say, in addition, to being anti-human, the slave trade was anti-family, deliberately demoralizing its victims with the forceful imposition of an irrevocable and unbreachable separation of family members. The transatlantic slave trade fragmented rather than linked family members through its transnationalism.

European settler families gradually began migrating to colonize the Americas from the sixteenth through the eighteenth centuries. Besides the freedom to return to their European-based families, the general prevalence of literacy amongst them facilitated communication with relations albeit infrequently. With the onset of formal European colonialism first in North and South America and later in parts of Asia, elite transnational families of a new sort emerged. In the late eighteenth and nineteenth centuries, men in the colonial civil services increasingly ventured abroad with their families (Allen 1979). Being relatively well endowed with wealth, communications and transport, they could retain family links with their home countries, where they eventually planned to return, tropical fortune and health permitting. However, these early colonial settlers and civil service personnel represented a trickle in comparison to the flood of people who left Europe and crossed the Atlantic in the nineteenth century, particularly during the latter half of the century.

Mass Settler Movement, 1840–1910

An estimated 52 million people left Europe between 1860 and 1914, most heading for the Americas (Moch 1992). The European influx was analogous to a tidal wave engulfing the American hemisphere. Although political unrest gripped mid-nineteenth-century Europe, historians are generally agreed that the mass movement was spurred primarily by economic rather than political factors. The industrial revolution in northern Europe profoundly altered family livelihoods in rural and urban areas and smallholder farming populations experienced a wide range of push and pull forces on their agrarian ways of life (Livi-Bacci 1997). Peasant families' time-honoured ties with the soil loosened as they failed to compete successfully with cheap grain imports from the American prairies and urban factory work beckoned their youth.

Increasingly, people, even those resident in rural areas, earned their income from non-agricultural sources, and youth were particularly attuned to avenues for alternative higher-paying work. International migration was one such avenue but it was not always a straight road. While some migrated directly from farms, others went first to nearby towns or the national capital before boarding the ocean liner to cross the Atlantic (Baines 1994). Early migrants tended to leave their farms as just-married couples or young families, hoping to resume their farming occupation in a country with abundant land resources. Over time, an increasing number tried their luck in a nearby town, giving the labour migration flow a much more industrial flavour. Migrants were leaving European cities with glutted labour markets in search of urban jobs in the newly industrializing cities of the North American seaboard.

As the nineteenth century progressed, migrants were typified by their status as young adults in the peak economically active age group between 20 and 40 years of age. A majority were male, most being single at the time when they migrated.[1] Their mobility rested on being unmarried and free of direct dependants, and eager to find viable forms of employment. Economists have claimed a direct correlation between migration rates and wage differentials between sending and receiving countries (Hatton and Williamson 1994). This would infer a finely tuned flow of information between populations in sending and receiving countries. In fact, migration decisions were contingent on a wide range of circumstances pertaining to the individual and the specific region and country from which he or she migrated.

Differential rates of emigration between European countries (Table 2.1) and individual country rate variations over time provide clues to some of the forces at play.

The devastating famines experienced in Ireland during the late 1840s, launched the transatlantic exodus of tens of thousands of tenant farmers. They were the first *en masse* migrants to the US, whose exodus peaked in the 1870s. The Scandinavian countries of Norway, Sweden and Denmark evidenced a similar pattern but not in such volume. Southern European migration started a decade or more later peaking in the first two decades of the twentieth century. Other countries like France and the Netherlands evidenced very low levels of migration indicative of more successful industrialization and alternative employment generation.

Return migration varied a great deal between different ethnic groups with less than 10 per cent of Jewish and Irish migrants ever returning versus roughly 60 per cent of Southern European Italians, Croatians and Slovenians doing so (Sowell 1996). When American-bound migration of Southern Europeans peaked, trans-Atlantic voyages had become faster and cheaper with the introduction of progressively larger steamships (Nugent 1992).

Differential migration rates applied both between as well as within European countries. Irish emigration was remarkable for its widespread

Table 2.1: European Emigration Rates by Decade (per 1,000 mean population)

Country	1851–60	1861–70	1871–80	1881–90	1891–1900	1901–10
Austria-Hungary	2.9	10.6	16.1	47.6	–	–
Belgium	–	–	–	8.6	3.5	6.1
British Isles	58.0	51.8	50.4	70.2	43.8	65.3
Denmark	–	–	20.6	39.4	22.3	28.2
Finland	–	–	–	13.2	23.2	54.5
France	1.1	1.2	1.5	3.1	1.3	1.4
Germany	–	–	14.7	28.7	10.1	4.5
Ireland	–	66.1	141.7	88.5	69.8	–
Italy	–	–	10.5	33.6	50.2	107.7
Netherlands	5.0	5.9	4.6	12.3	5.0	5.1
Norway	24.2	57.6	47.3	95.2	44.9	83.3
Portugal	–	19.0	28.9	38.0	50.8	56.9
Spain	–	–	–	36.2	43.8	56.6
Sweden	4.6	30.5	23.5	70.1	41.2	42.0
Switzerland	–	–	13.0	32.0	14.1	13.9
Average*	**16.0**	**30.3**	**31.1**	**41.1**	**30.3**	**40.4**

Source: Fenenczi and Willcox 1929 cited in Hatton and Williamson 1994: 7

* average of reporting countries

character throughout the country although the western and southern parts of Ireland were known to be the most heavily affected. In most countries, the bulk of emigration emanated from marginalized regions lacking labour-absorption capacity, areas with backward agriculture and restricted urban growth. Most migrants from the British Isles emanated from the desolate hill-farming areas of Scotland. In the Netherlands, it was the outlying regions, Friesland and Groningen in the north, Zeeland in the south and Gelderland in the east, which recorded the highest emigration rates (Swierenga 1985). These were often farming areas where population densities were not higher than average but land for cultivation was limited nonetheless by ownership and inheritance practices. The lack of farms subdividing constrained the growth of independent farmers and family formation (Blink 1915 cited in De Vries 1985).

The US was the major destination of European emigrants. There is an abundance of evidence to suggest that intra-familial communication was the central channel through which information was transmitted thereby spurring 'chain migration'. Migrants already settled in the US goaded those they had left behind to take the risk and join them. They sent letters through the postal services or word-of-mouth messages with go-betweens containing general information about living conditions, employment prospects, agricultural land availability and crop harvests.[2]

After finding viable occupations, some migrants were able to save sufficient sums of money to pay the ocean passage for family relations to follow. When European-based relations were facing acute distress this help was all the more forthcoming.[3] Whether or not extended families were involved in financing the ocean passage, migrants tended to settle in places where they knew their relations or fellow countrymen would be on hand. The need for help in finding housing, work or farmland in unfamiliar surroundings using a foreign language, and the lack of other institutional support, led most migrants to rely heavily on family relationships in the settlement process.

Not surprisingly, chain migration contributed to the formation of strong ethnic neighbourhoods with relational networks based on extended family ties. However, any general characterization of these ethnic neighbourhoods would be misleading. Their form and content depended on the migrants' countries of origin, cultural legacies and religious affiliations, their history of settlement, and whether they were located in rural or urban areas.

European Paralysis: World War I and Political Checks on Mass Movement, 1910–1950

The onset of World War I marked the end of European mass migration to the Americas. Military action interfered with the well-established passenger shipping businesses that plied the Atlantic. Adverse public opinion and national barriers to migration played their role. Significantly, the American government, bowing to mounting anti-immigrant pressure, imposed a literacy test on migrants in 1917 followed by legislation to restrict immigration during the 1920s.[4] But it was not just the demand-side of the migration equation that had changed. On the supply-side, migration to the US consistently fell short of official quotas from 1921 onwards.

A fundamental change had taken place in Europe. Hatton and Williamson (1994) argue that rates of natural increase were declining in Europe from 1870s onwards. Many men of migrating ages were killed or maimed during World War I, and communications between American and European family branches, which had fuelled the process of chain migration, had broken down due to the disruption of war and were not easy to resuscitate.

Meanwhile, the mood of the times had radically altered. Ultra-nationalism in the form of Nazism and fascist thinking was gaining sway with 'cultural purity' rather than 'cultural blending' as part of this philosophy. Ethnic groups that were known to have operative transnational family ties, notably Jews, were highly suspect. Even more liberal governments that did not espouse such views were enacting policies promoting isolationism rather than international migration. Economic emigration tapered off in the 1920s and virtually disappeared in the 1930s at the time when political refugees from fascist regimes were beginning to surface. It was replaced with the forced migration of Jews to concentration camps during World War II. Like the period of the European slave trade, transnational family formation during this period was inflicted from above and was designed to decimate rather than accommodate familial and network ties over long distances.

It is estimated that 30 million people were displaced between 1939 and 1945 (Moch 1992). As is common during war, World War II soldiers left behind 'love-children' where they fought, returning home often not knowing that they were fathers, or preferring not to know. Meanwhile, the children of these liaisons were often shunned as bastards, derided and denied their transnational family heritage.

Turning the Tables: Europe as a Major Destination for Immigration

In the wake of such extreme cultural isolationism and political tension, Western Europe began opening up to multiculturalism and transnational family existence during the latter half of the twentieth century. Having experienced net emigration for the major part of the two preceding centuries, European countries witnessed a rising tide of immigration which can be roughly periodicized as: 1950–75 when various European countries actively encouraged immigration, 1975–90 when immigration laws for labour recruitment became less relaxed but family reunification and political asylum seeking were legitimatized, and the 1990s to the present when the supply of potential migrants has surged forward and European immigration has become a hotly contested public issue with strong political lobbies for and against. In setting out this broad periodicization, there are several caveats. The timing of each phase varies from country to country. Rather than being sharply demarcated, the periods overlap and may be operating simultaneously in some places. However, most countries within the European Union have displayed some semblance of this sequence to greater or lesser degree.

Europe's Turning Point: From Source to Migration Destination, 1950–1975

World War II catalysed drastic realignments of political and economic power balances in the world. The writing was on the wall for European colonialism. Britain and France dismantled their colonial empires during the course of the 1950s and 1960s, but Portugal was slower to react and only gradually conceded independence to its colonies from the 1970s onwards.

As the major site of military action during the war, Western European countries' experienced heavy destruction of their economic infrastructure. The Marshall Plan was an important boost that helped lay the foundation for regional economic prosperity during the latter part of the 1950s. The economic boom led to labour shortages, especially in northern European countries, prompting them to open their doors to the migration of selective groups notably: southern Europeans including Italians, Spaniards and Portuguese, as well as the recruitment of Turks for work in West Germany, Magrebians in France, and West Indians and Asians in the UK.

There was a tendency for ex-colonial powers to recruit from their former colonies, but the recruitment had a progressively widening pattern. As Southern Europeans achieved better living standards, they were less impelled to migrate. Turks and North Africans replaced them.

Given the labour supply purpose of the migration, it is not surprising to find that the majority of the migrants were unskilled, single men. As Erel and Izuhara and Shihata (Chapters 6 and 8) demonstrate in their case studies, single women were, however, also part of this migration stream. In the case of the Japanese women migrants interviewed by Izuhara and Shihata, social rather than economic objectives spurred their migration.

Germany, France and Great Britain were in the forefront of labour recruitment in drives to reassert their industrial power in the post-war setting. Thus, many of the jobs entailed factory work. In Britain, along with the recruitment of South Asians to work in the country's textile mills, British Rail and the London Underground targeted West Indians for the transport sector. Meanwhile, low-paying domestic and service-sector jobs in Northern Europe attracted Italians, Spaniards and Portuguese, who were responding to the wage gap between Northern and Southern Europe.

The migrants entered the job market on the bottom rung of the ladder, obtaining low-paid jobs that nationals avoided. Labour recruitment procedures tended to assume that the worker would return to his/her home country in due course, as described by Erel (Chapter 6) and Kane (Chapter 13). In Germany, this was made explicit with the term 'guest-workers'. A migrant worker's remuneration package often included hostel accommodation and the fare home at the end of his contract. It was assumed that he was a target worker very much along the lines of colonial mining and plantation labour policies, which had entailed paying bachelor wages to migrant workers who returned to their families and villages after completion of a work contract. Despite these circumstances, migrant labourers renewed their contracts time and again and laid down roots and a sense of residential permanency that they strove to legalize (Blotevogel et al. 1993, Ogden 1993).

Family Togetherness and Security in Europe: Migrant Families' Reunification and Political Asylum-seeking, 1975–90

The oil crisis of 1973–74 brought the period of active European migrant labour recruitment to an abrupt end. In July 1974, France denied entry to North Africans and West Germany closed its labour recruitment centres abroad and encouraged large numbers of workers to return to their countries of origin. With the exception of the Netherlands, most European countries' migration rates showed a marked downward trend (King 1993).

As European countries drastically curtailed migrant entry and banned permanent immigration, they conceded to the reunification of migrant families, making it, along with political asylum, the main legal means for foreigners to settle permanently in the country. Many international conventions guarantee the individual's right to family life. France instituted its family reunion policy in 1975. It also became prevalent in Germany although it was of a *de facto* rather than of a *de jure* nature (Blotevogel et al. 1993).

In all the European countries of receiving immigrants, the definition of family included the spouse and children under 18 years, but in some cases was extended to include older relatives and other family members. The type of marriage was, however, a thorny issue. Most countries now demand proof that migrants have not contracted a marriage of convenience in order to gain national entry. Also, most rule out polygamous wives and families. There has been vacillation about this in France. In 1993, more than one wife could be brought into the country but this was rescinded in 1997 (OECD 2000). Conditions for family reunion include stipulations regarding the length of stay of the original family member and the provision of adequate means of subsistence and accommodation for the family. Not surprisingly, as European migration policy became grounded on family reunion, women's presence in the migration stream strengthened markedly. On the separate but related issue of 'mixed marriage', the same stipulations did not apply. Marriage between a

European national and a non-European national however created gender-biased legal anomalies in some countries like Germany (Breger 1998). Residence and citizenship rights accorded to a non-European woman married to a European man tended to be superior to that of a European woman given the patriarchal basis of civil law.

The 1970s witnessed a number of political crises throughout the world that catapulted people into a refugee status: the East African Asian crisis engendered by Idi Amin's regime in Uganda, Pinochet's power seizure from Allende in Chile and the fall of the Shah of Iran. European countries were often the first port of call for refugees seeking asylum. In the case of the Ugandan Asians, many found that their British passports did not afford them the easy entry they had hoped because Britain had started limiting Commonwealth immigration from the 1960s, downgrading their residence and citizenship rights (Mamdani 1973 and Barot, Chapter 10). Many Chileans claimed European nationalities on the basis of descent. As increasing numbers of refugees and their families sought asylum, European governments wrestled with the humanitarian ethics of exclusionary immigration laws. These issues as well as geo-political considerations came to a head in 1989 when the Berlin Wall fell and the communist regimes of Eastern Europe unravelled, spurring millions of East Europeans to escape poverty and strife and seek a better life in Western Europe. Between 1988 and 1991, 1.2 million East Europeans arrived in West Germany alone (Skeldon 1997).

Fortress Europe: Rising Immigration Pressure, 1990s and Beyond

As the increasing globalization of commodities and capital was heralded as a sign of a new era of world prosperity and democracy, the logical attendant free flow of labour across international boundaries was not part of the development agenda of post-industrial nation states during the 1990s. International financial institutions argued that cultural barriers and political dangers were harboured in an unimpeded flow of labour (World Bank 1995). In Europe, the supply of potential migrants far exceeded labour demand. European labour markets were in the process of restructuring and downsizing throughout the 1990s. Deindustrialization and the impact of information technology caused labour demands to contract, especially for unskilled, manual labour. Europe's unemployment rates were higher relative to its major trading partners (Skeldon 1997). However, there was a growing demand for highly educated, skilled labour, especially in the field of information technology.

Much has been said about 'Fortress Europe' in recent debates but the fact is that it is far from being an impenetrable fortress. European migration statistics record that the population of 'legal foreigners' increased by roughly 70 per cent over the course of the 1990s. SOPEMI[5] statistics, collected by the OECD and widely considered to be the most reliable statistics on migration, are problematic in that they rely on data collected by individual nations, which vary in their data-collecting methods and analytical criteria.

The national counts of 'stocks of foreigners', the most widely available statistic, do not report total numbers that have migrated to a country for two reasons. First, many incoming foreigners are reclassified and no longer counted as foreigners when they gain citizenship. Individual countries' citizenship requirements vary widely so it is impossible to make any general deductions about the influence of this on the total number of foreigners.[6] Second, the published statistics do not encompass the rising numbers who have migrated illegally, especially to the larger countries like Germany and Britain (OECD 2000). Organized long-distance smuggling networks are contributing to the increase. Tens of thousands enter overland through Eastern Europe or by boat along the Mediterranean and North Atlantic coasts. Others enter and apply for political asylum. As Table 2.2 shows, grants of political asylum have stayed relatively static throughout the 1990s whereas applications have skyrocketed. The asylum application process can take a long time in some countries. It is believed that those whose applications are rejected rarely leave but join the ranks of illegal immigrants (Fielding 1993).

By the late 1990s, the recorded legal flows and numbers of foreign-born across Europe reveal a complicated pattern (Table 2.3). While 'traditional' migrant groups such as North Africans in France, Turks in Germany and Indians in the UK are still salient, there is now a more varied mosaic of countries represented in the migration stream. Diverse nationalities, especially from developing countries, have surfaced. Somalis, for example, have become prominent in the Nordic countries. Some nationalities have joined the migration stream to Europe recently, arriving illegally, and therefore are not reflected in these statistics. They include increasing numbers of West Africans, notably Ghanaians, Nigerians, Senegalese and Congolese, and people from the Far East, especially China. Many of these migrants are poor and relatively unskilled. Economic liberalization policies promoted under the aegis of international financial institutions such as the World Bank in Sub-Saharan African, Asia and Latin America have had a profound effect on the livelihood prospects of people within these regions (Bryceson, Kay and Mooij 2000, Stalker

Table 2.2: Stocks of Foreign Population and Asylum Seekers in Selected European Countries, 1978–98

	Stocks of Foreign Population						Inflows of Asylum Seekers		
	Total numbers ('000)			1989–98 %-/+ Change	% of total pop'n		Total numbers ('000)		1990–99 %-/+ Change
	1978*	1989**	1998		1989	1998	1990	1999	
Austria	851	387	737	90	5.1	9.1	22.8	20.1	–11.8
Belgium		881	892	1	8.9	8.7	13.0	35.8	175
Denmark		151	256	70	2.9	4.8	5.3	6.5	23
Finland		21	85	301	0.4	1.6	2.7	3.1	15
France	3700		2875				54.8	30.9	–44
Germany	3981	4846	7320	51	7.7	8.9	193.1	95.1	–51
Greece							4.1	1.5	–63
Ireland		78	111	42	2.3	3.0	0.1	7.7	7600
Italy		490	1250	155	0.9	2.1	4.7	33.4	611
Luxembourg		107	153	43	27.9	35.6	0.1	2.9	2800
Netherlands	435	642	662	3	4.3	4.2	21.2	39.3	85
Norway		140	165	18	3.3	3.7	4.0	10.2	155
Portugal		101	178	76	1.0	1.8	0.1	0.3	200
Spain		250	720	188	0.6	1.8	8.6	8.4	–2
Sweden	424	456	500	10	5.3	5.6	29.4	11.2	–62
Switzerland	898	1040	1348	30	15.6	19.0	35.8	46.1	29
UK		1812	2208	22	3.2	3.8	38.2	91.2	139
Average				**73**	**6.0**	**7.6**	**438.0**	**443.7**	**1**

Source: OECD 1979, 1990, 2000, SOPEMI

* Figures for Belgium are for the year 1977, and for France for the year 1976
** Figures for France in 1990 were 3,597

2000). Exposed to world market competition of large-scale transnational corporations and the subsidised agriculture of the European Union and North America, developing countries' industries and peasant family agricultural units have struggled to survive. The vulnerability and lack of labour-absorbing capacity of developing country economies at the turn of the twenty-first century has generated circumstances similar to those that prompted European migrants' exodus to the Americas during the nineteenth century. Mass migration is under way with the difference being that the destination countries are less open to their entry.

It would, however, be a mistake to assume that current European immigration is solely characterized by mass migration of the economically displaced poor. Flows of highly educated migrants are also in process. East European migrants, notably those from the Former Yugoslavia and the Russian Federation, are often professionals able to speak several different European languages. Their emigration from Eastern Europe has been propelled by a mixture of political and economic factors in the wake of the demise of the communist bloc, as Al-Ali (Chapter 11) describes with reference to refugees who were faced with the carnage of the Bosnian war and its aftermath. The boundary between refugee and labour migrant is hazy.

Globalization during the 1990s represented labour opportunities for specially trained people in many occupations throughout Europe. This generated a supply response from existing and new international labour circuits. Intra-OECD migration flows followed some well-entrenched patterns, notably Scandinavians gravitated to neighbouring Scandinavian countries and Australians, South Africans and New Zealanders, using their commonwealth ties, migrated to the UK. Possibly indicative of closer European economic integration and new migrant flows, Luxembourg, Switzerland, the Netherlands and Ireland, all known for their banking, business service infrastructure, information technology and/or more lenient tax regimes recorded a majority of legal foreigners from other European or OECD countries. As capital and commodity flows become increasingly globalized, migrant populations have become highly hetero-geneous. Migrants, not only represent an increasing array of ethnic groups, they also cover the full class spectrum.

Over the past half-century, the OECD's post-industrial countries have become more uniformly prosperous while increasingly diverging from the national economies of the rest of the world. 'Globalization' is not global – in fact it has a very narrow base. As Europe and other OECD countries have 'globalized', the world's non-OECD economies have become increasingly marginalized. Since the early 1990s, developing

Table 2.3: Relative Importance of Top Five Countries in Total Immigration Flows in 1998 and Stocks of Foreigners and Foreign-Born in 1997

Receiving Country / Top Five Sending Countries	A Inflows Foreigners in 1998 Percentage of total	B Stocks Foreigners in 1997 Percentage of total	A/B
BELGIUM			
France	14.6	11.5	1.3
Netherlands	12.3	9.1	1.4
Morocco	8.5	14.7	0.6
Germany	6.3	3.7	1.7
United States	5.6	1.4	4.0
Total ('000)	50.7	903.2	
DENMARK			
Somalia	8.6	4.1	2.1
Former Yugoslavia	7.1	13.5	0.5
Iraq	6.3	3.4	1.9
Germany	5.5	4.8	1.2
Norway	5.3	4.8	1.1
Total ('000)	20.4	237.7	
FINLAND			
Former USSR	29.8	23.6	1.3
Sweden	9.6	9.3	1.0
Estonia	8.1	12.0	0.7
GERMANY			
Poland	10.9	3.8	2.8
Former Yugoslavia	10.2	9.8	1.0
Turkey	8.0	28.6	0.3
Italy	5.9	8.3	0.7
Russian Federation	4.7	2.3	2.0
Total ('000)	605.5	7365.8	
GREECE			
Russian Federation	12.6	n.a.	
Bulgaria	7.6	n.a.	
Albania	7.1	n.a.	
Egypt	5.8	n.a.	
Romania	5.5	n.a.	
Total ('000)	38.2		
IRELAND			
United Kingdom	36.6	n.a.	
United States	11.6	n.a.	
Other countries	51.9	n.a.	
NETHERLANDS			
Morocco	6.5	20.0	0.3
Turkey	6.3	16.9	0.4
Germany	5.8	7.9	0.7
United Kingdom	5.8	5.8	1.0
United States	4.0	1.9	2.1
Total ('000)	81.7	678.1	
NORWAY			
Sweden	22.4	11.0	2.0
Denmark	8.0	11.5	0.7
United Kingdom	4.7	6.9	0.7
Germany	4.0	3.2	1.3
Somalia	4.0	..	..
Total ('000)	26.7	157.5	
SWEDEN			
Iraq	15.1	4.5	3.4
Finland	8.4	18.4	0.5
Former Yugoslavia	5.4	6.1	0.9

Receiving Country / Top Five Sending Countries	A Inflows Foreigners in 1998 Percentage of total	B Stocks Foreigners in 1997 Percentage of total	A/B
Somalia	4.3	6.5	0.7
Iraq	3.2	3.0	1.1
Total ('000)	8.3	80.6	
FRANCE			
Algeria	14.3	16.4	0.9
Morocco	13.8	16.9	0.8
Turkey	5.8	5.2	1.1
China	4.9	0.3	17
Tunisia	4.6	6.3	0.7
Total ('000)	116.9	3315.0	

Receiving Country / Top Five Sending Countries	A Inflows Foreigners in 1998 Percentage of total	B Stocks Foreigners in 1997 Percentage of total	A/B
Total ('000)	21.6	n.a.	
ITALY			
Albania	10.1	n.a.	
Morocco	6.6	n.a.	
Romania	5.3	n.a.	
Former Yugoslavia	5.1	n.a.	
United States	4.2	n.a.	
Total ('000)	111.0	n.a.	
LUXEMBOURG			
Portugal	18.7	n.a.	
France	18.7	n.a.	
Belgium	11.2	n.a.	
Germany	7.5	n.a.	
Italy	5.6	n.a.	
Total ('000)	10.7	n.a.	

Receiving Country / Top Five Sending Countries	A Inflows Foreigners in 1998 Percentage of total	B Stocks Foreigners in 1997 Percentage of total	A/B
Norway	4.6	5.6	0.8
Iran	4.1	4.8	0.9
Total ('000)	35.7	552.0	
SWITZERLAND			
Former Yugoslavia	15.4	n.a.	
Germany	12.4	n.a.	
France	7.2	n.a.	
Italy	7.1	n.a.	
Portugal	6.8	n.a.	
Total ('000)	74.9	n.a.	
UNITED KINGDOM (1997)			
United States	17.9	n.a.	
Australia	11.2	n.a.	
India	6.8	n.a.	
South Africa	5.5	n.a.	
New Zealand	5.1	n.a.	
Total ('000)	236.9	n.a.	

Source: OECD 2000, *Trends in International Migration* (SOPEMI), Paris

countries have conceded to WTO injunctions to remove their trade barriers, international communications and media have expanded, and the Western tourist industry has made new inroads into the developing world, the 'have nots' have become acutely aware of the 'haves'. Is it any wonder that Europe is an attractive destination for migrants and their families?

Contrasting Family Networking in the Nineteenth and Twentieth Centuries

As the preceding historical outline has argued, transnational families in Europe and from Europe are not new. However, at present, a more polarized world economy and more pervasively felt economic and political deprivation propel migration and transnational family formation. Have transnational families assumed radically new forms and contents under these circumstances? Have their means of self-definition, cohesion, emotional and economic interaction and relational dynamics altered in the current era of yawning economic disparities starkly juxtaposed by instantaneous global communications and jet travel?

The following is intended to be merely suggestive of some of the lines of convergence and divergence that have taken place over the past century when comparing two transnational families: the Onninks, Dutch emigrants to the US in 1865, and the Ouarrouds, Moroccan emigrants to the Netherlands in 1974.[7] The intention is not to claim historical or geographical representativeness for these two families. Rather they are two examples amongst millions of migrant families with transnational networks. They are chosen for comparison because they come from similar smallholder farming backgrounds and share the same motivation for migration. Both were intent on building a better life for themselves. Their experiences are roughly a century apart and involve the Netherlands as the point of departure in the nineteenth century and as the point of arrival in the twentieth century. The Onnink case study derives from the author's family geneology records and the Ouarroud study is based on the author's seven-year acquaintance with the family and in-depth interviews with two family members in 2002.

The US-bound Onninks from Gelderland, Eastern Netherlands, 1865–1940s

In September 1865, Jan Hendrik Onnink at the age of 27, just a day after marrying Hannah Berendina Lefferdink, set off with his new wife and his two younger brothers, Gerrit Jan and Herman Jan for America. Their reasons for migration from Gelderland were undoubtedly many, not least the farm tenancy system that prevented young men from establishing independent farms. No doubt the news of the end of the American Civil War combined with the letter that had arrived earlier that year from their great uncle, Gerrit Willem Walvoord who had settled in Gibbsville Wisconsin, were taken into account when they decided to emigrate. In January 1865, Walvoord wrote the following to Jan's father:

we inform you of the circumstances in which we are: the yield was rather successful except for the summer wheat and the hay, which suffered a lot due to the persistent drought; all the food articles for cattle and people are expensive, particularly the bacon: 14 cents a pound; beef: 10–12 cents; butter 32 to 34 cents, this also makes good cattle so expensive . . . The days wages are also much higher than before because in March there has been a war [American Civil War] going on for 4 years and such involves a lot of expenses and brings poverty to many because surely you must have heard that they must draw lots here and the last time they cast for conscription, Tobias drew a bad number . . . you know what the Lord says . . . a house or country that is divided against itself will be destroyed and it is the same over here about it . . . we let you know that we enjoy rather good health . . . J.W. Wilterdink and his wife are also well, as are Dulmes and his wife and children. And we also let you know that we have a family of 6 children: 2 boys and 4 girls (one little boy is deaf) and they all look good, fresh and healthy . . .

On 26 November, 1865, Harmen Jan describes their journey and arrival in Gibbsville, Wisconsin:

We . . . arrived here on the 6th of this month at the Walvoord home . . . yes, all friends and acquaintances who heard of our arrival came speedily to see us, to hear out of our mouths some news again out of Holland. And thus we were asked if there weren't any more people who had put their minds to coming to America. We told them that there were indeed a few who would like to do so, but who sometimes lacked the money. And others who could afford it, did not want to, because they were worried about the trip and consequently there were not many who did come. So they told us here that those people would be crazy to bring the landowners so much yield and to toil from dawn till dusk and yet have barely enough bread to eat. I will not write anything further about this, for we really cannot say much about America as yet.

About the 17-day ocean voyage from Liverpool to New York, he writes:

Yes . . . there were all sorts of people: Frenchmen, Englishmen, Irishmen, Germans, Italians, and only 33 of us were Dutchmen. There were also three blacks, but those are mainly to be found in New York over here . . . we were in the company of 2 Americans. One by the name of J. Vogel who had fetched his family from Holland. The other had been to Holland just for fun. Those two were of great use to us that way, for they had a good command of English . . . and told us what we should do . . . So we sailed slowly on and after travelling for 17 days we arrived in New York . . . Yet we had to stay off-shore from that Sunday afternoon until Monday afternoon when we were taken to Castel Garden and there we had to pay again for the remaining stretch to Milwaukee 46 and a half dollars as well as 6 dollars for the excess weight of the luggage.

The Onnink brothers farmed in Wisconsin for five years, then the three brothers and their wives set out for Nebraska in ox-drawn covered wagons. They were responding to the Dutch-language American news-paper that advertised the opening of new prairie land for farming. Under the Homestead Act, the American government allocated 80-acre plots per family. After farming the plot for five years, the family received title deeds to the land. They moved to Firth Nebraska where another brother joined them from the Netherlands. Although there is no record of any one of the four brothers or their wives ever returning to the Netherlands to visit their families, they continued corresponding with them. Over the period 1865 to 1911, 30 letters from the brothers were preserved by their Netherlands-based relations, giving an insight into their lives. In 1878, after a visit from his elderly mother, Jan Hendrik wrote to her and his four remaining brothers in the Netherlands, giving his views on the necessity for settler farming on America's great plains:

it pleased us . . . that Mother just once came and visited us in her old age, and made this 'little trip' over the Atlantic ocean. And then travelled an additional 1400 or 1500 miles overland in America by railroad.

As far as the crops are concerned, everything grows and stands very nicely . . . Oats are extraordinarily good. I didn't sow much oats, only 8 acres or 20 *schepelzaat* in Gelderland. That is, however, a lot by your standards! . . .

The United States are less dependent on any other country. Gold, copper, iron, cotton, tobacco, etc. are found or grown here. We are, however, dependent on Europe as such, because if we would not export all of these goods, then we would have everything in excess and we would not get good prices for these goods. And still there are thousands of acres of fertile land which is not cultivated.

The natives of America were called Indians by Columbus. Copper-colored or redskins they are mostly called. They live off hunting, fishing, and stealing. But the same will happen to them as to the Cananites. They will be removed by the whites. They cannot be taught how to farm, and they don't even want to. As far as religion is concerned, they are hopeless, because they are very hostile to the missionaries . . . Our government always has soldiers (mercenaries) handy in areas where Indians dwell in order to protect whites and settlements, because sometimes they rob and murder tremendously.

Thus, their farming settlement in the American Midwest was seen as God-ordained. North American Indians' use of the prairies for hunting was considered to be a gross waste that had to be corrected. The Onnink family, having made Nebraska their base, continued to reside there from generation to generation and identified themselves as Americans. Their Dutch community settlement spanned three small villages: Firth, Pella and Holland. A Dutch Reformed church was established immediately following the migration of Dutch families. There they raised their children.

Jan Hendrick and his wife Janna had 10 children, 8 of whom survived to adulthood. In 1885, their oldest born Jane Gertrude married another second-generation Netherlander David Lensink. They raised 13 children amongst whom Albert, their third son married Jenny Liesveld in 1914 another third-generation Netherlander who traced her roots back to Gelderland. They raised 7 children, three girls and four boys, but it was in the fourth generation that the agrarian and linguistic roots of the family began to loosen.

This generation was the first that was not Dutch speaking. Services in their local Dutch Reformed church began to be delivered in English in the mid-1930s. This generation married just after World War II. The girls were sanctioned by their parents to marry outside the local community if they wanted to because there was concern that there had been too much inter-marriage in the small rural community. All three girls married men with non-Dutch ancestry. The boys all started farming in the area, but American farming changed in the decades that followed. Small family farms were being edged aside by larger, agro-industrial farms. By the time of their retirement, only one of the four brothers had managed to hold on to his farm and make it prosper.[8]

This is therefore a story of a transnational migrant family that lost its direct transnational connections in the second generation due to the long duration and high cost of transport between the US and Europe during the nineteenth century. Yet, for all intents and purposes, the Dutch-speaking rural community with its heavily interlaced Dutch social networks, transposed a rural Netherlands community into the American Midwest, retaining its cultural and religious coherence for over 60 years. Two American-born generations were raised in tightly knit social networks centring on the Dutch Reformed Church.

The Netherlands-bound Ouarrouds from Northern Morocco, 1970s–90s

In 1980 at the age of 30, Fatima, a Berber-speaking woman from a small village in the Northern Rif mountains of Morocco, migrated to the Netherlands. She came with her five children following her husband Hassan who had already obtained a job and had been allocated a house by a municipal government authority. It had taken six years for Hassan to establish this base for his family. As Fatima explained:

> My husband went to Toulouse because he had a friend who had already gone to France and was working in a vineyard there. He told my husband that the vineyard was looking for more people to work . . . Hassan left because there was no money. Life was very hard in our village. There was not enough water. One had to walk kilometres for water. Hunger was frequent and women died in childbirth because there were no medical facilities and no schools. None of us had the chance to learn to read. It wasn't that things were getting worse, it was just that we knew there was a better life elsewhere. That's why he left . . .

Hassan had in fact migrated to France in 1974 just when the government was reacting to the international oil crisis and economic recession with a clampdown on immigration. Through family networks and luck he found his way to the Netherlands.

> After harvesting grapes for 6 months, my husband's contract was up. There was no more work. He then went to my mother's uncle who had already settled in Lille some years before. Hassan stayed with my uncle but he found it impossible to get work there. However, Hassan heard from some other Moroccans that there was work in the Netherlands and that that country was issuing visas. He took a bus to Holland. He knew no one in Holland. He arrived in Den Haag where he found a community of Moroccans and Turks near the railway station . . . He asked around and heard that there was an area of glasshouses not too far away, about 25 kms, called Schipluiden where they were hiring people. Hassan arrived in that area and went from place to place asking for work. He eventually found a farmer in Den Hoorn near Delft who was growing roses in glasshouses. He agreed to hire my husband for 3 months.

Hassan worked two consecutive three-month contracts before his boss hired him permanently. His boss agreed to write a letter in Dutch to Fatima, and Hassan then had this translated into Arabic by friends in Den Haag. He posted it to Fatima's uncle who could read Arabic and verbally translated it into Berber since Fatima could not read. As Fatima recalls:

My uncle was so happy that my husband had a permanent job . . . In the letter Hassan promised to come home after two months. In fact, he did so, bringing lots of presents: clothing for my daughters, a radio for me as well as European underwear which I found very strange and was rather embarrassed to wear because no woman wore underwear in my village. He also brought money for us to live on . . . This was the first of three annual visits when he brought money and presents to me for housekeeping.

Hassan was fortunate to find work in the Netherlands just before family reunion policies and measures to improve migrants' access to housing were implemented (Dieleman 1993). This provided the green light for Fatima and her children to join Hassan. Fatima vividly recalls her arrival in the Netherlands.

In 1979 I received a letter from my husband saying that he had been allocated a house in Schipluiden [located between Den Haag and Rotterdam] by the Dutch social housing department. He got a terraced house because he told the social services that he had a family . . . When I succeeded in getting a passport in Casablanca and knew that I was really going to the Netherlands I was ecstatic. At Oujda, I boarded the plane bound for Amsterdam with Hassan and my 5 children . . . I told my children that 'I'm born again. I'll never starve again.' The flight was about three and a half hours long. We arrived at Amsterdam airport and it was another world. I was immediately conscious of how different I looked. I was wearing a long skirt whereas all the women around me were wearing short skirts. Hassan took me to the house in Schipluiden. My first thought was that the house had so many big windows in all the rooms. I didn't feel comfortable with the idea that people could look in and see me and my family. It was so different from Morocco, shameful by Moroccan customs. But I was very happy to be in Holland where I could raise my family without hardship.

However only a year after her arrival, Fatima encountered hardship made all the more traumatic by her immigrant status, her inability to speak Dutch and lack of extended family support:

I remembered Morocco but I didn't want to remember. I wanted to make a new start in life but then within a couple of months of my arrival I was pregnant with Nazim, my sixth child. After Nazim's birth I kept bleeding and bleeding. The doctor said he had to operate. I had a hysterectomy and had to stay in the hospital for one month and 8 days. When I returned home I was still very sick. My husband soon rejected me. He told me I was no longer a useful wife and that he wanted to get a new wife. He ordered me to return to Morocco and started beating me when I refused. Things were very bad. Under Dutch law he was not allowed to have a second wife as would be the case in Morocco. He was very angry with me for not giving him a divorce and returning with the children to Morocco. We continued to live in the same house, but daily life was a nightmare.

Samira, Fatima's youngest daughter, currently 23 years of age, takes up the story describing the distressing events that ensued in 1983 which she remembers clearly although she was very young:

I was five years old and playing outside in the front of the house with my little brother Nazim . . . I was three years older than him and he always stayed close to me . . . My older brother Habit who was nine years old at the time was also outside. I remember my father driving up in his Mercedes. It was a very old but big car. He said to us: 'Come, I'm going to the market in Den Haag' . . . there was a big open market in Den Haag, with lots of nice things to eat and buy. Habit and I were keen to go. Nazim wanted to come with me, so I told my mom I would look after Nazim. She didn't like the idea, but we children so wanted to go, so she had to agree. In fact even then my mother was very apprehensive that something was going to happen to us. I remember that my dad gave all of us kids something to eat soon after we got in the car. The next thing that I remember was waking up and not being in Holland. Habit knew it was Spain. My father told us we were going on vacation. We were on our way to Morocco. In fact my father had stolen my mother's passport which had all of her children's names in it. He took the ferry to Morocco and then drove to . . . the house of his brother . . . My father left us there because he had to go back to his job in the Netherlands. It was awful. My uncle beat us. We stayed there for six months before my mother could rescue us.

Fatima continues the story:

Three of my children had been kidnapped. I was in a terrible situation. I had no money of my own. I couldn't go to Morocco to get them and leave my other three older children in the Netherlands. I wasn't able to speak Dutch yet. I was mostly at home. Most of the people I knew were other Moroccans living in Den Haag or Rotterdam. There were no Moroccans resident in Schipluiden other than us. I had learned a bit of Dutch here and there . . . from my interaction with Dutch people and my neighbours. This really helped me when my troubles began. Nonetheless I was really alone. The person I had to rely upon primarily was my daughter Hordia. She was fluent in Dutch because she had attended a Dutch school for two years. Although she was only 12 years old, she was my go-between with the Dutch social service people who took up my case. They helped me to get my children back. Six months after the kidnapping I went to Morocco with the Dutch social worker and Hordia and got my children. This was my first time to return to Morocco. It was a very disturbing time, but I got my children back and we all returned to Holland. Thereafter, I divorced Hassan. There was a lot of red tape, but my children and myself were allowed to stay in the Netherlands and continue living in the little house in Schipluiden. I raised my six children on my own.

Fatima's determination and force of personality have made her a focal point for extended family network activity. She has extended family relations in France and Belgium but most are settled within a 25 km radius around her home in the Netherlands. The various branches of the family keep in close telephone contact. Frequently, at weekends, there are big extended family feasts with Moroccan dishes of couscous, chicken, lamb and vegetable tagins. These occasions take place annually at Ramadan and for commemoration of the Prophet Ibrahim's sacrifice of his son Ismail marked with the slaughter and roasting of a whole sheep. In addition to religious holidays there are births, engagements, weddings and funerals. The feasts involve a great deal of work for the women. Fatima confesses to sometimes hiring another Moroccan woman to cook for her because she does not have the big cooking pans nor a kitchen large enough. Despite the work and the expense, these extended family occasions are vital to the family's continued unity and functioning as a mutual support network.

Since Fatima's children and nieces and nephews have all reached marriageable ages, engagement parties and wedding feasts have become frequent, but the selection of marriage partners is fraught. Various extended family members may intervene and exert pressure on the young female family members to marry specific men in Morocco. Merolla (Chapter 5) alludes to these pressures within the Dutch Moroccan community.

Fatima's associational ties are not restricted to Moroccans. Elke, a German woman that she met at the time of her divorce, has become like a sister to Fatima and an aunt to her children. Elke has offered advice and material support at critical times. In her block of flats, Fatima's female neighbours, mostly Moroccans and Turks, network daily, borrowing foodstuffs and helping each other with childcare.

Fatima fervently feels that life is about offering mutual support to family, friends and neighbours, which is the way people interact with one another in her Moroccan home area. She jokes about the contrasts between Morocco and the Netherlands. 'Living in Holland sometimes makes me feel like a mushroom. It's so dark, wet and cold here for so much of the time, I become very pale. In Morocco, there is sun and openness and people interact with one another more. They have to because people are poor and need each other's help whereas in the Netherlands people are busy making money and rushing about to their appointments.'

She has managed to purchase a house in a town near her home village, which she rents out. But opportunities for her to visit Morocco have been few. The five relatively short visits she has made over the past 10 years have all been connected with marriage arrangements for her children or illness amongst family members still living in Morocco. At 52 years of age and after nearly 20 years of residence in the Netherlands, Fatima's life is firmly planted in the Netherlands with her grown-up children and grandchildren who need her daily presence.

A Century Apart: Similarities and Differences

There are remarkable similarities between the two cases cited above. The Onninks and the Ouarrouds both emanated from agricultural backwaters where they saw no hope for their families' futures. Both used chain migration to ascertain work and resource availability in their destination countries. Both were involved in stepped migration, before they arrived at their final settlement point. Both moved in the wake of major economic turning points, namely the cessation of the American Civil War in 1865 and the international oil crisis of 1974. Both took advantage of economic opportunities in the destination country. The Onnink family benefited from the award of agricultural land under the Homestead Act whereas the allocation of social housing made it possible for family reunion and the settlement of Fatima and her five children with her husband in the Netherlands. Within only a couple of decades both families were surrounded by extended family networks in which they could interact along lines similar to those they knew from their home areas.

There are, however, significant differences that relate to family structure as well as changes in international communications. Whereas the Onninks migrated as a couple and retained a strong patriarchal tradition, in which divorce was virtually unthinkable, Fatima and her husband had had to live apart for several years prior to family reunion. Fatima's divorce was painful, made worse by her lack of financial means, but she coped and her extended family network as well as friends she made along the way helped her as a single parent.

The comparative ease of travelling to and from Morocco in the late twentieth century as opposed to the US in the late nineteenth century is significant. Bearing in mind that the distances are different, the migrant's journey is now easy thanks to air travel. Fatima spent less than four hours travelling by plane as opposed to the Onnink's sea and overland journey of almost a month. Furthermore, the possibility of going back and forth to one's home area provides a range of spatial choices and family residential arrangements that would not have been entertained a century earlier. When Hassan proposed sending his sick wife and children back to Morocco, his calculations were based on assumptions regarding the ease of international travel, the ease of divorce for men in Morocco, and his years as a single migrant worker free from the ups and downs of daily family life. Fatima adamantly refused to return because she saw the Netherlands as a better environment for herself and her family in contrast to the daily hardships of life in the Rif Mountains of Morocco. Although Morocco and the Netherlands are not far away in travel time they were worlds apart in her mind. Now she enjoys returning because she visits without the same threat of material want hanging over her. When she goes back to Morocco to facilitate her daughters' marriages, she is never empty handed. She can offer people material goods from the Netherlands.

The Onninks also experienced material success. They came to own farms far larger than they could have ever hoped to have in the Netherlands. They lost contact with their Dutch relations over the generations and eventually gave up speaking the Dutch language but they conserved their family's farming tradition over several generations in the American Midwest. Fatima, on the other hand, regrets the loss of her agrarian traditions. She loves growing plants, and used to have a small front garden at her house in Schipluiden where she cultivated maize, tomatoes and fig trees, somewhat to the annoyance of her Dutch neighbours who all had well-tended flower beds and bushes. However now that most of her children have left home, she lives in a high-rise block of flats without a garden and misses her maize crop and trees. Her hope is to return to Morocco once all her children have married.

Forging New Frontiers in Europe: Transnational Families and their Networks

This chapter's schematic overview of European transnational family formation through time has concluded with some nineteenth- and twentieth-century case study contrasts, serving to highlight the changing nature of family structures, the role of networking in migrant flows to Europe and the embeddedness of transnational families in mutual support networks following residential settlement. The tension between Europe's predilection for ethnic consolidation and its growing global multiculturalism has also been observed.

The comparative case-study material in this chapter illustrates the conceptual utility of frontiering and relativising. Relativised family relationships are apparent when contrasting the two families. The Onninks were male headed and patriarchal in form, whereas the Ouarrouds became female headed. Generally, patriarchal family structures, traditionally ordained by religious communities, governments and other collective authorities, are increasingly giving way to more varied constructions of family. Family roles are becoming less ascriptive. The younger generation and the female sex are no longer necessarily found in dependency roles. Traditional dependency roles may be reversed or mixed and matched at different stages of the life cycle. Part of this may relate to the physical absence of transnational family members, although this is not necessarily the case. In this process, family construction results from an attitude of mind, but one that is nonetheless tested and confirmed by interactive emotional and material exchange between family members.

In terms of frontiering, transnational families initiate and extend their geographical dispersion through networking. Chain migration is nothing new, as demonstrated by the Onninks' migration to the US. Nonetheless, the rate of chain migration may be hastened now by technological advance. Instantaneous telephone and email communication contrasts with the slower uncertain postal deliveries of the nineteenth century. However, it is transnational family networking following migratory movement that is of most interest here. In the 19th century, migrant families' networking with their home areas was largely precluded by the second generation due to travel costs and the physical distances involved. A century later, although second and later generations increasingly veer away from cultural conformity with the home area, they nonetheless may visit on holiday, or for marriage or study purposes. During this contact, they may influence the home area as much as the home area influences them through a cross-fertilization of attitudes towards marriage, childcare, politics and so forth (Merolla Chapter 5, Salzbrunn Chapter 11). For example, Fatima's daughters wanted weddings in Morocco because they were more festive and fun than weddings in the Netherlands, but in so doing they had to conform to many of the norms of their Moroccan home area.

It is apparent that patterns of neighbourhood networking may be diverging. The Onninks lived in an extremely tight-knit community of Dutch-speakers. They held self-righteous views about native American Indians who they deemed were not capable of farming and were considered to have criminal tendencies. By contrast, the Ouarrouds live amongst other Dutch Moroccans, but theirs is a more multi-ethnic society with friends and contacts that are Dutch as well as Turkish, German, English, Belgian, Italian and French. They have a sense of cultural relativity and see both pros and cons concerning their customary beliefs. Fatima, for example, views the position of women in Moroccan society and arranged marriages between close families as sometimes problematic. She observes her grown children becoming more and more Westernized and believes that this is inevitable, hoping however that they retain an outward-directed socially interactive attitude towards people, that she feels is lacking in wider Dutch society.

While this is just one example, amongst a wide spectrum of attitudes ranging from tolerance to intolerance, there are many indications that the cultural mixing of ethnically diverse people in Europe is contributing to broader social understanding. Ethnic tensions remain in many places and may even flare into violence in isolated instances, but current attitudes in Europe represent enormous attitudinal change when contrasted with the attitudes of European settlers in the Americas a century ago. Their settler communities tended to be modelled on their home areas and the common assumption was that cultural displacement, even cultural annihilation of the original inhabitants of their host country, such as American Indians, was inevitable to make way for them. Seen in this light, attitudes have become far more tolerant. Nonetheless, multiculturalism in Europe has to be safeguarded from historical retrogression by conscious state policies and by the heightened awareness of every individual, migrant and non-migrant, to the economic and social vitality of cultural exchange. From being a continent of emigration to one of immigration, Europe's role in world history has experienced a profound turnabout with which it is still coming to terms.

References

Allen, C. (1979), *Tales from the Dark Continent*, Aylesbury, Macdonald Futura.

Baines, D. (1994), 'European Labor Markets, Emigration and Internal Migration, 1850–1913', in T.J. Hatton and J.G. Williamson (eds), *Migration and the International Labor Market 1850–1939*, London, Routledge.

Breger, R. (1998), 'Love and the State: Women, Mixed Marriages and the Law in Germany', in R. Breger and R. Hill (eds), *Cross-Cultural Marriage*, Oxford, Berg.

Blink, H. (1915), 'De Landverhuizing uit Nederland', *Vragen van den Dag*, 30: 177–94.

Blotevogel, H.H., Müller-ter Jung, U. and Wood, G. (1933) 'From Itinerant Worker to Immigrant? The Geography of Guestworkers in Germany', in King. R. (ed.), *Mass Migration in Europe: The Legacy and the Future*, London, Bellhaven Press.

Bryceson, D.F., Kay, C. and J. Mooij (eds) (2000), *Disappearing Peasantries? Rural Labour in Africa, Asia and Latin America*, London, Intermediate Technology Publications.

Dieleman, F. (1993), 'Multicultural Holland: Myth or Reality', in King, R. (ed.), *Mass Migration in Europe: The Legacy and the Future*, London, Bellhaven Press.

Ferenczi, I. and Willcox, W.F. (1929), *International Migrations*, vol. 1, New York, National Bureau of Economic Research.

Fielding, A. (1993), 'Migrations, Institutions and Politics: The Evolution of European Migration Policies', in King, R. (ed.), *Mass Migration in Europe: The Legacy and the Future*, London, Bellhaven Press.

Hatton, T.J. and Williamson, J.G. (1994), 'International Migration 1850–1939: An Economic Survey', in Hatton, T.J. and Williamson, J.G. (eds), *Migration and the International Labour Market 1850–1939*, London, Routledge.

Hatton, T.J. and Williamson, J.G. (eds) (1994), *Migration and the International Labor Market 1850–1939,* London, Routledge.

Hopkins, A. (1973), *An Economic History of West Africa*, Longman, London.

King, R. (ed.) (1993), *Mass Migration in Europe: The Legacy and the Future*, London, Belhaven Press.

Laslett, P. (1965), *The World We Have Lost*, London, Methuen.

Livi-Bacci, M. (1997), *A Concise History of World Population*, Oxford, Blackwell.

Mamdani, M. (1973), *From Citizen to Refugee*, London, Francis Pinter.

Mitterauer, M. and Sieder, R. (1982), *The European Family*, Oxford, Blackwell.

Moch, L.P. (1992), *Moving Europeans: Migration in Western Europe since 1650*, Bloomington, Indiana University Press.

Nugent, (1992), W. *Crossings: The Great Transatlantic Migrations, 1870–1914*, Bloomington, Indiana University Press.

Ogden, P. (1993), 'The Legacy of Migration: Some Evidence from France', in King, R. (ed.), *Mass Migration in Europe: The Legacy and the Future*, London, Bellhaven Press.

Organisation for Economic Co-operation and Development (OECD) (2000), *Trends in International Migration: Continuous Reporting System on Migration*, OECD, Paris.

Saueressig-Schreuder, Y. (1985), 'Dutch Catholic Immigrant Settlement in Wisconsin', in Swierenga, R.P. (ed.), *The Dutch in America*, New Brunswick, Rutgers University Press.

Skeldon, R. (1997), *Migration and Development: A Global Perspective*, Harlow: Longman.

Sowell, T. (1996), *Migrations and Cultures*, New York, Basic Books.

Stalker, P. (2000), *Workers without Frontiers: The Impact of Globalization on International Migration*, Boulder, Lynn Rienner.

Swierenga, R.P. (1985), 'Dutch Immigration Patterns in the Nineteenth and Twentieth Centuries', in Swierenga, R.P. (ed.), *The Dutch in America*, New Brunswick, Rutgers University Press.

Swierenga, R.P. (ed.) (1985), *The Dutch in America*, New Brunswick, Rutgers University Press.

Vries, H. de (1985), 'The Labor Market in Dutch Agriculture and Emigration to the United States' in Swierenga, R.P. (ed.), *The Dutch in America*, New Brunswick, Rutgers University Press.

Woodham Smith, C. (1962/1977), *The Great Hunger: Ireland 1845–9*, London, Hamish Hamilton.

World Bank, (1995), *World Development Report 1995: Workers in an Integrating World*, New York, Oxford University Press.

Notes

1. Sixty-four per cent of immigrants to the US between 1851 and 1913 were men (Hatton and Williamson 1994: 7).
2. Saueressig-Schreuder (1985) notes that the volume and timing of Dutch emigration to Wisconsin in the US revealed a pattern of short-term emigration waves separated by two to three years, about the time it would take for information to arrive in the Netherlands and be acted upon by eager migrants.
3. During the Irish famine of the late 1840s, desperate appeals were made to American-based kin: '"For god's sake don't let us die of hunger", wrote a small farmer in Sligo to relatives in North America, asking for the loan of passage money.' One estimate was that Irish Americans sent the remarkable sum of about a million dollars to relations during the height of the famine in 1847 (Woodham Smith 1977: 237).
4. The Emergency Quota Act of 1921, the Immigration Act of 1924 and the National Origins Act of 1929.
5. French acronym for the 'Continuous Reporting System on Migration'.
6. Citizenship is difficult to acquire in countries like Germany, which have until recently based citizenship solely on blood ties rather than residence (see Erel, Chapter 6).
7. Family and personal names have been altered in this section.
8. Currently, Nebraska as well as other Midwestern states are experiencing depopulation, as family farming and the small towns that supported such farming gradually disappear ('Fare thee well, Iowa', *Economist* 18 January 2001). Ironically vast tracks of land are being used for buffalo grazing.

Part II

Families Straddling National Boundaries and Cultures

3

Transnational Families: Imagined and Real Communities

Ulla Vuorela

Families living simultaneously in and between different nation states, which can include both migrant and ethnic minority families, may be a source of sensitivity and uncertainty for the nation state, as was manifest, for instance, in the forceful expulsion of Asians from Uganda in 1972. Likewise, governments may perceive loyalty to multiple countries as a threat to their national economy and coherence. On the other hand, from the perspective of individuals and their families, it is the nation states and the restrictions on movement they impose that may be the problem. This has been demonstrated in the frequently shifting ways immigration laws and policies have defined families and regulated family reunions.

In this chapter, it is argued that living transnationally is not necessarily a problem from the point of view of families and individuals; nor does it have to conflict with the 'making of nations'. Both nations and families can be seen as imagined and real communities: belonging to a nation and belonging to a family are constructions with political and emotional underpinnings, and do not necessarily implicate each other.

An encounter with an Asian[1] family living in Tanzania led me to consider the notion of transnational families. How do people create a unity of kinship and family feeling when living apart? What kinds of networks are formed within and through the formation of transnational families? What processes have resulted in them living apart? How have people with transnational life stories adjusted to the receiving nation-state? What issues arise regarding citizenship, gender and generation in the 'fission and fusion' of households? How do individuals leading transnational lives negotiate their sense of belonging? How do they think about their belonging to a family and their belonging to the places where they have lived? This chapter focuses on a family that has, over four generations, spanned four continents: Asia, Africa, Europe and North America.

One methodological problem in dealing with a family as dispersed as the one discussed in this chapter is that the members of the family live so far apart, and the story differs depending on who is recounting it. Some may suggest that the research should follow as many members of the family as possible to establish a complete picture, but an understanding of a 'multi-sited' family in terms of the issues that arise when thinking about transnational families, however, does not necessarily demand a multi-sited ethnography.

Telling the story here, primarily from the vantage point of only one of its members, adequately reveals the complexities of transnational family dispersal and reunion. The story is based on interviews held with Fawzi, a woman in her late forties who lectures in English and world literature at a university in New York City. Her account is supplemented with a few interviews with other members of the family and their published autobiographical material. These 'stories' are situated in a historical context to give additional explanation as to how family members have negotiated the global and the local. Emphasis is placed on the kind of assets and symbolic capital that they have employed through this historical timeline. The significance of place and national belonging is explored by centre-staging Fawzi.

The ways in which a family's branches and offshoots connect and become anchored to new places provide a myriad of stories of different life paths and processes of identity construction. In these stories, the identifications and loyalties are as varied as the families themselves.

Fawzi's Family

Discussions with Fawzi have been nurtured by the fact that I have shared some of her personal history with her family since the mid-1970s. I came to know Fawzi in 1979 when I was working in Dar es Salaam, Tanzania, with her brother on a Finnish-Tanzanian research project. I became and have remained an adopted member of her family to the extent that I could sometimes, just like a relative, announce my arrival and expect to be well received and vice versa. After living in Tanzania for 10 years, I moved back to Finland, my home country. All of us have now dispersed in various directions around the globe, but we still remain in close contact.

The story of Fawzi and her familial and national loyalties is a story of a post-colonial scholar living in New York City, a Tanzanian and second generation East-African Asian, a US citizen who was educated in Kenya, Pakistan, England and the US. Fawzi was born into an Asian family in Arusha, in the then-British colony of Tanganyika, now Tanzania. Even though Fawzi has never lived in Tanzania for more than a year at a time, this is the country she most strongly identifies with. Tanzania became her home country both as a place of birth and as the place where her parents lived longest. There is also a 'particular, perhaps even sentimental affiliation' as Fawzi describes her sense of being a Tanzanian:

> The practice of saying that I am Tanzanian has been consistent throughout my life. In different contexts within which I make that claim, sometimes it is inaccurate in as much as I am not a Tanzanian citizen. I haven't lived there for a major portion of my life, and there are no rooted ways in which I belong to any sort of national entity that is called Tanzania. Yes, it's always been . . . but it is a mediated sense of being something. Initially it was associated with my place of birth, and as a child I put an enormous amount of importance on that. Family, home is where the parents are. A combination of sentimental ties along with a growing sense of other kinds of socialized loyalty.
>
> But at the same time, there was also a more alienated sense, alienated in the sense of it being really distant from one's own experience. An alienated sense that we belonged in a loose way to some kind of ethnic group, though the word ethnic was not really part of our vocabulary. So we understood that we had a kind of affiliation of lineage and inheritance with the Asian communities, but that we in fact did not belong to any of them. Within the East African setting and in the Tanzanian setting they were very insulated, with self-defining and coherent groups among themselves, and we were not part of the larger community. There is always this notion that originally we came from these distant places like India and China, but it was never a visceral, real feeling.

Fawzi's mother, Sophia, was born in the Punjab of India, when her parents, who otherwise resided in Nairobi, were there on home leave from Kenya. Sophia had spent her childhood years in Kenya while her husband, Abdulla, was born in Hong Kong, of a Chinese mother and a father from Jammu, an area bordering Punjab and Kashmir. His father worked as a civil servant when Queen Victoria's son Edward was the King Emperor of India. Fawzi's mother Sophia explains the complex origins of Fawzi's paternal family:

> As the British used to take suitable people from one colony to another when needed, so was Abdulla's father taken to Hong Kong which was then a British Colony. He was first married to a cousin and had four children with her. This wife died when he came for a holiday to India. He remarried, his new wife soon died and he did not get married for a long time until he married a Chinese lady, Abdulla's mother. Abdulla was the oldest of the children from this marriage. When Abdulla was seventeen, his father retired and went to India where Abdulla studied at the University of Punjab and did his BA Hons in English and Political Science and Economics at the Government College in

Lahore. In 1938 he came to East Africa. After having spent some time in Zanzibar and Kampala he arrived and settled in Nairobi. (Interviewed 1999)

Abdulla met Sophia in Nairobi where they married in 1941. Nairobi was the family's original home in East Africa, where they all settled from different corners of the British Empire in South and South-East Asia. The presence of Sophia's natal family in East Africa dated back to the 1910s. Her grandfather worked as a clerk for the British colonial government in India and after surviving the trauma of the Amritsar massacre he went to Kenya to visit an old school friend. He enjoyed the country and exhorted his sons to immigrate there. His son, Sophia's father, moved to Kenya and worked in a company installing the country's first electricity supplies and later in a construction company where Jomo Kenyatta[2] also worked. He returned to India to marry Sophia's grandmother. The couple set up house in Nairobi where they gave birth to five sons and one daughter, Sophia.

During World War II, Abdulla studied law in Kenya and worked for Nairobi City Council. After the war, Abdulla completed his law degree in England while Sophia went to India to visit her husband's family. She found herself unwittingly embroiled in the partition of India in 1947 and became part of the millions who were relocated to Pakistan. Abdulla returned to Nairobi to join the law firm of a well-known lawyer who enlisted Abdulla to run the firm's office in the neighbouring country of Tanganyika. Reunited, Sophia, Abdulla and baby daughter Hana set up home in Arusha, Tanganyika in 1948. There Sophia gave birth to a son, followed by Fawzi, their second daughter and the couple's last child.

Fawzi's elder sister, who, like Fawzi, was sent to school in England, returned to Kenya after her schooling to marry a pharmacist and make her career as a trained nurse. She and her husband had a daughter before deciding to move to Canada and later to the US. Fawzi's brother, Mali, was also sent to an English boarding school at the early age of five, 'before he was even able to tie his shoelaces'. After studying at a public school and Cambridge University, he returned to Tanzania to gain a further degree at the University of Dar es Salaam where he eventually became a lecturer. Later he settled in England due to the residential preferences of his British wife. He then started a transnational career in the service of a UN organization and has lived in different African countries in connection with his job ever since.

Jumping ahead, if we look at Fawzi's immediate family in the year 2000, we find her brother living in Namibia with his wife and son, her sister and husband as Canadian citizens residing in the US and her parents

Sophia and Abdulla living in Canada. Rather than remaining in Tanzania, they decided to move to North America in their old age to be near their granddaughter and their eldest daughter. Canada's medical care system also influenced their decision to move from East Africa.

A Far-Flung Polyglot Extended Family

The dispersal of Fawzi's extended family has been even more widespread. Fawzi's mother had four brothers, all raised in Nairobi. One of them settled in Dublin having married an Irishwoman. Two other uncles moved to London and the fourth has become a resident of Islamabad, Pakistan, and is a high-ranking officer in the Pakistani air force.

To give a glimpse of further dispersals in the next generation, one of the cousins, the son of Fawzi's 'Irish uncle', enthusiastically embraced Swedish culture, its language and residence, and has become a much-talked about character within the family. Having had a public career in the Swedish music business, he was infamously accused of being involved with adolescent girls. To defend his case, he published his memoirs in Swedish, a book that I accidentally found in a Helsinki bookshop. He concludes:

> But the green island is no longer my 'home' [Ireland]. It is here in Sweden that I have found my true self – my real self. It is therefore that I think of my life in this dark but wonderful country with its Jantelag, its jealousy and its incomparable quality of life. Exactly in the same way that my father took little Ireland to his heart some 50 years ago, I have taken Sweden to mine. He lived and died in Ireland. History will repeat itself – because I will live and I will die in a Nordic country. (Butt 1997: 333)

In its dispersal, the family is not only multi-sited, but within two generations has become multi-lingual and multinational. Being mult-inational means simply that various family members have become citizens of different states, carry different passports and need to move across borders for larger family reunions. While some may see transnational family loyalties over-riding the individual's sense of loyalty to the nation, in fact it is national loyalties that may get in the way of family loyalties. The most immediate and practical difficulty is that of family members' non-overlapping language capabilities.

Studying the scope of home areas and languages shared within Fawzi's nuclear family one can form an idea of the multiplicities of family life. Growing up in Nairobi, Fawzi's mother learned Swahili and English in addition to the Urdu and Punjabi of her parents. Fawzi's older sister Hana shares the languages of Urdu, Punjabi and Swahili with her mother, whereas her brother speaks English and Swahili with his mother. Fawzi, who spent most of her childhood away from her parental home, speaks only English, although her first language was Swahili and she still remembers some words of Swahili. As none of them ever learned their father's school language, Chinese, and English was the only language common to them all, English became the family members' basis for communication with each other. In the East African context, this made the family distinct in the midst of other Asian families in East Africa. Fawzi reflects:

> I'd say almost without exception, every single East Asian spoke whatever the mother tongue was, whether it was Gujarati, Punjabi, Urdu, Hindi; whatever the language happened to be of the group they belonged to, they would speak at home. And just about everybody was multilingual as well, both in terms of Swahili and English.

At times this posed communication problems within the extended family. Fawzi's mother, as the most multilingual member of the family, had to act as translator between her children and relatives. When Fawzi first visited Pakistan and met her parental aunts and uncles and their families, there was at first virtually no communication other than amongst the children because only her cousins knew English.

Family as an Identity and a Community

Living apart across long distances does not prevent Fawzi from speaking of her parents and siblings as her 'immediate family':

> Well, I think of it [my family] in terms of the immediate family, my parents, my brother and my sister. But then we've always been conscious of the extended family. I have 21 first cousins on my father's side and my mother's side, which is really extensive. There are some cousins on my mother's side that I've never met. But many of them I have, and I'm the one until recently who knew my father's side of the family and my cousins there, but they recently came to the US and so met my brother and my sister. My sister only met them two years ago. She never knew her cousins on my father's side.

In its immediacy it is simultaneously a multi-local or multi-sited entity, extended across nations and continents. It is also multinational in terms of the variety of passports its members carry. National loyalties are multiple within the immediate family.

Fawzi's family has, in two generations, experienced the continental dispersal of the nuclear family. Sophia and her brothers set up homes in England, Ireland, Kenya, Tanzania and Pakistan. Not all of the family members have kept in contact all the time and sometimes a long time has elapsed between reunions even with close relatives. Despite the distances between family members on the level of everyday life, there has always been a strong family feeling. Fawzi elaborates:

> Well, [we have] a very strong sense that is possibly even over-determined, because [we have missed] the customary and usual processes that families go through, when they cohabit and live together . . . So therefore it means that in many ways we still need to work out our relationships with each other in ways that other families have been able to do. . . . Certainly my parents completely invested in what their children were doing and defined themselves . . . In many ways they lived their lives through their children. Yet we all lived very separate existences, but there is a very strong sense of loyalty both healthy and unhealthy in many ways.

Likewise, Fawzi is very conscious of her place in the chain of historical events. The ways in which she has introduced herself to other people has varied along with the circumstances.

> If the people in that part of the world where I was had no knowledge on the kind of diaspora colonialism created, I had to explain that I am part of that movement. The phrasing I used to use – I don't use it so often now – is to just simply call myself a second-generation East-African Asian.
>
> You know, from the age of consciousness I always understood myself to have been somebody, a product of a historical process and that in many ways I am a very early and very thorough example of someone who was Anglicised.

Family in the British Colonial Project: Schooling and the English Language

In Fawzi's narrative, the process of Anglicization is central. It takes us back to how Fawzi grew up between families and nations. As was common among the educated classes in the British dominions of the 1950s and faced with the intransigence of racial segregation in the organisation of colonial education, the family's three children were sent to boarding school in England. While her two older siblings were already in boarding school, Fawzi at the age of two was sent to live with one of her maternal uncles, who had settled in Ireland, because her mother was hospitalized for an extended period in London. From Ireland Fawzi was sent to Britain to stay with a landlady. Between the ages of two and three, the ambitious lady, who was not happy with the child's Irish accent, forcefully turned Fawzi's English into a 'proper accent'. Her efforts were so thorough that Fawzi's mother did not recognize the accent when she returned home from hospital. Fawzi recounts:

What I remember of that experience is – I remember quite vividly . . . Apparently what happened there was that the English I had been speaking in Ireland was not acceptable to those people. So they retrained me and kept focusing on my pronunciation to such a degree that by the time my mother came home from hospital I was speaking the kind of English I speak now, which was a total transformation from what she had seen before she went into hospital.

Fawzi looks back on that reunion as highly significant because she and her mother then returned to East Africa, whereas her older sister and brother remained in England at their boarding schools. The child had to cope with her new East African environment alone:

Apparently my reaction on going back to our home in Arusha which I did not remember was having to be told again and again by both my mother and my father that yes, this is really my home. There was no landlady who told me to be quiet. Yes, this was really my home, it was my very own. I could go anywhere in the house and no landlady was going to come and get me into trouble. And also apparently it took me some time to accept that this was my father, I simply did not recognise [him]. This all happened to me before the age of four.

At the age of six, Fawzi was also sent to boarding school. Despite the fact that for most of her childhood thereafter Fawzi was separated from her parents and her siblings, she holds a strong sense of her immediate family. To my question as to whether she was always clear about who her parents were, Fawzi replied:

As far as I know yes. Subsequently when I went off to boarding school at the age of six, there were times when I wasn't quite sure what my parents looked like other than from the photographs I had, and I could not remember what my mother sounded like.

Given the expense of international transport and communication during the 1950s and 1960s, sending children to school abroad meant that parents saw their children only during the longest school holidays during the European summer months, if that. Residence at foreign boarding schools created an enormous physical separation of children from their parents and also often created another world in the mind of the child. Among her siblings Fawzi was the only one who had ever lived at home and attended a day school and this was only for two school terms in Tanzania. This time was exciting for the child, but especially for the parents who were not used to having their children at home.

> Going back to Africa was peculiar, because I was not used to having my parents around and my parents were not used to having children around, and we all had to become accustomed to each other. And there are some funny stories from that time about when I brought my homework back, you know they did not know what I was doing and nobody could help me with the arithmetic and the mathematics. According to my mother, my father used to sneak up to the doorway of my room where I had my desk. And he used to come and look at me doing my homework because it was such a pleasure for him to actually see one of his children at home agonizing over their homework; it was such a novelty for them.

That family interlude was brief, however. From the day school in Arusha, Fawzi moved to a boarding school in Kenya because Kenyan schools were perceived to have higher academic standards that more closely approximated the public schools in England. The school where she spent five years turned out to be a grim experience as it also provided her first exposure to racism. She was the only coloured student and on completion of her schooling there she told her parents that she was unwilling to continue her education at white schools in Kenya.

Family members recount different versions of what happened thereafter and whether it was Fawzi's or her mother's idea for her to attend a girls' college in Pakistan. Whatever the case, the family agreed on the decision. There was an additional benefit to Fawzi's schooling in Pakistan. It introduced her to the Pakistani branch of the extended family and gave her parents the opportunity for a family reunion. Her parents accompanied her to Pakistan to settle her in the new school and they toured the country visiting a number of relatives. Her father saw his sisters for the first time in 20 years.

At Kinnaird College in Lahore, Fawzi confronted another version of racial prejudice. Her classmates quickly classified her as a 'brown European'. However, the students' initial hostility towards her in Lahore soon melted and was transformed into acceptance because Fawzi excelled in the areas that the school held in high esteem. Her abilities in sport and her British accent, so painfully acquired, contributed to her acceptance and elevated her position among the students. However, she always had a sense of being considered a serious oddity, something she played upon at times. Her ability to imitate a cockney accent in a school play, which, in Fawzi's words, 'anybody who had spent some time in Britain could easily do', gave her a cachet all her own.

In the Anglicising environment of Kinnaird College, she was 'authentic' as someone who had actually lived in Britain. The British connection was to continue to help her in later life. As Fawzi herself jokes, her unfailing British accent was one of the factors that assisted her, when it came to the final choice, in being offered the position as a professor of English literature in New York City.

Her formative years at Kinnaird have been remarked upon by Sara Suleri in her autobiography *Meatless Days* (Suleri 1987). Suleri gave Fawzi, her former schoolmate and long-time friend, the nickname 'Mustakor' and made the 'surprise of Mustakor' the subject of her story. A chapter is devoted to the unsettling effect Fawzi had on her classmates in a women's college in Lahore, Pakistan:

> Known variously in her Western manifestations as Congo Lise, Fancy Musgrave, and Faze Mackaw, Mustakor of Tanzania is a woman who amazed her coterie of friends . . . So oh, poor Mowgli! What must it have been like to lope into Lahore fresh from East Africa and then, let alone Lahore, to lope into Kinnaird! . . . Kinnaird signified a magical arena containing a few hundred very eligible women in an architectural embrace remarkably reminiscent of the old days of the *zenana khana*, its room after room of unenterable women's rooms . . . Kinnaird College! For Women! On Jail Road! In Lahore! The college was indeed on Jail Road as was the jail, and the racecourse, and the lunatic asylum, too: daily we found it hard to believe ourselves, but it was true
>
> She came with all the tentative innocence of one who returns, seeking to understand the geographic reality of her forefathers and waiting to locate herself in an unknown mode of speech to wraith of an intuitively familiar cadence. Those who travel curiously imagine that returning is somehow sweeter, less dangerous, than seeking out some novel history, and Mustakori evidently had such nostalgia encoded in her genes. Of course, she was disappointed in Lahore, arriving as she did like an eager pony and finding instead of a warm welcome a deep historical dislike, which placed her cheek to cheek with the term 'brown European', another name to vex her need of equanimity. (Suleri 1987: 45–9)

After seven years at Kinnaird College and Punjab University, both Fawzi and Suleri moved to the US, where they lived together and studied English literature. Both subsequently became professors of English literature at different universities in the US.

Family – Nation – State

Fawzi, the quintessential English speaker, carries a strong sense of being a Tanzanian, in defiance of her British colonial origins. She persistently defines herself as a Tanzanian, but has never carried a Tanzanian passport, nor has she lived in the country for longer than the one year that she spent at school in Arusha. She carried a Grade D British passport, which in the event of the war that separated Pakistan and Bangladesh in 1971, was not effectively recognized by the British authorities. After a number of years with a stateless status, she has recently become a US citizen. Fawzi relates:

> The British have been issuing passports to people, different statuses given to people from different parts of the British dominions. And the gradations had to do with the limited rights of access you had. To work in Britain, abode in Britain and abode in former British colonies. The most troubled aspect of which has been both the status and non-status given to British subjects of Asian descent in Africa and to British subjects of Chinese descent in Hong Kong, both of which applied to me. The last British passport I had when I got it renewed in the early 1990s was one that gave me the right of abode in Hong Kong. It made me Chinese in a sense and – my father was born in Hong Kong – so they were patrilineal in their definitions of who was who. And that was one of the reasons why I basically decided that I would become a US citizen [on the basis of long-term US residence]. And the reason was not only because of the anomalous status of my non-British status because travelling on the British passport was problematic in as much as some countries would not allow me entry . . . Nationality and citizenship have a very different meaning now than they had in the mid-twentieth century at the time of decolonization, so I have been able to circumnavigate many problems, even though I spent the bulk of my life in a stateless situation.

In Tanganyika, a marginalized part of the British colonial empire, Fawzi's mother, Sophia, took her sentiments further and actively engaged in Tanganyika's independence struggle against British colonial rule during the 1950s. Sophia joined the Tanganyika African National Union (TANU), the African nationalist party led by Julius Nyerere, touring the country in a rainbow coalition agitating for the cessation of British rule. After Nyerere became the first president of Tanzania at independence in 1961, Sophia was elected as a Member of Parliament and served in this capacity during the first years of independence. Visiting Tanzania during the school holidays, Fawzi became part of a family environment deeply devoted to the nationalist movement and the construction of the nation of the post-colonial era as indicated by her remark:

by extension ... as Sophia's children we felt that sort of political affiliation as well. There was a very sentimental kind of affiliation; it was something that you gave a lot of importance to, something you held on to.

There was a difference, however, between the children. While the two younger ones developed a strong sense of belonging to Tanzania, the eldest sister became more anchored in Kenya. For Fawzi, who spent a considerable portion of her youth in Pakistan, the identification with Tanzania remained strong:

When I went to Pakistan it complicated matters in many ways because I never felt a sense of belonging there. Even though this was culturally and in terms of the lineage of my parents where I was supposed to be from, I never felt a sense of closeness. In some ways I became even more aligned to the notion of being Tanzanian rather than being Indian or Pakistani.

In 1958, Sophia agreed to stand as an independent candidate in the elections and won the Arusha Asian-reserved seat in the Legislative Council. In 1963, she became the first Asian Member of Parliament in independent Tanzania. In her work, she appealed to Asians to forget their various sects and communities and to consider themselves as Tanganyikans. As Sophia recounted in her book:

I told them that in achieving this, the first step for the Asians must be the reorganisation of their way of thinking of themselves as separate and distinct groups, whether based on language, religion, caste or sex. I meant that Asians must first attempt to remove the distinctions and classes among themselves and, after doing so, should proceed further and identify completely with the country as Tanganyika citizens. They should aim at the creation of Tanganyika citizenship and Tanganyika loyalty. (Mustafa 1962: 80)

This was in line with those who emphasized the necessity for a non-racial Tanganyika as a guarantee of political stability. She saw that the Asians had a significant part to play in assisting the general political development in the territory.

She also spoke of the 'sickening' differences in wealth between Africans, Asians and Europeans (Seidenberg 1996, Mustafa 1962). In her politics, Sophia was a keen supporter of African aspirations in Tanganyika's struggle for independence and during the post-independence years. She considered that the majority, i.e. Africans, should play the dominant role in Tanganyikan politics. Subsequently she worked for the undoing of racial segregation. It was thus through Sophia's activities, and living in

Tanganyika-cum-Tanzania that the family became closely connected to the nationalist cause and came to identify themselves as Tanzanians.

Sophia's siblings, however, did not share the same national affiliations. One of her brothers, who had grown up with her in Nairobi, moved back to the Indian subcontinent when Pakistan was created as an independent nation. His daughter explained to me in Lahore:

> Surprisingly, he was the only sibling who actually chose at that time (in 1947) to come to Pakistan. He stayed with Sophia for a few years. She was actually much more than an elder sister to him; you know, she was like a mother, a teacher, a mentor.
>
> Then he just chose to find his own way of life. [As] he was very fond of flying; this was the real reason that brought him to Pakistan. [For him] the thrill was ... here was this new country; this new Islamic country had been made. And all the Asians and all the Muslims even in Africa were proud and jubilant and very emotional about the partition. And everybody wanted to go to Indian Pakistan, you know, to sort of fight for the new homeland. So Muslims all over the world, including those in East Africa, were highly charged and motivated to come here. My father was about 16 or 17 when he ... I think. He told us that he saw a little advertisement in the newspaper for the Pakistan air force because they were wanting to recruit young pilots and cadets, Muslims, from all over the world. So it was really this, like two inches of an advert or one inch of an advert in a newspaper in East Africa which made him decide. OK, here it is, I'm going.

Thus, Sophia became an active participant in the construction of the emerging nation of Tanganyika/Tanzania, whereas one of her brothers felt equally strongly about the making of the nation state of Pakistan. Both became deeply involved in the processes of decolonization and the struggle for political independence. One of the brothers became a committed Irish citizen, and the remaining two settled in England with their families. In the next generation, the two daughters and the son carried different passports: Kenyan, Tanzanian, British (different classifications), Canadian and American. Throughout these phases, the sense of a closely knit immediate family was never forsaken.

The Intangibles of Family Unity

In the time span of three generations, the family that Fawzi belongs to has made several moves between Asia, Europe and Africa. Having arrived in Kenya as an outcome of labour migration within the British Empire, the family has dispersed in a variety of directions. Sophia's natal household with its five Nairobi-based children varied in its composition through fission and fusion over the years. After the death of her mother, it was Sophia who took on the mothering role *vis-à-vis* her younger brothers in the 1940s, when she was already married herself. Since then, the family members have crossed national boundaries and anchored themselves in their new countries so that a community has come about that is multi-sited and multinational. Despite the physical distance, there has been a very strong sense of familyhood or kinship, albeit not one shared by all family members:

> we have not only the cousin marriage, but it's acceptable to marry first cousins, too. So there is a lot of this, which in other countries would be seen as incestuous combinations. Yes, it is very clannish; it's very clannish . . . I think there's some importance attached to the kinship that finally defines itself in the network that I would define as clan. That's very strong on my mother's side of the family. So many of my uncles . . . my cousins, they have invested in maintaining, in finding out more about the connections between the various branches of the [clan] . . . I'm amazed, I'm amazed. I have no interest whatsoever in that.

Nevertheless, the idea of a close connection between parents, children and grandchildren living far apart has required particular ways of working out the sense of intimacy and togetherness. Imaging and narrating have constructed a sense of a community that is both imagined and materialized through various practices, both as a presence and *in absentia*. A sense of togetherness is reproduced through correspondence, greetings and presents carried by visitors. It is anchored in photographs and objects that become talismans of home and belonging. For Fawzi, it was her mother's letters, the book written by her mother that mentioned the children by name, family photographs and the picture of Mount Meru in Tanzania. For her brother, it was the fruitcakes and *chevra* to be enjoyed at teatime as a reminder of the teatime as a family ritual, sent to him in Dar es Salaam, carefully packed in tin containers from Nairobi. For the mother, it was the ritualistic narration of the birth of each child on his or her birthday.

During the years at boarding schools the mother's letters arrived like clockwork, once a week, wherever the children were, creating a strong sense of family bonding. The mother conscientiously paid attention to each of the children by sending them individually addressed letters. And the mother kept the letters conscientiously as a way of maintaining the presence of her children even in their absence. That went on until their adult years so she kept all 52 of Fawzi's letters posted to her during Fawzi's 18-month stay in China. The practice of saving the letters has only disappeared with the availability of e-mail as Fawzi explains:

> You know, a curious thing Ulla, not only has she kept many of my letters, if not all of them from the very first to the last, but a lot of my childhood memorabilia . . . What it tells me is the kind of battle my mother must have lived through being separated from her children, and how she found these ways to keep our presence around her. A lot of the stuff she has redistributed to each of us.

The story of the family also takes new twists and turns with the life paths of each generation. A careful mapping would be needed to illustrate the entire dynamics during different decades. Another dimension is created by centre staging Fawzi as the single professional living in New York – a single person who is not alone but is an integral part of a vibrant family network that meets whenever their paths physically intersect. In this sense, New York City is an ideal location for intersection. In New York, Fawzi has settled on her own and her apartment has become a central node in the family's transnational hospitality network. Fawzi has arranged her household such that visitors can be easily accommodated. And they come, not unlike the way Suleri described it years before:

> And if she has not been able to visit Meru for a while, then the mountain periodically comes to Muhammad, bringing the clan of Mustakoris to her door. Great families of cousins suddenly arrive – Andy, Pandy, Hoola, Hoopa, Rusti, Brusti, and Tim – drenching the streets with Mustakori look-alikes, the kitchen sunlight band. (Suleri 1987: 71)

This open-door policy intersects with Fawzi's local neighbourhood network to create jumbled multi-ethnic encounters of goodwill and fun, as I personally experienced when I visited Fawzi in New York. I enjoyed Christmas lunch served by Fawzi's neighbours, a Guatemalan family, who opened their doors to a company of 'strangers' coming not only from Finland but from other distant places too. After lunch, we joined New Yorkers wandering around the huge Christmas tree (a Norwegian donation) in the Rockefeller Center where, according to tradition, it is customary to skate under the tree on Christmas Day. The surrounding neighbourhoods were filled with food and clothing vendors who were capitalizing on the presence of the crowd. 'If you look at people more closely', I was told, 'you will realise that most of them are newcomers to

New York'. In contrast to the closed Finnish Christmas that I was accustomed to, strictly confined to the nuclear family in their homes, Christmas in New York City was outward-oriented and composed of an anomalous collection of people from different families, different ethnic backgrounds, different religions all celebrating different meanings of togetherness on a national holiday.

Conclusion: Transnational Families in Post-Coloniality

I have related the story of Fawzi and her transnational family to explore transnational ways of living. The family is highly dispersed but has a unity of an imagined and real kind. What it shares amongst its members is both material and spiritual. The story is both of volatility of locations and of a historically changing nature of identification and nationality. The family map that would have only included India, Hong Kong, Kenya and Britain in the 1930s had extended to include various European and North American nodes by the 1980s. In the 1990s, none of the members of the immediate family, which had so closely identified with Tanzania's decolonization, actually resided in Tanzania. The presence of the family and kin in East Africa lasted only for two or at the most three generations, to ebb away completely by the end of the 1990s. This occurred to such an extent that when Fawzi started planning a return to the area as a researcher, she turned to me as her 'closest relative' in terms of connections back in Tanzania. Once in Tanzania, she was warmly welcomed by former colleagues and friends of her brother. The colonial period provided particular conditions for transnational mobility. In post-independence Tanzania, the 'era of development' created another form of transnational encounter with development workers from a variety of nations entering a previously colonial space. This context provided me, as a Finnish national, with the opportunity to connect with, participate in and observe a whole set of contemporary transnational practices.

With hindsight, European colonialism appears as a historical moment of globalization. Robertson (1992) sees the colonial instigation of nation states and their national societies roughly a century ago as an aspect of globalization. This process involved the incorporation of a number of non-European societies into international society. It explains the highly stratified social impact of Europe's colonial empires. More to the point, Western Europe's colonial expansion created its own space for the movement of capital and people, centrally and forcefully governed from European metropolitan centres. Within this space, access to resources became dramatically split along class and racial lines. There were enormous physical movements of people within this colonial project related to labour recruitment for the construction of colonial economies. What was then an imperially generated spatial movement of people has continued to the present as a transformative cultural process. This is evident in the histories of families and communities and the ways in which their stories have continued to be elaborated.

Education and social skills associated with the British colonial empire have been a pillar in the construction of the *modus operandi* of Fawzi's family and countless other families in Asia and Africa that were incorporated into Europe's colonizing projects. Viswanathan (1992) has demonstrated how the curriculum for the English language and the study of English literature were created in the process of establishing schools in Europe's colonies, both for the children of the colonizers and those of the colonized upper classes. Not only were the families of colonizers separated through the educational arrangements made for their children, but, as Fawzi's family demonstrates, the same applied to families in the colonies, who started sending their children to be educated in colonial centres. This was one aspect in the construction of transnational colonial elites. The role of boarding schools in training people to live apart from their families is an under-researched area. This separation did not occur only in terms of separating children from parents; it also uprooted children from the traditions of their parents. It is in this process that transnational elites have found a nurturing ground, different in spaces dominated by each of the metropolitan centres, be they British, French, Belgian or Portuguese. Pieterse and Parekh (1995) view this process as a contribution to the collective human repertoire for colonial rulers as well as select colonial subjects. But in the latter case, there were bound to be multiple loyalties and a need to become conscious of the colonial experience and the kind of complicity it involved. These are factors that have contributed to the making of Fawzi as an intellectual embracing post-colonial studies with a desire to critically examine and evaluate the story of colonialism.

Bourdieu's (1998) notion of *habitus* may be apt here to describe how particular people have held positions in a colonial space and how their *habitus* reflects this. In cultural terms, traces of their colonial history have symbolic manifestations such as the habit of having an English breakfast and afternoon tea with Kashmiri and Punjabi lunches and dinners in between. In the colonial legacy, the emphasis on elite school education, European language proficiency, a particular social etiquette and choice of sports, leadership skills and an engagement in local politics, in addition to family and kinship networks, metaphorically 'blood ties', contributes to the making of one form of transnational *habitus* found today. A diasporic space, to use the term by Brah (1996), was in fact created whereby the colonial encounter and its educational policies contributed to the making of a 'transnational elite' that came to share a similar education and a *habitus* that would make it easy to find common ground in the formerly colonial space.

Despite long physical separations and deep cultural ruptures, the dispersed family seems to be multi-centred: each new family creates its own sense of belonging and loyalties. Family members centre their stories with a different starting point and a different anchorage. What is striking in the case of Fawzi's family is the absence of a sense of family belonging to either a house or land. It seems that attachment to these was antithetical to the family's high level of mobility. A house was simply a dwelling at a particular time and place. It did not carry any symbolic reference to one's origin. Nostalgic memory was not associated with a place of origin, but rather with a history of family and kin: their achievements, their foibles and their moments of bonding.

In Fawzi's family both multinational and transnational elements are salient. In her parents' generation, her mother and her uncles became anchored in different nation states and eventually began to carry different passports connected to different nations: in Fog-Olwig's (1997) words, they 'localized' differently. In her own generation, Fawzi and her two siblings have carried different passports at different periods of their lives. Their mobility continues to be prompted by professional and marital considerations, as in the colonial era when the family inhabited 'colonial space', defined to a large extent by colonial interests in recruiting educated and skilled employees to serve the needs of the colonial empire. For the aspiring elite, or the people with upwardly mobile interests, education became the most valuable symbolic and social capital, worth investing in even at the expense of home life and a family environment, which would see children grow up in its confines. As in the case of migrant families, family lore, exchange of correspondence, holidays and significant symbolic objects contributed to forging a sense of belonging and togetherness.

In conclusion, the kind of transnational family highlighted in this chapter can also be seen as a manifestation of the post-colonial problematic. The trajectories of the individual family members carry traces of colonialism and its undoing in their very lives. It could be said that the colonial and post-colonial experience is inscribed in their lives. Thus, the transnational family history manifests some of the futility of debates about the 'timing' of the post-colonial. It is the colonial project and its globalising dimensions that have enhanced the dispersal of the family over three generations.

The colonial project gave impetus to the making of imperial-cum-transnational elites with a wealth of symbolic capital, who experienced a relatively wide scope for transnational and cosmopolitan movement and lifestyle. However, personal and familial deprivations were inherent in the project in terms of long-term familial separation, a fact that seems to have been accepted more or less philosophically. There were both seductions and strictures.

Learning from the story of the family discussed here, one can observe that there are impacts and continuations of colonialism that cannot be reversed. Likewise, one can say of families, few return to their sites of family origin once the movement is under way. A return can be only thought of through imaginings and attachment to the histories and the social relations that have been part of such histories. In this sense, the transnational family is continually onward and outward bound, quite different from diasporic communities that instil social imperatives for going back to their places of origin. Diasporas of transnational families only refer to the dispersal, not to the idea of return.

References

Bourdieu, P. (1998), *Practical Reason: On the Theory of Action*, Cambridge, Polity Press.

Brah, A. (1996), *Cartographies of Diaspora: Contesting Identities*, London, Routledge.

Butt, B. (1997), *Vem f-n är Billy But? Min egen berättelse*, Stockholm, Wahlströms.

Fog-Olwig, K. (1997), 'Cultural Sites: Sustaining a Home in a Deterritorialized World', in Fog-Olwig, K. and K. Hastrup (eds), *Siting Culture: The Shifting Anthropological Object*, London, Routledge.

Mustafa, S. (1962), *The Tanganyika Way*, London, Oxford University Press.

Pieterse, J.N. and Parekh, B. (eds) (1995), *The Decolonization of Imagination*, London, Zed Books.

Robertson, R. (1992), *Globalization: Social Theory and Global Culture*, London, Sage.

Seidenberg, D. (1996), *Mercantile Adventurerers: The World of East African Asians, 1750–1985*, New Delhi, New Age International.

Suleri, S. (1987), *Meatless Days*, London, Collins.

Viswanathan, G. (1992), *Masks of Conquest: Literary Study and British Rule in India*, New York, Columbia University Press.

Notes

1. Calling people of South Asian descent 'Asians' was adopted in Africa after the partition of India. This avoids the need to specify whether one's roots lead to India, Pakistan or Bangladesh.
2. Jomo Kenyatta was Kenya's first president after national independence.

4

Loss of Status or New Opportunities? Gender Relations and Transnational Ties among Bosnian Refugees

Nadje Al-Ali

A series of long and bloody wars in Bosnia devastated what was hitherto a popular vacation spot in Europe. The 1990s shattered images of war-torn refugees as people from remote far-away countries as thousands of refugees from the former Yugoslavia poured into Western Europe. The Dayton Peace Agreement negotiated at Dayton, Ohio, and signed in Paris in November 1995 brought an end to this terrible war, but in the view of many it was not a solution as much as 'an uneasy temporary truce' (Bojicic and Kaldor 1999: 92). Return remains one of the most vexed issues in post-Dayton Bosnia, this chapter takes a very different angle on the theme of reconstruction and nation building. It challenges the commonly held view that refugees have to return in order to contribute positively to the reconstruction of a war-torn society.

The focus here is on transnational links between Bosnian refugee families living in either the UK or the Netherlands and their family members who remained in Bosnia. 'Transnational links' refer to regular long-distance cross-border activities (Portes 1998, Vertovec 1999), which connect Bosnian refugees to their families and friends in Bosnia. My exploration of transnational activities challenges strictly political economy approaches, which tend to stress processes related to the globalization of capital at the expense of other motivations such as family ties and the social obligations implied in them.[1]

Before the question of how family structures and gender relations are developing among Bosnian families in the receiving countries is addressed, I will discuss some of the emerging issues by focusing on one specific family, while occasionally referring to other examples. The scope of this chapter does not allow for a detailed comparison of various case studies yet it is necessary to stress the diverse levels of heterogeneity among Bosnian refugees who, like many other refugees, are often presented in an homogenized and essentialized manner.

An Uncivil War and its Immediate Aftermath

Among the warring parties – Serbs, Croats and Bosnians – the latter particularly became the victims of horrendous killings, so-called 'ethnic cleansing', mass rapes and destruction from 1992 to 1995. In what is often misleadingly described as a civil war, multi-ethnic Bosnia-Herzegovina[2] was initially involved in a defensive war against Serb aggression that was channelled through the Yugoslav Army (JNA) as well as Bosnian Serb paramilitary forces. The Bosnian government's military alliance of Bosnian Croats and Bosnian Muslims fell apart in 1993 due to nationalist ambitions by some Croats within Bosnia as well as Croatia itself. Subsequently a war within a war unfolded with the aim of creating a Croatian mini-state called 'Herzeg-Bosna'.

The Dayton Peace Agreement, brokered and drafted by North American politicians, diplomats and lawyers, and aided by input from some Europeans, was signed by Muslim, Serbian and Croatian leaders. It called for the creation of a single state and the return of over two million refugees and displaced people to their homes. In reality, Bosnia-Herzegovina is now divided into a Muslim-Croat Federation and a Serb entity (Republika Srpska). Within the Federation, tensions between Croats and Muslims run high, particularly in areas dominated by Croat nationalists. Many of the political leaders of the nationalist parties who were in power during the war still hold government positions, even if their authority has been severely restricted by the Organization for Security and Cooperation in Europe (OSCE) and the Office of the UN High Representative (OHR). To the present, political instability and human rights violations translate into fear for personal security, especially for those refugees who would become minority returnees in their places of origin.

In the course and in the aftermath of the war, over half a million Bosnians have been displaced to countries in the European Union (Black et al. 1997: 1). Although every EU member state has been affected by an influx of refugees, the distribution of Bosnians was very uneven. Almost 60 per cent of all Bosnian refugees were located in Germany and a further 30 per cent in Austria, the Netherlands and Sweden (UNHCR 1997 cited in Black et al. 1997: 7). Despite significant efforts by international organizations such as UNHCR to implement Dayton's stipulations concerning the return of refugees in general and minority return in particular, numbers have not yet matched expectations. Even in Germany, the country that has devised a forced repatriation scheme, more than half of the 342,000 Bosnians have so far remained.[3] In Britain, about 7,000 Bosnian refugees (widely dispersed over 55 different cities) are hoping to have their temporary protection extended into the right to reside permanently within the country. The vast majority of the 25,000 Bosnians who live in the Netherlands were granted refugee status shortly after their arrival, entitling them not only to residence but also to citizenship after five years.[4]

Bosnian refugees in the UK and the Netherlands differ most obviously with respect to their gender and age, their ethnic background (Muslim, Croat, Serb),[5] their education and professional backgrounds, their political views as well as their attitudes towards religion. Another significant element differentiating people, especially in terms of their actual and potential links with Bosnia, relates to their place of origin. Some Bosnians escaped from areas in which they would now constitute a minority (for example Bosnian Muslims in towns of the Serb entity called Republika Srpska, such as Banja Luka), whereas others originate from areas in which their ethnic group now constitutes a majority (for example Bosnian Muslims in places belonging to the Muslim-Croat Federation, such as Sarajevo).

Specific experiences of the war in Bosnia and the circumstances of flight present a pivotal factor. About half of the Bosnian refugee population in the UK arrived through international programmes run by organizations such as the Red Cross or UNHCR. Many of them had only just been released from concentration camps or were close relatives of those who had been released and brought to the UK. Among the refugees I interviewed in the Netherlands, most had arrived independently of organized programmes. Those refugees who came individually to the Netherlands as well as the UK tended to report less immediate experiences of terror and war crimes.

The difficulties of implementing Dayton's stipulations concerning the return of refugees is linked to problems and failures related to democratization, inter-ethnic cooperation and the protection of minority rights. Moreover, the reconstruction process has been slow and unsystematic. The economy continues to be in crisis or, as Bojicic and Kaldor (1999: 93) put it, 'abnormal'. Lack of housing, inadequate health care and education characterize post-Dayton Bosnia. Dependence on humanitarian assistance is coupled with widespread unemployment. Industry has faltered and investment is virtually absent. The transition from a command to a market economy poses challenges in itself. It comes as no surprise then that refugee return is not only minimal, but that Bosnians are still continuing to leave the country or at least express their wish to do so.

Ruptures and Ties within Extended Families

For most Bosnian refugees, the war, ethnic cleansing and the circumstances of their flight have destroyed the families they used to know. The narratives of Bosnians speaking about the significance of their home-based extended families and neighbours concur with the few anthropological accounts of pre-war Bosnia that exist (Balic 1992, Bringa 1995). Although socio-economic changes in the former Yugoslavia after World War II radically changed the composition and organization of the patrilineally based household, extended family ties have continued to be significant in structuring social ties and support networks (Bringa 1995: 41). As Meliha, a young Bosnian Muslim woman from Tuzla, currently living in Amsterdam remembers:

> When I think about my childhood and even my teenage years, I always think of my aunts, uncles and cousins, and, of course, both of my grandparents. I seemed to spend more time with them than with my parents, but maybe this is just the way I remember it now, because I miss them so much. I sometimes discuss this with my friends here and they feel the same way. For us, families were important and much bigger than they are for Dutch people. My friend Selma is lucky because she has two uncles and four cousins here as well as her parents. They were working here before the war.[6]

The disruption of extended-family relations constitutes the most obvious break with pre-war family patterns and structures. Women in particular are affected by the absence of a support network provided by relatives, especially with respect to childcare.

Throughout my interviews with Bosnian refugees the memory of home was regularly associated with an intertwined conceptualization of geographical space and extended family. The majority did not have the privilege of choice – it was in fact the extended family which influenced the decision-making process in terms of departure times and country of refuge. In this context, links between two separate yet not entirely independent migration waves can be observed.

Bosnian refugees in the European Union experienced a drastic rupture in their existing migration order.[7] From the 1960s and prior to the war in Bosnia, Bosnians of all ethnic backgrounds were part of a large-scale labour migration from former Yugoslavia to countries of the EU, particularly to Germany. Extended family ties could link labour migrants and refugees in a specific host country or across national boundaries. However, Bosnian Muslims, like most southern Europeans, did not generally choose the UK as a destination for labour migration.[8] A combination of geographical and economic factors rendered the Netherlands a far more attractive destination for labour migration than the UK. Networks of Bosnian Muslim labour migrants in Germany, and to a lesser extent in the Netherlands, helped in the reception of thousands of refugees during and after the war. In the Netherlands, labour migrants had previously not only established informal networks but also created more formal community associations. Some of these early labour migrants tried to provide assistance to refugees, as well as sending material help to Bosnia during the war. Such networks were not available in the UK, where reception programmes initially found it difficult even to find interpreters who could speak the Bosnian dialect as opposed to detectable Serbian or Croatian dialects.

For those who remained in Bosnia, current links with extended family members tend to be limited to occasional phone calls, letters and, increasingly, visits home by the refugees to Bosnia, especially during summer months. Often images of struggling refugees and well-to-do labour migrants become blurred when talking about extended family abroad. This appears to be particularly the case for those who are not immediate family members or close friends and who are in occasional contact only. The specific relations between Bosnian-based families and the refugees and their contact with one another cannot be generalized because objective factors, such as the circumstances of flight and the social, economic and political conditions within the receiving country are coupled with subjective factors, such as relative sentiments of closeness or remoteness, the regularity and intensity of the contact with relatives.

Living Like a Piece of Wood

What has emerged, inside and outside of Bosnia, is the increasing shift towards reliance on members of the immediate nuclear family. Numerous refugees have been subjected to losses, disruption and break-up within the context of the nuclear family. As Weine, a psychiatrist who has worked extensively with Bosnian refugees in Chicago notes: 'There are husbands without wives, wives without husbands, parents without their children, children without their parents, and all other possible configurations after an irreparable rupture or hole in the family that was' (Weine 1999: 69–70). For many refugees, the loss of loved ones presents the core of their existence, and the thought of family evokes a gaping absence.

Those who were more fortunate and managed to reach a safe haven together with their immediate families, or were later re-united with them, have nonetheless experienced a tremendous break with their previous lives. Edin and Amra, a UK-resident middle-aged Bosnian Muslim couple with one daughter Selma, sum up their current situation as 'living like a piece of wood'. The first time I visited Edin and his wife Amra, in their council flat north of London, I was introduced to the rest of the family. Photographs taken before and after the war showed the couple with family members in Sarajevo and their native Gorazde. On my next visit I watched two videos recorded during a recent visit to Bosnia. While watching the family walking through the old town in Sarajevo, having lunch with Edin's brother in Sarajevo and socializing with Amra's family in Gorazde, Edin and Amra did not cease to comment on the many family members visible on the video. Both talked about the life they missed back home. Edin pined:

> I really want to go back. I think I would find work, especially now that I have completed several computing courses. Before the war I was an economist, but that would not help much these days. Computer skills are needed and I am really working hard on it. What worries me more is the political situation. It is still very unstable especially in Gorazde.[9] If SFOR [Stabilization Force] left, the war would start again. I want my daughter to be safe. But look at us, we live as if we were pieces of wood. (Al-Ali forthcoming)

In the course of my interviews, several people expressed a similar feeling to Edin's metaphor of 'living like a piece of wood'. This was an inanimate state in which one was dependent on income support, had no regular employment or alternatively worked in an unskilled job unrelated to what one had been trained for. The lack of regular socializing with neighbours and relatives, missing friends and the good old times in general all contributed to a feeling of inaction.

Amra was very apologetic about her poor English and hesitated before she spoke:

> It is very boring for me here. I have no work. I stay at home most of the time. I tried to look for a job but I could not find anything. It is partly because of my English. It is still not good enough. I was a lawyer in Gorazde. People in Gorazde always ask when I am coming back to resume my work. But because of our daughter's education and my husband's health we have to stay.

Edin was medically evacuated by UNHCR in 1994 after being wounded in fighting in his hometown. Amra and their daughter Selma were not allowed to join him initially and were only able to enter the UK when his medical condition started to deteriorate rapidly and doctors feared for his life. Despite a series of medical problems that still seriously affect his well-being, Edin has to a large extent recovered.

As Anna's and Edin's comments indicate, although loss, alienation, uprooting and helplessness are part of their refugee existence, empowerment, creativity, increased self-confidence and the sense of new beginnings may also appear as part of a refugee's experience. Despite Edin's bleak description of his current life, he has managed to acquire new qualifications and skills. During the preceding two years, he concentrated on improving his English language skills and has attended several computing courses. He is also involved in a Bosnian community association in London that organizes social events and collects money to send to Bosnia.

Gender Dynamics among Bosnian Refugee Families

Frequently changes and transformations within nuclear families result in conflict and tensions across generational and gender lines. The latter was evident between Edin and Amra. Despite his medical condition, Edin has been able to spend much more time outside the house than Amra. While he has been taking courses or socializing with other Bosnians, she has been taking care of Selma and the house. It is not surprising that her English is not as good as Edin's, a fact that makes her feel reluctant to venture outside the house.

Instead Amra spends her time writing letters to friends dispersed around the world. She has kept in touch with them through what one informant called 'Telefonitis Bosanska':

> I used to call my friends and relatives in Bosnia, Germany and the States a lot. Every three months we had to pay about £300. Now I am trying to restrain myself, but I get very lonely at times. Edin is out a lot and when Selma is in school I am on my own. I know we need the money. Edin bought a computer so that he can practise what he learns in his courses. And we are also sending some money home.

The pattern of wives feeling more isolated than their husbands and trying to compensate by maintaining contact with friends and family worldwide was widespread among the couples I interviewed. Many women had been professionals in Bosnia but found themselves relegated to the home upon arrival in the receiving country. Several women described a perpetual train of trauma and culture shock related to the war, circumstances of flight, separation from family and friends, insecurities related to language barriers, the perceived strangeness of their physical and cultural surroundings, and a general sense of isolation.

However, in other cases, women proved to be more resourceful and adaptable while their husbands suffered from isolation, loneliness and the sense of living in limbo. This was particularly true for several women in the Netherlands who reported that it had been much easier for them to find work than for their husbands. Many worked as cleaners or nannies despite the fact that most of the jobs were not related to their former professions. They stressed that their work enabled them to leave the house, improve their language skills, come into contact with the local population and gain some financial independence and decision-making power.

Nermina (45), who came to the Netherlands with her husband in 1994, laughs in response to my question about the way her relationship with her husband has developed in recent years:

> It is strange, but despite all the trouble we have been through and my sadness about all that has happened, Marko and I get along better than before. When we were in Bosnia I used to fight with him a lot because he did not help me in the house. Now he is doing much more housework and also plays much more with our two children. I think it is because he only has a part-time job. But he also sees and hears how men behave in this country. It is very different from back home. He knows that he cannot get away with things anymore as he used to. We know many couples who got divorced because the wives were fed up with their husbands' behaviour. Here they have seen that it could work differently.

The women are not alone in having contrasting experiences of changing gender relations. Bosnian men also express a broad range of attitudes and perceptions. For the majority, being refugees has meant a break with their traditional role as head of the household and as the main breadwinner. Being dependent on income support or engaging in low-paid work different from their actual profession is often interpreted as a loss of identity and manhood. The alleged emotional attachment and commitment to Bosnia sometimes appears to fill the gaps within the domain of identity previously occupied by a range of factors including profession, family ties, and local officialdoms. In other words, ethnic, national and political identities become especially significant in light of the loss of other identifiers traditionally associated with the 'male sphere'.

It is important to stress that public versus private spheres cannot be equated with male versus female domains. As shown in the case of Amra, women also experience a great loss of identity and self-esteem with the disappearance of their professional work. However, as has been widely demonstrated in numerous case studies, women tend to be less conscious of status deprivation because of their responsibility for maintaining household routines (Buijs 1993). Perhaps even more important, the home as an everyday, tangible and natural conceptual unit, as Giles argues in the context of nationalist ideologies, 'is frequently mapped into the intangible abstractions of nation and state' (1999: 85).

Most Bosnian refugee men, however, are by no means obsessed with a sense of loss or nationalist feelings. In fact, many husbands living with their families abroad are much more concerned with their immediate family than political or cultural questions. Some men, like Osman, who used to be the manager of a car factory outside Sarajevo, profess that they enjoy the time they spend with their children and are much more involved in childcare and household chores:

When I was working I used to come home late. I never touched anything in the kitchen, except food that was already prepared. I just knew how to make coffee. You know our coffee. It is much more work than the coffee they make here. Saliha [his wife] never complained but she tells me now that she was often upset about having to go out to work and then come home and take care of everything. What I enjoy most these days, is spending time with our daughter. She is so smart and I like to teach her all kinds of things.

Osman also feels closer to his wife and acknowledges that he speaks to her much more regularly than he used to in the past: 'She and my daughter are all that I have. In the beginning I talked to her, because there was no one else to talk to. Then I realised that I could discuss many things with her I would have never raised before.' The couple also socialize more together than they used to at home, partly because most other Bosnian families they know live relatively far away.

Negotiating across Generational Lines

Amra's decision to enrol in English classes coincided with steps that she took to spend more time with Selma improving her daughter's Bosnian: 'Selma speaks perfect English. She sometimes corrects me. Her teachers all say that she is doing really well. But her Bosnian was getting worse with time. So now I am spending a few hours almost every day reading

Bosnian stories to her, practising writing and talking. I don't want her to lose our language.'

Language skills are highly valued with regard to children's education and many Bosnians fear that their children will lose their mother tongue as time passes. A Bosnian language teacher described the level of Bosnian language skills as being very low among most of the children she has been teaching. During the past few years, several communities in the UK established Bosnian weekend schools. The Bosnian Embassy provided an official curriculum issued in Bosnia which includes the Bosnian language, history, geography, music and art. Currently there are about 10 schools in the UK with more than 250 pupils aged between 6–16 years attending classes. The teachers are professionals who used to work in Bosnia. Most work on a voluntary basis, although some receive a small stipend. The need for more schools was expressed by many people, but due to a lack of premises, funds and professional teachers, the numbers have been restricted. In the Netherlands, some associations organize informal language and art classes for children, but the Bosnian consulate has not been involved in help with their curricula (Al-Ali forthcoming).

Some parents expressed disappointment over the fact that their children refused to attend Bosnian supplementary schools at weekends. Saliha stopped sending her two children to the school after she and her husband got fed up with the children's opposition:

> I know they just want to play at weekends. Every weekend we used to drag them there and it was a terrible fight. Two months ago my husband and I gave up. We discussed it for a long time. We both think that they do not want to be different from the other children in their school. Even at home they speak English to each other. But Mirsad and I force them to speak Bosnian to us.

Children and adolescents generally find it much easier than their parents to adapt to their new environment. In some cases they start rejecting their alleged state of being different, their parents' strong emotional links to Bosnia, and the constant references made about returning home. Several adolescent Bosnians told me that they would stay behind if their parents ever returned to Bosnia. They complained about their parents' inability to start a new life and their constant mention of a past life left behind. However, other teenagers, like 15-year-old Anisa, feels that she misses Bosnia all the time. She said:

> Bosnia is so different from the Netherlands. I am looking forward to the summer when we will go back to Sarajevo. It is so much more fun there. I go out with

my friends and cousin all the time. People are so much nicer and warmer there. Most of my best friends here are from former Yugoslavia, not just Bosnians. We try to have fun here as well. But here everything is so expensive and my parents won't let me stay out as late as in Sarajevo. And the food . . . I hate Dutch food! Have you tried our pies?

Tensions across generational lines can be found among middle-aged refugees and their elderly parents. For many of the elderly refugee population, the wish to die in their native homeland overrides all practical and security considerations. In cases where elderly parents have remained in Bosnia, refugees feel particularly compelled to send remittances and visit Bosnia.

Financial Strategies

Amra's dilemma about spending too much money on phone calls to Bosnia or other places raises the wider issue of financial budgeting and security. Like many other refugees interviewed, Amra and Edin have to constantly negotiate how much money to invest in their life in London, how much money to send back to Bosnia and how much to save. Unlike those refugees whose only source of livelihood is income support and who need to juggle with an extremely tight budget, however, Edin and Amra have more flexibility thanks to his disability allowance.

Refugees in the Netherlands appear to be more satisfied with state allowances than refugees in the UK, although there are variations in perceptions about the amount of income support in both countries. Most of the people sending remittance money to Bosnia, however small the amount might be, stated that the money was usually in direct response to the basic needs of their relatives, such as for food, housing, medicine and clothes.[10]

Edina and her husband Namik, Bosnian Muslims from Brcko, arrived in the UK in 1993. They both had to leave their respective parents in their hometown. Since their arrival they have been sending them small sums of money, varying between £50 and £100, every two or three months. 'Edina is very good at saving money,' says her husband. 'She even started to bake her own bread.' Sometimes the couple argue about whose parents to support at a specific point. Namik says: 'We try to help them financially as much as we can. My parents were forced to flee from their house and now they have to rent an apartment even though they used to own a big house. It is very humiliating to see your parents live in poverty now and you can do so little to help them.' Edina's father, on the other hand, suffered a stroke a few years ago and needs expensive medicines. He is also supported by Edina's brother, Ahmed, who has been in Sweden since 1994.

Employment providing a regular salary and the possibility to save is the single most important factor in increasing the capacity of refugees to assist their relatives financially. Chances of employment, in turn, are related to factors such as language skills (English or Dutch), education, professional background and experience, possibilities of having professions officially recognised, the level of difficulty in obtaining necessary qualifications, and the specific job-market situation in the host country. However, there are also a number of subjective factors that increase or decrease employment possibilities among refugees. Traumatic experiences during the war have often been the cause of depression, insecurity or emotional instability and decrease the refugee's chances of finding employment. In other cases, the perceived limbo-like situation of being neither here nor there can be a paralysing force and prevent refugees from actively seeking employment.

In addition to employment or the lack thereof, another important factor influencing the capacity to send money home is an individual's skill at economizing and saving. Several women refugees reported that they managed to save a little money from their household expenditures by finding bargain shops, baking their own bread and cakes, and buying less meat than is common for their diet despite living on income support. Those with additional income, either due to a war pension from Bosnia or because of employment in the host country, are often faced with a choice between saving money to return, supporting their families in Bosnia, or starting to build a new life in the host country (Al-Ali forthcoming).

This dilemma was very apparent with Amra and Edin. Amra's wish to go back to Bosnia has not changed but practical and economic considerations have forced her to improve the very tools needed to start a new life in the UK. This strategic shift in home-base focus is not unique. Many other Bosnians share Amra's recognition that their stay in the UK or the Netherlands will be long term, if not permanent. In this context, it becomes apparent that boundaries between the category of refugee and labour migrant become blurred. Many Bosnians who initially came to the UK or the Netherlands as war refugees have decided to stay on for primarily economic reasons, often to seek employment. This applies more to well-educated refugees. Many others lack language skills and higher education, and therefore find it nearly impossible to study in either English or Dutch to acquire the new skills they need to find jobs.

Visiting Home

More than half the Bosnians I talked to in each receiving country reported having visited Bosnia for a short period of time. A considerably smaller number had returned twice or more in order to see family and friends. These visits often take place during the summer months, especially for families with children. Those who return on a regular basis tend to think more seriously about the option of returning than those who have visited only once or even not at all. However, others stated that their initial wish to return changed after a visit to Bosnia due to the continuing unstable political situation, the economic crisis and the poor health care facilities. For many of these refugees, disappointment with the ongoing crisis in Bosnia has led them to a decision to remain where they are and, like Edin and Amra, to shift their home-base focus to the receiving country.

Questions regarding their legal status and travel restrictions impede movement between the UK or the Netherlands and Bosnia. Both countries offer a three-month 'testing the waters' scheme,[11] which allows refugees to visit Bosnia, check out the possibility of return and re-enter their country of refuge without legal difficulties. Yet, the fear that participation in the test-the-water scheme might endanger someone's possibility of obtaining permanent residence status in the receiving country prevents the majority of refugees from making use of it. A much more common practice is to visit Bosnia by circumventing travel restrictions – entering Bosnia via Croatia on a Bosnian passport.[12]

Refugees in the UK who have been granted temporary protection and who are anxiously waiting to receive permanent permission to remain are often reluctant to travel to Bosnia or to display any interest in possible return. Until recently, refugees in the Netherlands felt more secure about their right to remain in the country. Their refugee status allows the possibility of Dutch citizenship after five years of residency. During the past year, however, several political parties in the Netherlands have challenged the justification of this status. Prior to recent local elections, the Liberal Party led calls for the return of all Bosnians arguing that their country was now safe. This call triggered a political debate in the Netherlands, which received significant press coverage and reached the wider population. Some refugees felt unsettled and betrayed by their host country, which had initially seemed to welcome them. Others stressed that the government's position has not changed and dismiss the debate as a political game that should not be taken seriously. In any case, insecurities have been raised and seem to have had an adverse effect on the confidence of some refugees.

A number of people initially felt uneasy about or were even opposed to visiting Bosnia, but felt compelled to do so due to circumstances like the need to attend to elderly parents, a sick family member, a death in the family, or bureaucratic matters related to property issues and housing. Others revealed that they had wanted to visit for a long time before they finally dared to visit the place they had fled. Experiences of these visits vary greatly. The majority of refugees perceive their visits to Bosnia as essential for maintaining links with their family and friends, and general social ties.[13] Most people describe reunions with their families as positive experiences, but some mentioned encountering resentment and envy in those who had remained in Bosnia.

Maja and Ferid, for example, felt ambiguous about their visits to Bosnia. Being a mixed-marriage couple in their forties, they arrived in the Netherlands in 1993. Both left behind close family and friends in their hometown of Sarajevo, with whom they had kept in close contact throughout the war. Maja missed her family, more so than Ferid, and for a few months even fell into a depression. While she wanted to visit her family as soon as possible, Ferid was hesitant, mainly because of a fear of resentment by those who had not left, but also because of changing attitudes towards mixed marriages. In 1996 they went back for the first time and both felt ambiguous about the visit. They were overjoyed to be reunited with their families, but were hurt by comments from neighbours and friends who accused them of taking the easy way out and of escaping during the war. They both went back again in 1998 but have now given up the idea of ever returning permanently.

Their experience differs greatly from Edin's. As he was medically evacuated after being wounded while fighting for the Bosnian army, he does not meet the resentment that other refugees who escaped during the war now experience. Especially in places that were under siege and where heavy fighting took place over a long period of time (such as Sarajevo and Gorazde), male refugees are often perceived as cowards and deserters by the population who remained behind. Others believe that refugees have been accumulating wealth abroad while they themselves have had to struggle with an ongoing economic crisis in Bosnia. By and large, refugees belonging to the same ethnic group as those who remained behind are perceived in a more sympathetic light than those of a different ethnic group.

During my visit to Bosnia I detected a whole range of attitudes on the part of Bosnian residents related to specific experiences of the war, the refugees' departure, the nature of the family relationship be it extended or immediate, and the kind of contacts and links people have with friends and family who are refugees. Indeed, attitudes towards refugees constitute one of the most precarious and sensitive issues in post-Dayton Bosnia. Despite the enormous flight of refugees to other countries and the subsequent 'brain drain', Bosnian politicians have not encouraged the involvement of refugees in current developments. Some people would even suggest that the leaders of Bosnian nationalist parties have propagated resentment against refugees in the national media and are partly responsible for the negative attitudes towards refugees held by many inside Bosnia.

Conclusion

Acknowledging that women could gain or lose status depending on their specific migration context and cultural background, the prevailing literature appears to group migrant and refugee women in either category: those who have gained in status and importance within the family due to new economic and social responsibilities, and those whose role in the family has been undermined (Buijs 1993). However, in the context of Bosnian refugee families, gender relations and family dynamics have shifted in various directions, accounting for empowerment and increased opportunities as well as impediment and loss among Bosnian refugee women and men. It should be emphasized that gender relations should not be equated with women *per se*; instead they include the power relations between men and women as well as the underlying notions of femininity and masculinity.

Kosmarskaya (1999) demonstrates in the context of post-Soviet Russian migration that there is a theoretical concentration on women's opportunities and reversed gender relations created by their refugee situation. She quotes Hollands' (1996) remarks about refugee integration in Dutch society:

Refugee men tend to refer longer to a past in which they *were* somebody. Due to male dominance in most societies, they more often than women had positions of power and status, in the field of work, in the field of politics and also as men . . . refugee women on the other hand seem to refer sooner to the present and to a future in which they hope to *become* somebody . . . For women this might create some space to escape from oppressive social codes concerning female roles, female behaviour and female identity. Their position as women has not been self-evident as it had been for men . . . This can be also basis of solidarity, with other refugee women, migrant women, but also Dutch women. (Hollands 1996: 11–12)

Some of my own findings concur with this assessment. Yet what seems to be missing in Kosmarskaya's account is a discussion and analysis of differences within specific refugee communities. Migrants who originate from the same country and belong to the same ethnic group constitute a 'community' but in making this assumption there is the danger of homogenizing and essentializing a diverse group of people (Rouse 1991, Smith and Guarnizo 1998). Paradoxically, the concern with and campaign against essentialism, which has dominated feminist scholarship over the past decade, seems to have barely touched the study of refugees and migrants. Yet refugee women, just like other women, vary in terms of class, education, political and sexual orientation, and so forth. And the same holds true for Bosnian men.

It comes as no surprise that many Bosnian women who *were* someone in Bosnia, either in terms of profession, public office or family background, think about the past with a sense of loss and regret. Just like Bosnian men, professional women suffer from lack of self-esteem and a sense of frustration since, aside from all other losses, they are unable to practice their previous professions. On the other hand, other Bosnian men and women stressed their sense of new opportunities despite facing hardships and losses. This was particularly true for refugees in the age group between 20 and 30 who might be able to acquire the kind of education or training they would not have been able to receive in Bosnia.

An analysis of changing family dynamics helps to shed light on how gender relations and links to the home country are shaped with respect to the circumstances of flight from a war-torn country, becoming a refugee and trying to create and maintain everyday life in the receiving country. Family relationships and their disruption are linked to conceptualizations of home. In turn, 'home' relates to a particular nation, place, and dwelling. Bosnian refugee households tend to diverge from more traditional extended family ties and frequently create strong nuclear family units. Many refugees experience tensions in their loyalties to extended family members who have remained in Bosnia and their wish to optimize their capabilities and improve the living conditions of their nuclear families within their country of refuge.

It could be argued that forced migration sometimes leads to forced transnationalism. Family responsibilities may push refugees to a greater involvement with their home country than they desire. In the context of labour migration to the US, the possibility of obtaining social status and improving one's social position is mentioned as a significant factor in encouraging transnational practices, such as sending home remittances (Goldring 1998). Rather than seeking to gain social status, many Bosnian refugees wish to keep a low profile, trying to avoid or diminish the resentment of those left behind in Bosnia. Assisting family members financially or with goods such as medicines and clothes is generally perceived to be a responsibility, occasionally even a burden. Even when this attitude is not prevalent, the element of social pressure needs to be taken into account when exploring relationships between households and families.

Developments in post-Dayton Bosnia as well as factors within their current country of residence shape refugees' shifting strategies and practices. A sense of political and economic security within the respective country of refuge can give rise to the confidence needed to create and maintain transnational links between households and families. The sense of security or anxiety that arises in relation to the question of the legal status of refugees plays a significant role in creating or hindering the space from which transnational practices can occur. As long as refugees are not certain about their legal status, they will tend to avoid anything that might jeopardize their position. In this context, it became clear that prior to the recent political debates about sending Bosnians back, the Netherlands provided more secure legal conditions than the UK, thereby creating a more conducive space from which transnational practices could occur.

The motivations for engaging in transnational activities have to be sought in the specific circumstances of being a Bosnian refugee and cannot simply be assumed or explained in terms of globalizing capital, time space compression and the internationalization of labour (Portes 1998). Aside from the unresolved dilemma of deciding which place to call home, other factors also come into play. Even those refugees who have decided to remain in their country of refuge often feel close emotional, social and cultural ties to the place from which they were forced or decided to flee. Most significantly, their displacement and the specific history and background of the war leading to it are directly linked to nationalist aspirations and struggles. If people were killed, raped and ethnically cleansed because of their religious and ethnic backgrounds, it comes as no surprise that the sense of being Bosnian, and more specifically Bosniak (Bosnian Muslim), very much governs people's sense of identity and of belonging.

The level of identification with the state has to be perceived in terms of a continuum with a total rejection at one end being contrasted with strong nationalist feelings at the opposite end. High levels of nationalist sentiment are momentous in motivating transnational activities. On the other hand, identification with former Yugoslavia as opposed to present-day Bosnia and Herzegovina might prevent the desire to create and maintain transnational practices. Nonetheless, individual links to relatives and friends may override wider political and economic considerations.

After all, a sense of 'home' and its transnational supports are constructed in one's mind and not on the solid, or not so solid, soil of nation states.

References

Al-Ali, N. (forthcoming), 'Transnational or A-National: Bosnian Refugees in the UK and the Netherlands', in N. Al-Ali and K. Koser (eds), *New Approaches to Migration: Transnational Communities and the Transformation of Home*, London, Routledge.

Balic, S. (1992), *Das Unbekannte Bosnien: Europas Brücke zur Islamischen Welt*, Köln, Bohlau Verlag.

Black, R., Koser, K. and Walsh, M. (1997), *Conditions for the Return of Displaced Persons from the European Union*, Brussels, European Commission and Brighton, Sussex Centre for Migration Research.

Bojicic, V. and Kaldor, M. (1999), 'The "Abnormal" Economy of Bosnia-Herzegovina', in C-U. Schierup (ed.), *Scramble for the Balkans: Nationalism, Globalism and the Political Economy of Reconstruction*, Basingstoke, Macmillan.

Bringa, T. (1995), *Being Muslim The Bosnian Way: Identity and Community in a Central Bosnian Village*, Princeton NJ, Princeton University Press.

Buijs, G. (1993), 'Introduction', in G. Buijs (ed.), *Migrant Women: Crossing Boundaries and Changing Identities*, Oxford, Berg.

Giles, W. (1999), 'Gendered Violence in War: Reflections on Transnationalist and Comparative Frameworks in Militarized Conflict Zones', in D. Indra (ed.), *Engendering Forced Migration: Theory and Practice*, Refugee and Forced Migration Studies, vol. 5, New York and Oxford, Berghahn Books.

Goldring, L. (1998), 'The Power of Status in Transnational Social Fields', in L.E. Guarnizo and M.P. Smith (eds), *Transnationalism from Below*, New Brunswick NJ, Transaction Publishers.

Hollands, M. (1996), 'Of Crowbars and Other Tools To Tackle Dutch Society: The Integration of Refugees and the Multicultural Society', Paper presented to the Second International Conference, 'New Migration in Europe: Social Constructions and Social Realities', Utrecht, 18–20 April.

Kosmarskaya, N. (1999), 'Post-Soviet Russian Migration from the New Independent States: Experiences of Women Migrants', in D. Indra (ed.), *Engendering Forced Migration: Theory and Practice*, Refugee and Forced Migration Studies, vol. 5, New York and Oxford, Berghahn Books.

Portes, A. (1998), 'Globalisation from Below: The Rise of Transnational Communities', ESRC Transnational Communities Programme Working Paper No. 1.

Rouse, R. (1991), 'Mexican Migration and the Social Space of Postmodernism', *Diaspora*, 1(1): 8–24.

Smith, M.P. and Guarnizo, L.E. (1998), 'The Locations of Transnationalism', in L.E. Guarnizo and M.P. Smith (eds), *Transnationalism from Below*, New Brunswick NJ, Transaction Publishers.

Smith, R. (1998), 'Transnational Localities: Community, Technology and the Politics of Membership Within the Context of Mexico and US Migration', in M.P. Smith and L.E. Guarnizo (eds), *Transnationalims from Below*, New Brunswick NJ, Transaction Publishers.

Van Hear, N. (1998), *New Diasporas: The Mass Exodus, Dispersal and Regrouping of Migrant Communities*, London, University College London Press.

Vertovec, S. (1999), 'Conceiving and Researching Transnationalism', *Ethnic and Racial Studies*, 22(2): 447–62.

Weine, S. (1999), *When History is a Nightmare: Lives and Memories of Ethnic Cleansing in Bosnia-Herzegovina*, New Brunswick NJ and London, Rutgers University Press.

Notes

1. This chapter is based on findings from the project entitled 'The mobilisation and participation of transnational exile communities in post-conflict reconstruction: a comparison of Bosnia and Eritrea' by Richard Black, Khalid Koser and Nadje Al-Ali, University of Sussex, University College London and University of Exeter, and funded by the ESRC Programme on 'Transnational Communities'.

2. Prior to the war, about one third of the population of Bosnia-Herzegovina was of Orthodox (Serb) and one sixth of Catholic (Croat) background. The majority of the population were of Muslim origin, but many identified themselves as Yugoslavs rather than 'Muslim in the sense of nation' (Bringa 1995: 28).

3. Between 1996 and 1998 a total of 161,985 Bosnians returned from Germany (UNHCR Sarajevo, 1 July 1999).

4. Between 1996 and 1998, 257 Bosnians living in the Netherlands and 102 Bosnians residing in the UK returned in the framework of assisted repatriation programmes.

5. Most of the Bosnians refugees I interviewed are Muslim, although I also interviewed people in mixed marriages and of different ethnic backgrounds. I interviewed 26 Bosnian women and 24 men in both the UK and the Netherlands, as well as 18 women and 13 men within the Federation of Bosnia and Herzegovina. The majority of those interviewed were between 30 and 50 years old, but I also spoke to 11 teenagers and 21 people over 50 years of age.

6. Quotes and excerpts from interviews are based on notes taken during interviews. If the interview took place in Bosnian, my research assistant translated it for me. Throughout this chapter I try to maintain the original 'flavour' of the interview. I have edited only in those cases where the original quote would have been too difficult to understand due to grammar or syntax mistakes.

7. Here I use Van Hear's (1998) conceptualization of 'migration orders' and their changes. In his conceptualization, specific migration orders comprise individual and household decision-making, economic and political disparities between countries, the development of migrant networks and institutions, national and international legal and policy institutions as well as macro-political economy developments (Van Hear 1998: 14–16). A 'migration transition' refers to a fundamental change in a given migration order (Van Hear 1988: 21–2).

8. Historically, the UK did not offer access to migrants originating from Europe as other countries (Germany and France, for example) did.

9. The status of and access to Gorazde were among the many points of fierce contention during negotiations in Dayton, Ohio. The town, which suffered terribly during the war, belongs to the Federation but is surrounded by villages and towns under Serb control (Republika Srpska). The remaining, predominantly Muslim, population feels isolated and lives in a constant state of fear and insecurity.

10. Most people did not provide me with any concrete figures with respect to the frequency and amount of money they send to relatives in Bosnia.

11. In the Netherlands, this scheme is called 'look and see'.

12. The Home Office tends to turn a blind eye to this practice.

13. A small number of Bosnians interviewed in the UK and the Netherlands reported that they have been visited by relatives or friends from Bosnia. A slightly larger number stated that they had managed to be reunited with their families – including wives, husbands, parents or siblings – who had followed them to their country of refuge.

5

Deceitful Origins and Tenacious Roots: Moroccan Immigration and New Trends in Dutch Literature[1]

Daniela Merolla

Generational relationships in immigrant families and the 'deceitful deed' of looking for one's family roots are approached in this chapter through the writings of two Dutch authors from the Moroccan immigrant community in the Netherlands: a short story by Hafid Bouazza, 'De verloren zoon' ('The Lost Son'), and the novel by Abdelkader Benali, *Bruiloft aan zee* (*Wedding by the Sea*). These narratives ironically question individual trajectories as well as major social issues such as (failing) attempts to renew links between 'sending' and 'emigrant' families through marriage. At issue is the constitution of individuals through the negotiation of their identities in the Netherlands.

Approaching immigration and other social processes through literary narratives can be criticized, as indeed it has been, from the point of view of both social disciplines and literary studies. The possibility and adequacy of studying novels as a form of anthropological research is controversial. The sociological approach to novels in literary studies is also contested. In the Netherlands, extensive discussion took place around the publication of a collection of articles entitled *Romanantropologie* (Bremen, van der Geest and Verrips 1979, 1984). Without probing too far into disciplinary quarrels, it is however useful to recall a few aspects of encounters between anthropology, literary studies and the reading of literary narratives.

Undisciplined Encounters

Anthropology and other social sciences construct descriptions and interpretations on the basis of data that are considered more objective than literary writings. The differences in objectivity between literary materials and social data have been of great importance in the debate even if the degrees of abstraction and of objectivity of social and cultural data have always been under scrutiny in the social sciences. This scrutiny became even sharper after the criticism raised by Geerts (1973, 1988) and Cliffords and Marcus (1986) as to how ethnographic writings construct and interpret the social reality that researchers are studying.

When anthropological research was connected to literary productions, attention was focused on oral productions whether they were defined as myths, oral traditions or verbal art.[2] The specific attention paid to myths was initially linked to the idea of oral production as a collective activity. Thus oral productions were opposed to writing and to written texts that were seen, in a perspective still influenced by Romanticism, as individualistic and artistic production.

The difference between oral and written productions has been undermined by the criticism raised in the study of ethnopoetics (Hymes 1974, 1981; Tedlock 1983) and the ethnography of speaking (Bauman and Sherzer 1974). These approaches criticize the dichotomy between literacy and orality in terms of the opposition between individualistic and collective creation. Instead, they pay attention to the individual (re)creation and variations of oral productions and to the uniqueness of oral performance. Conversely, in the field of literary studies, the works of Bakhtin (1976, 1986) shed light on the social and cultural constraints of the language of novels.

Rethinking disciplinary interactions, literary studies in the 1960s were influenced by structuralism and the analysis of oral productions developed in anthropology. Conversely, a new interest for written narratives and discourse analysis developed in literary studies has ballooned in anthropology since the 1980s. This interest has involved two broad areas of discussion: self-criticism concerning the objectivity of ethnographic writings, and the so-called shift from orality to literacy.

A number of scholars have made use of tools developed to analyse novels and narrative texts in literary studies: Geerts (1973, 1988) and Cliffords and Marcus (1986), Crapanzano (1980), Rosaldo (1989) and Rabinaw (1988). They argue that the use of narrative techniques in ethnographical writings has traditionally affirmed the authority of the discipline and of the ethnographers themselves. Such writing obscures processes of abstraction and the reconstruction of social data resulting in seemingly objective descriptions of the studied social and cultural systems. On the basis of this critique, post-modernist approaches see anthropology as an activity much more similar to literary writing, a position that many anthropologists do not willingly accept. Marcus urges the inclusion of autobiography as a mode of writing in anthropological research (Clifford and Marcus 1986).

As to the famous shift from orality to literacy, several studies have considered the interactions between oral and written productions and between 'high' and 'popular' literatures. These studies focused on contexts in which orality and literacy have coexisted for a long time, for example in Europe and in the Middle East, and on contexts in which the acquisition of literacy has developed since the colonial period. There are, for example, the discussions stimulated by Goody's work (1977, 1987) on the interaction between orality and literacy in terms of hegemony and subordination among groups and social classes and by Ong's (1982) study on the mental implications of the acquisition of literacy.

The spread of print literacy in the construction of nations is another important area of study. Anderson (1983) discusses how novels and autobiographies contribute to the narrative construction of the nation as an 'imagined community'. In particular he considers the production of novels and autobiographies as genres in which readers are constructed as collectives that experience a special kind of time: a homogeneous flow of time in which different characters are seen to be performing independent actions at the same clocked time. Such a perception of time is, according to Anderson (1983: 26), homologous to the homogeneous time that he recognizes as characterizing the nation 'conceived as a solid community moving steadily down (or up) history'.

Anderson's work has been influential in both anthropology and literary studies and has contributed to interdisciplinary discussion and encounters around questions concerning nationalism, gender and cultural productions (Appadurai 1991, Bhabha 1990, Brinker-Gabler and Smith 1997, Parker, Russo, Sommer and Yaeger 1992, Wilford and Miller 1998). These works indicate that a new interest in novels and autobiographies is coalescing in the social sciences (Alvarez 1995, Moore 1999, Ortner 1991, Thomas 1999).

Turning to literary studies, the question about how to read and analyse literary works is still open. The central criticism emanating from literary studies regarding the socio-anthropological reading of written texts is that 'form and content' are indivisible and that the artistic qualities of literary works go beyond a mere proposition of society and culture. Literary works, and elements of socio-cultural 'information' embedded in these works, are not to be considered as social and anthropological data. Nonetheless, scholars of literature representing other approaches argue that literary productions take place in the framework of expectations conjured up by cultural constraints and historical contexts (Culler 1975,

Eco 1979, Zima 1981, 1985). They stress the context of the literary as evidenced by Even-Zohar's (1979) theory of polysystems, which refers to the canonization or marginalization of literary works and their authors in the dynamics between the 'centre' and 'periphery' of literary and cultural systems. A literary work is conceived as a system within a larger system that is synchronically and diachronically heterogeneous and open (Rinner 1998). Another direction of research has been stimulated by Gramsci (1950, 1975), Said (1979, 1984) on orientalism, and Deleuze and Guattari (1986) on minority literature which, however differently, all highlight power relationships inscribed in history.[3] Post-colonial and post-modern studies focus on links between writing and power based on colonial, gender, class and ethnic divides. Other authors investigate the internal heterogeneity and divergence of literary work in contrast to the coherent unities of structuralist readings.[4]

In conclusion, from initial disciplinary opposition there has recently been a trend towards inter-disciplinarity. This is not intended as eclecticism but rather as an attempt to integrate tools developed in different disciplines to capture the multiplicity of social and cultural processes and to determine how these processes are individually experienced and constructed. As centuries of censure on literary writings forewarn, literary attention to the singular, the particular, the one case, can strongly express collective questions. Thus, literary production has become relevant in social studies, while the context intended as the sociological system of literary creation and production becomes essential in textual analysis. In other words, literary texts must be viewed in the context of their production, and specific elements within the texts must be understood within the framework of the narrative discourses and techniques of each novel.

Dutch Literary Space of a New Generation of Writers of Moroccan Background

Immigrants from Morocco, and in particular young male immigrants, are mainly seen by the Dutch public as a group caught up in criminal activities (Adriaansen 1996, Coppes, de Groot, and Sheerazi 1997, Eddaoudi 1998). This negative image becomes representative of the Moroccan community, while older men and women and young women simply disappear from the picture. Moreover, age and social differentiation among young immigrant men is not taken into account. According to Lucassen and Pennix (1994: 165), immigrant children who move to the Netherlands when they are too old to become fully integrated into the Dutch school system encounter serious difficulties. Without a good knowledge of the Dutch language and without educational qualifications they have difficulties getting a job and find themselves marginalized by society. Children who come to the Netherlands at a younger age or who are born in the Netherlands have a better chance of succeeding economically.

If we consider the new generation of authors from the Moroccan immigrant community who are active in the different artistic fields of literature, theatre and music,[5] we see that they mostly belong to this latter group[6] of immigrant children, or they are immigrants or refugees themselves.[7] It was only in the mid-1990s that a few young Moroccan immigrant writers first succeeded in publishing their novels and short stories, with some winning literary prizes in the Netherlands and in Flemish-speaking areas of Belgium.[8]

These works, initially labelled 'allochthonous' literature, catalysed debate in the Netherlands concerning immigration and were alternatively welcomed as a new trend in Dutch literature or criticized as being over-hyped and a temporary fashion with no solid literary basis (Merolla 1998). Either way they are acknowledged, sometimes feared, and often welcomed as the fulfilment of a multicultural society, expressing the present *métissage* between 'allochthonous' and 'autochthonous' cultures in Dutch society. Such a position, however, assumes that recent flows of immigrants make European societies multicultural, inferring the existence of distinct ethnic and culturally 'pure' hidden heterogeneity (Amselle 1990/1999).

Interviews with writers such as Bouazza, Benali, Stitou and Al Houbach reveal their rejection of the term 'allochthonous' and the labelling of their writing as such. They are critical of the sociological and anthropological reading of their works, refusing to be grouped together as artists and seen as separate from the Dutch literary field.[9] Each writer asserts his or her unique position and rejects being considered as a spokesperson for the immigrant group. The uniqueness of the writer is upheld although the texts treat experiences that can be recognized by many immigrants, especially young Dutch Moroccans.

Hafid Bouazza confided that definitional questions about writers and literature were forcing him to rethink his Moroccan roots and to what extent those origins inspire him.[10] For example in an interview about the themes of his work, he explained:

Both my feet are in the Dutch culture. By this I do not deny that I was born in Morocco and this fact plays a role in my stories. Childhood is always a good background for stories. (*Volkskrant*, 25 August 1995).

About the term 'allochthonous', he commented:

A French writer writes in French, an Allochthonous writer writes in Allochthons and a Dutch writer writes in Dutch. (*NRC*, 21 June 1996).

I write in Dutch and I have a Dutch passport. What else can I do to be a Dutch writer? (*De Roskam*, 31 January 1997).

The writer Abdelkader Benali initially dismissed the debate on allochthonous literature. In an interview given in 1996 he said:

Oh, this so-called *hype* concerning allochthonous writers is passing. And what now? Do you know what is going to happen with such a literature? The more it is published, the less it is special or strange. (*Karavan*, August 1996, no. 1).

Yet one year later, amidst the debate surrounding allochthonous literature and his work, Benali hardened his position:

No, I do not feel the allochthonous of my publications. The division allochthonous-autochthonous has no sense at either literary or human levels. What is important is the credit paid to my work, not to my origins. (*Het Parool*, 5 April 1997).

More recently, Benali (2000) gave his own definition of the new generation of writers of Moroccan origin in the Netherlands:

A new literary stream has developed during the last five years. It is not entirely Moroccan, it is not entirely Dutch. Neither. It is something in between, which would be too easy. No, *it* is an *action*.

To me migration means story-telling, telling stories to the world. After all we are Mother Migration's impatient children who could only become quiet thanks to stories.

Questions about the criteria of inclusion/exclusion in the Dutch literature are still unanswered. However, when we look at the history of European literatures, new contributions linked to long-term migration are not a new experience. Dutch literature has never been monolithic. Many enriching intersections have taken place in the past associated with the displacement of peoples within Europe, including the immigration of Jews from Spain and Eastern Europe, and displacements caused by Dutch colonial expansion since the sixteenth century.[11] During the nineteenth and twentieth centuries, linguistic, literary and social interactions linked to migration opened up the canonical Dutch literature contributing to form a new space for literary creation that I provisionally call 'Dutch literary space'. In the Dutch literary space, both 'canon' and 'margins' tend to be reconfigured selecting and partially including new contributions linked to recent migrations, as the 'canonization' of the diary of Anna Frank shows and the literary prizes won by Benali and Bouazza seem to confirm.[12]

Significantly, Bouazza's recent novella (1998) and a play by Benali (1999) do not have an immigrant context any more, although elements of their previous works are recognizable in their styles and themes. In his novella, Bouazza treats the delicate story of a child who is different and unique because of his bizarre qualities. Benali's play pivots around the encounter between King Boabdil and Queen Isabelle in Granada during the last hours of Moorish rule in Spain. This work makes room for a post-modern mixing of genres, literary references and historical anachronisms.

Conversely, when migrant contexts and themes are touched, the literary works by Bouazza and Benali ironically and sometimes sarcastically infer consequences of Dutch multiculturalism. This is the case in the two texts presented below.

Immigrant Families and Deceitful Origins: De verloren zoon[13]

We can look at discourses on the immigrant family, marriage, and their origins in the short story 'De verloren zoon' ('The Lost Son') by Hafid Bouazza (in *De voeten van Abdullah*). As the title forewarns, this short story presents a troubled relationship between the older and younger generations in an immigrant family. The son has fled to Amsterdam and to another kind of life but he decides to come back home. The beginning of this story is *in media res*:

> After seven years I was again at my parents' door. It wasn't raining.
> Mirianna did not know about it. I had left her lying in bed, after she had wiped off the traces of our rhythmic lovemaking and had wanted to draw herself close to me (one of those bad habits of Dutch women). Yet I had stood up, washed myself, got dressed and told her I was going out to buy cigarettes. As I closed the door behind me I caught a glimpse of her eyes, freckles and breasts in which breathtaking beauty was the canvas for hurtful wounds. (p. 121)

> She was not to blame. It had already happened once. Seven years had passed since I fled from my family womb that I never knew well. I now realise this.

Now I find myself going to catch the train to my parents' house. What did I flee from and what am I going back to? I had decided that understanding the past was the only way to accepting the present. My life in Amsterdam has never been free from doubt and trouble, and I needed my parents to expel these two demons. (p. 121)

Bouazza refines and invents the Dutch language with his rich descriptions and the interplay between present time and memory that modify the linear sequence of the narration. The assemblage of sequential adjectives, which gives rhythm and richness to his sentences by creating new words and refreshing old ones, creates a particular literary effect. Readers and reviewers found Bouazza's style excessively baroque or poetic (Anbeek 1999).

Whether their verdict is positive or negative, all reviewers noted his highly refined style, contrasting markedly with the Dutch language of daily life. Language invention has a double effect on the reader, offering both distance and proximity. Proximity because the terms are in Dutch and the reader can usually understand them even if they are new or 'refreshed', but at the same time a distance is created by their novelty. A sense of strangeness is introduced into the language and a 'deterritorialization' is obtained by working on the Dutch language without recourse to the insertion of foreign words. The use of Arabic is restricted.

Human physicality is a central theme and detailed descriptions are given of the characters' sexual encounters. A second relevant theme is that of 'difference', illustrated by the narrator's comments on 'the bad manners of Dutch women', emphasizing the narrator's distance from all that is Dutch. The salience of difference is reflected in the narrator's questioning of his relationship with his parents. Having fled from them, he now returns, troubled by cultural disloyalty and searching for meaning in his life.[14]

Elements can be recognized of the classic dilemma of immigrants stretched between two worlds: the world of the Moroccan family and the world of Dutch society, with gender behaviour highlighting the differences. The Dutch world, characterized by unrestrained sexual behaviour, is summarised by the sexual approachability of Dutch women (see p. 124). Yet the story dislocates simple oppositions and distinctions.

This is most evident in the character of the mother, who, as expected, personifies cultural conventions and traditional attitudes. She urges her son to return home and marry into his own group. The words of his mother resound in the thoughts of the narrator as he lives a 'free' life in Amsterdam:

Did you flee to have a good time with women of this misbelieving land? . . .
You will only waste your youth with girls who cannot get a man from their
own country. If you want a woman so much, we will find you a bride, a girl of
your own clay and faith. (p. 122)

I had never been able to chase my mother's words away from my memory as I
passed from embrace to embrace during those seven years. (p. 124)

The reader discovers in passing that the mother's call upon ethnic and
cultural continuity is ironic. She is in fact a Dutch woman, who became
Muslim and married the narrator's father, a Moroccan immigrant. This
woman, Moroccan only by marriage, assumes the role of the defender of
Moroccan 'roots'. She has acquired not only the most stereotyped
traditionalist attitudes of immigrants but also all the outward appearances
of Moroccan women: their gesticulation and the use of Arabic words and
sayings when speaking Dutch (see p. 122). The narrator takes pains to
explain the Arab translation of his mother's Dutch name. 'Maimuna' is
said to be the name of a type of primate, which prompts him to criticize
her religious faith as a step back in human evolution seeing her as a
'sanctimonious hypocrite as converts are' (p. 123).

This revelation about his mother's background and his harsh attitude
towards her destabilizes what at first seems a classic discourse on
immigration, and casts suspicion on the narrator's desire to return to his
parents. The notion that family history is essential in revealing one's 'true'
self is a literary frame utilised in European classic literature as in post-
colonial parents' mixed marriage. How does it not lead to a sequence of
social and emotional problems that the reader would normally expect in
a family of mixed cultural backgrounds? Problems of communication and
misunderstanding between spouses and negative social reactions from the
wider community do not surface. Quite the opposite, the complete
assimilation of the mother into Moroccan community norms and her
more-royalist-than-the-king attitudes subvert the 'expected'. Labelling his
mother as a hypocrite, the narrator discloses a critical appraisal of cultural
assimilation. Moreover the mother's character deconstructs the opposition
between allochthones and autochthones in terms of an essentialist ethnic
difference (see Amselle 1990/1999).

The juxtapositioning of origins resumes when the narrator accepts being
married off in Morocco and suddenly realizes:

with a shock of nostalgia I realised what I had left behind and what a deceitful
deed is going back to the origins when one does not know what and where
those damned origins lie. (p. 127)

The setting of the story changes when the narrator and his parents go to Morocco to arrange for a bride. The text indicates that going to Morocco is not 'coming back' for the young man. He ignores or misunderstands a great deal of what takes place in his father's village and in particular the marriage and sexual practices in the 'land of origins'. The marriage celebrations' exotic features are ambivalently couched in ironic tones, while the bride's name is mocked by slight changes of vowels in the string of three female ancestors' names: Fattúma bint Fátima bint Futayma bint Fattáma. It is at this point that the surrealistic plot of the story emerges. The reader receives an example of the 'mythical injection' that the narrator says 'could give meaning to his life' (p. 124): the bride disappears when the different layers of her dress are stripped off by the wondering bridegroom who remains with only pieces of material in his hands.

> In the end I decided to snatch her head veil off and, before I knew it, the rest of the dress fell to the ground. I still held the veil in my hands while the other part of Fattúma bint Fátima bint Futuyama bint Fattáma lay at my feet. (p. 132)

In 'De verloren zoon', the relationship between different generations in the family is presented in terms of a lifestyle conflict. The family conflict affects the self-perception and identification of the son, which can be overcome only when the young man goes back home looking for his 'origins'. However, looking for one's roots is a deceitful deed that ends with the disappearance of the bride. The story concludes on a paradoxical note: the impossible return to Moroccan 'origins' for the narrator and the short-circuiting of the family cycle. Refreshing the links between immigrants and sending branches of the family are as surrealistic as the disappearing bride.

Disappearing origins and the impossible 'return to tradition' are coupled with the ironic position of the narrator towards people, customs and rigid life convictions in the Netherlands as well as in Morocco, setting him apart from any group identity. The narrator does not speak for a group. This non-conventional position of the narrator intertwines the style of writing characterised by subversion and reinvention of the language and by the insertion of fabulous and surrealistic elements.

Immigrant Families and Tenacious Roots: *Bruiloft aan zee*

In the novel by Abdelkader Benali, *Bruiloft aan zee* (*Wedding by the Sea*), the narrator assumes a similar position, keeping his distance, often assuming the perspective of the central character Lamarat, a first-generation migrant. Lamarat is a young man who goes to the Moroccan Rif together with his family for the wedding of his sister and his uncle. But his young uncle flees to a nearby town and Lamarat is sent by his father to bring the bridegroom back to the house by the sea where the wedding is due to take place. The story is woven around an intricate sequence of events, past and present, narrated during Lamarat's taxi ride from the house by the sea to the town. The complexity of the narrative strategy is coupled with different literary styles, childlike in some episodes and a stream of consciousness in others, that flow from one to the other as the story tellingly shifts from external narrator to a character-bound narrator.[15] Such a post-modernist style allows the Dutch language to be submitted to strange forms of deterritorialization without the introduction of words or sentences from the author's mother tongue, as in the case of Bouazza's writing.

Interrelated themes that organize the narrative discourse are introduced at the beginning of the novel: migration and the return to the 'land of origin', men's fears of marriage, degrading villages, and the spatial-temporal distance of returning migrants represented by the tourist-like Lamarat.

The initial encounter between the young Lamarat and the all-knowing taxi driver Chalid allows a contrast between different points of view. On the one hand, the landscape and people are presented from the perspective of those who are 'ignorant', notably Lamarat, and possibly the reader. Lamarat's distance from his parent's homeland is signalled by his inability to recognize sounds like those of the cicadas, and local customs such as the driving mirror placed in a downward position as a form of respect to one's passengers. Both mark the landscape as southern and foreign. As expected, migration for a son of emigrants implies ignorance of and distance from Morocco. On the other hand, the encounter, seen from Chalid's perspective, poses the question of Lamarat's origins in a more meaningful form, using the metaphor of the tenacious roots of the local horseradish plant.

> Lamarat Minar was not an inhabitant of the Iwojen region unlike Chalid, the driver of the white Mercedes cab, who had brown teeth and a reversed rearview mirror, the taxi driver who knew, because of his profession, every hill, hogback ridge and gully in Iwojen; he who knew the source of all those chirring sounds. (p. 5)

> Somehow Chalid was able to catch on to what sort of person Minar Lamarat was, the son of the son of the father from that village by the sea, the young man who had not been back to the region since he was ten. (p. 5)

The taxi driver . . . (could have told) that the young man was linked to the region in a certain way, a kind of fat horseradish that oddly enough only got fatter the further it grew up from the root and tenaciously went on growing in a landscape that was otherwise bone-dry. (p. 5)

Nonetheless, cultural and affective roots cannot elude the estrangement of emigration. Migration is a turning point in time since it divides 'before' from 'after' in absolute terms. 'Before' is represented by Lamarat's birth and the social context of the love story between his father and mother, reminiscent of rural folktales and an agrarian context that is long gone, not only from the perspective of the young man but also for the Moroccan population. Spatial and temporal distance is underlined by the ironic tune of the narration and by the initial setting of the parents' love story in the fields where the family went to defecate:

Lamarat . . . had been born one sunny Saturday to a father and mother who, before they were married, had lived in two houses one on the top of the other in the centre of the village of Touarirt on the Mediterranean coast; at a faraway time for the one and only yesterday for the other, but far, far, far away from Thalidomide children and birth control. (p. 7)

The theme of distance created by emigration is further developed in the relationship between parents and son. Unlike in Bouazza's short story, the older and younger migrant generations are not in conflict. Yet a definite gap between generations is conveyed by the narration. This is particularly clear in the description of the encounter between Lamarat's father and a Dutch seller of plastic chairs. This encounter allows the narrator to satirize the Netherlands and Dutch people. But the profusion of stereotypes in the jokes about the Dutch seller is coupled with the portrayal of Lamanat's father as overly naïve in falling for the salesman's patronizing spiel. The son, and the narrator, perceive him as being different from the receiving land and culture, but also removed from the father's attitude:

Salaam mulaykum, keen bak vie dhar! 'What you mean is that I should understand Arabic,' Lamarat said, thinking out aloud, 'but unfortunately I do not understand that language of yours'. 'Well, then, I'll put it another way: *ehlel ye sehlel ouid wewesch e mis n tefkecht* (freely translated from Berber to Dutch: Good morning, go to fetch your father, son of a king-sized portion of spite). Floor knew that you always should treat Berbers somehow insolently, rudely, otherwise you do not get your message across.

'Thanks but no thanks.' Lamarat withdrew from the front door leaving his father to look at one garden chair after another and listen to Floris-Jan's jokes.

'Call me Floor, and I'll call you Abu Baker, you don't mind if I address you
on first-name terms, do you?' (p. 65)

Father, completely bewildered and impressed by the clever young man with
the Donald Dutch tie and wing-tip shoes who so easily 'assimilated to him',
bought the plastic chairs. Back in the living room . . . he called his wife:
'Darling, darling, what an experience! The perfect Dutchman was at the door!'
(p. 66)

Generational distance and the distance between emigrants and non-
emigrants are reinforced in this encounter when the reader remembers
the novel's opening scene in which the all-knowing taxi driver Chalid
remarks that garden chairs are for weak people (p. 5).

The ambiguous relationship between those who leave and those who
stay in Morocco is another recurrent theme in the novel. The term
'strangers' is used in Morocco for the immigrants who come back during
the summer or re-immigrate and who are liked and disliked at the same
time by those who have stayed. Social and economic links between
emigrants and those who stay behind are consummated in the construction
of houses and their children's marriages to one another. The name of the
town Nadorp is a play on words. Nadorp is a town favoured by migrants
for house building whereas Nadorp actually means 'after the village' in
Dutch.

There is a note of ironical distance in the narrative voice, as in the
reference to the emigrant 'model', the gender opposition in leaving or
staying at home, and the construction and demolition of houses:

If you go somehow further or you come from there, there is Nadorp, a migrant
boomtown with tight rows of houses . . . As could be expected in this town,
Lamarat's father, as behoves a model emigrant, has ordered the building of a
house. (p. 6)

And yet local residents in Nadorp 'loved the foreigners' (the emigrants). They
brought in hard cash (*doukou*), held weddings, facilitated young men's
emigration and encouraged young women to stay at home for the rest of their
lives, ordered houses to be built and tore them down again. (p. 44)

The central event of the narrative, the marriage-to-be between niece
and young uncle is framed in the context of the construction of a durable
house and the fragile links between migrant and 'sender' family. The
prestige-laden wedding is the tangible realization of links between the
two branches of the family and epitomises the social formula *do ut des*, a

reciprocal exchange that the character/narrator Lamarat only begins to understand during the course of the narrative:

> It was during that holiday that father began to talk about houses being built in cities . . . And the uncle said, 'Let me make you a proposition, my dear brother . . . I will do whatever your house needs, brother, if you will help me with something afterwards . . . something that helps me to get ahead too. (pp. 92–3)

> Lamarat did not understand what it was all about. But the one who understood him very well was his brother . . . actually, and I do not know why it has taken me so long to get it since it was so simple to think of: This was the beginning of the wedding. He (the uncle) would provide supervision for the work and in return the father would help in sailing him to Europe with a wife as his oar. A simple trade, but it benefited the house. (p. 93)

Marriage is a risky enterprise, however, as revealed by Chalid who is afraid of marrying and the young uncle's escape from marriage. Whatever reasons men may have for their fears, the bridegroom's choice of taking temporary refuge in the local bordello touches the bride, irreparably wounding the pride of Rebekka and leading to the story's paradoxical end.

Rebekka seems better integrated into the family than Lamarat. It is through her marriage that the bride's and groom's parents can renew family relationships and links with Morocco. Rebekka acknowledges her crucial role and agrees to marry her uncle (p. 95). Moreover, she speaks Berber while Lamarat finds himself linguistically handicapped when he wants to communicate with his grandmother in the Moroccan Rif.[16] However, it is Rebekka who, symbolically and literally, cuts the links between emigrant and sending branches of the family: her wedding night ends with the emasculation of the bridegroom. Rebekka becomes the pivot of delinking in the face of the traditional gender division that accords responsibility for cultural and family continuity to women. By contrast, Lamarat increasingly becomes a passive witness and narrator of events.

After the paradoxical conclusion to the wedding, Lamarat, his sister and his parents go back to the Netherlands and refuse to speak about what happened.

> Together they stood in the shallow sea. Rebekka turned and tugged at her bridegroom, who, together with his blood, was losing his honour, his strength, his everything that makes a man a man. (p. 155)

Everyone has gone home. Lamarat went back to Holland with his dear sister. She had come through the crash, but it was too terrible for words, thus she preferred to remain silent and she did so longer than her mother. (p. 159)

From the beginning of the novel the house that the father constructed in his Moroccan village is intended to cement the family's links to the land of origin. However, the house's deterioration is a thread throughout the novel, symbolizing the impossibility of recovery from the consuming consequences of emigration/immigration processes.[17] The house's final fall coincides with the failure of the wedding. The 'return to the origins' and 'refreshing' relationships between different branches of the family have failed: the uncle dies and the village is abandoned. Morocco becomes the place for the young man's summer holiday.

But ten years later, when Lamarat came back to the region . . . he was told by everyone that after his house had fallen down many others had followed: everything is empty, the houses are in ruins and everybody is busy in the town (which is much more enjoyable, with all those casual contacts etc.). (p. 160)

In *Bruiloft aan zee*, extensive attention is paid to the spatial, temporal and affective estrangement and distance caused by emigration. There are socio-economic links and even deeper 'horseradish' roots that counter migration estrangement, but what these roots are or mean in Lamarat's life remains unclear. The narrator keeps his distance from both sending and receiving lands and cultures, and the wedding's failure and the final abandonment of the village assert the impossibility of 'going back' to Morocco except as an occasional tourist.

Conclusion

The author's works cited in this chapter highlight the social and literary context of Dutch productions by writers from the Moroccan immigrant community in the Netherlands and literary perspectives on immigrant family relationships and the question of 'roots'.

Elements of 'information' in novels such as these are not and cannot be considered as social and anthropological data. However, the literary discourses point out intellectual trends and dissident voices when the discourses are set within their social context of production. The discourse on immigrant families in texts is embedded in a field in which writers and readers (public, literary critics, and anthropologists) interact, generating substantial anthropological insights into the migrant condition.

Examining the literary and social context of production, it is clear that Dutch writers from the Moroccan community in the Netherlands refuse the distinction between allochthonous and autochthonous and reject the role of intellectual mediators between these groups whatever social and ethnic boundaries these groups are attributed institutionally or in literary debates. Their texts treat experiences that are recognizable to many young Dutch Moroccans, but in interviews and public debates they assert their autochthonous position. Whether this position can be related to the social and cultural position of the writers themselves, and what the social and literary impacts are of the positions assumed by these young writers towards immigration and multicultural society, are aspects still to be studied.

Turning to Bouazza's (1996) and Benali's (1996) literary perspectives on immigrant families in the two texts considered, both main characters are the sons of Moroccan families who immigrated to the Netherlands. These 'sons', however, keep their distance from their immigrant parents and from their land of origin. This is linked to the disruption of the opposition between autochthonous and allochtonous. In Bouazza's story, the mother displaces discourses on origins in essentialist, ethnic, being and belonging terms, playfully stretching the implications of Dutch multiculturalism. In Benali's novel, the Moroccan families living in the Netherlands become the 'autochthonous immigrants in Morocco', reversing the equation.

The chosen perspective in these novels is that of young people who take their family as a cultural reference point but are not able to fit into the expected family pattern. The family conflict affects the self-perception and identification of the sons, which can apparently be overcome by looking for one's origins. However, it is unclear what these mean in the young men's lives. Conversely, it is readily apparent in both texts that parental attempts to strengthen family links between immigrant and sending branches of the family are not a viable option. Their efforts bring paradoxical and surrealistic results. There is no going back to whatever roots the young men imagined or hoped to find.

The literary strategies in these narratives allow the reader a glimpse of how individuals attempt to 'locate' themselves within the processes of migration and a new setting. The way out of family conflicts and cultural paradoxes in these narratives is through the use of linguistic deterritorialization and irony. Irony, affording critical distance from the cultural traditions of both sending and receiving lands, is entwined with the literary effect of a deterritorialized Dutch language created by highly refined style and reinvented language in Bouazza's story or by the mixing of styles and narrators in Benali's novel. Irony and linguistic deterritorialization become the main devices by which the narrators/sons attain their autochthonous 'location' in telling and acting. The narrative discourse on migration is embedded in these literary devices, providing an alternative to an essentialist and static approach to identity and origins. Immigrant families remain central to the narrative discourses of these texts, but their origins magically disappear or are neatly excised despite tenacious roots.

References

Adriaansen, F. (1996), *Een onderzoek naar de oorzaken en achtergronden van criminaliteit bij Marokkaanse jongens*, PW, Faculteit der Pedagogische en Onderwijskundige Wetenschappen.

Alvarez, R.R. (1995), 'The Mexican-US Border: The Making of Anthropology of Borderlands', *Ann. Review of Anthropology*, 24: 447–70.

Amselle, J.L. (1990/1999), *Logiques Métisses*, Paris, Edition Payot.

Anbeek, T. (1999), 'Fataal succes, Over Marokkaans-Nederlandse auteurs en hun critici', *Literatuur*, 6(16): 335–42.

Anderson, B. (1983/1991), *Imagined Communities*, London, New York, Verso.

Appadurai, A. (1991), 'Global Ethnoscapes: Notes and Queries for a Transnational Anthropology', in R. Fox (ed.), *Recapturing Anthropology*, Santa Fe, Mexico, School of American Research Press.

Bakhtin, M. (1976), 'Epos e romanzo. Sulla metodologia dello studio del romanzo', in V. Strada (ed.), *Lukács, Bachtin e altri, Problemi di teoria del romanzo*, Torino, Einaudi.

Bakhtin, M. (1986), *Speech Genres and Late Essays*, Austin, Texas, University of Texas Press.

Bal, M. (1985), *Narratology*, Toronto, Buffalo, London, University of Toronto Press.

El Barakat, A. (1999), 'Ach zakken meel', in *Smurfen en shadada*, Amsterdam, El Hizjra.

Bauman, R., and Sherzer, J. (eds) (1974/1989), *Explorations in the Ethnography of Speaking*, Cambridge, Cambridge University Press.

Benali, A. (1996), *Bruiloft aan zee*, Amsterdam, Vassallucci.

Benali, A. (1999), *Wedding by the Sea*, (translation by S. Massotty), London, Phoenix House/Butler & Tanner.

Benali, A. (1999), *De ongelukkige (The Unfortunate)*, Amsterdam, Vassallucci.

Benali, A. (2000), 'Introduction', *Koorddansers, Jonge Marokkaanse en Arabische auteurs in Nederland*, Amsterdam, El Hizjra.

El-Bezaz, N. (1996), *De weg naar het noorden (The Way to the North)*, Amsterdam, Contact.

Bhabha, H.K. (1990), *Nation and Narration*, London, New York, Routledge.

Bouazza, H. (1996), *De voeten van Abdullah* (*Abdullah's Feet*), Amsterdam, Arena.

Bouazza, H. (2000), *Abdullah's Feet*, (translation by I. Rilke), London, Review.

Bouazza, H. (1997), Interview, *De Roskam* (Amsterdam), 31 January.

Bouazza, H. (1998), *Momo*, Amsterdam, Prometheus.

Braidotti, R. (1994), 'Toward a New Nomadism', in C.V. Bundas and D. Olkowski (eds), *Gilles Deleuze and the Theatre of Philosophy*, London and New York, Routledge.

Bremen, J., van der Geest, S. and Verrips, J. (eds) (1979), *Romanantropologie: essays over antropologie en literatuur*, Amsterdam, UVA, CANSA.

Bremen, J., van der Geest, S. and Verrips, J. (eds) (1984), *Romanantropologie: essays over antropologie en literatuur, deel II*, Amsterdam, UVA, CANSA.

Brinker-Gabler, G. and Smith, S. (eds) (1997), *Writing New Identities: Gender, Nation, and Immigration in Contemporary Europe*, Minneapolis, University of Minnesota Press.

Cliffords, J. and Marcus, G.E. (1986) *Writing Culture*, Berkeley, Los Angeles, London, University of California Press.

Coppes, R., de Groot, F. and Sheerazi, A. (1997), *Politie en criminaliteit van Marokkaanse jongens: een praktijkonderzoek*, Deventer, Gouda Quint.

Crapanzano, V. (1980), *Tuhami: Portrait of a Moroccan*, Chicago, University of Chicago Press.

Culler, J. (1975), *Structuralist Poetics*, London, Routledge.

Deleuze, G. and Guattari, F. (1975), *Kafka: Pour une littérature mineure*, Paris, Minuit. (English translation: Minneapolis, University of Minnesota Press, 1986.)

Eco, U. (1979), *Lector in Fabula*, Milano, Bompiani.

Eddaoudi, A. (1998), *Marokkaanse jongeren : daders of slachtoffers?*, Rotterdam, Donker.

Even-Zohar, L. (1979), 'Polysystem Theory', *Poetics Today*, 1: 287–305.

Geerts, C. (1973), *The Interpretation of Cultures*, New York, Basic Books.

Geerts, C. (1988), *Works and Lives: The Anthropologist as Author*, Stanford, California, Stanford University Press.

Gilroy, P. (1993), *The Black Atlantic: Modernity and Double Consciousness*, London, Verso.

Goody, G. (1977), *The Domestication of the Savage Mind*, Cambridge, Cambridge University Press.

Goody, G. (1987), *The Interface Between the Written and the Oral*, Cambridge, Cambridge University Press.

Gramsci, A. (1975), *Quaderni dal carcere*, Torino, Einaudi. (English translation: *Prison Notebooks*, New York, Columbia University Press, 1991.)

Gramsci, A. (1950), *Letteratura e vita nazionale*, Torino, Einaudi.

El Haji, S. (2000), *De Dagen van Sjaitan*, Amsterdam, Vassallucci.

Haraway, D. (1991), *Simians, Cyborg, and Women: the Reinvention of Nature*, London, Free Association Books.

Hargreaves, A. and Mckinney, M. (eds) (1997), *Post-Colonial Cultures in France*, London and New York, Routledge.

Al Houbach, M. (1996), 'Ik weet, ik weet wat jij niet weet', in A. Ergün (ed.), *Het land in mij*, Amsterdam, Arena.

Hymes, D. (1974), *Foundations in Sociolinguistics: An Ethnographic Approach*, Philadelphia, University of Pennsylvania Press.

Hymes, D. (1981), *In Vain I Tried to Tell You: Essays in Native American Ethnopoetics*, Philadelphia, University of Pennsylvania Press.

Jameson, F. (1986), 'Third World Literature in an Era of Multinational Capitalism', *Social Texts*, 15: 65–88.

Literatuur (The Netherlands) (1999), Special Issue, vol. 6, 1 December.

Louwerse, H. (1999), 'De taal is gansch het volk? Over de taal van migranten-schrijvers', *Literatuur*, 6(16), 370–2.

Lucassen, J. and Pennix, R. (1994), *Nieuwkomers, Nakomelingen Nederlanders, Immigranten in Nederland 1550–1993*, Amsterdam, Het Spinhuis.

Merolla, D. (1998), 'Hafid Bouazza: "De voeten van Abdullah"' (Les Pieds de Abdullah)', *Le Maghreb Littéraire*, 2(3): 117–21.

Merolla, D. (2000), 'Poetics of Migration and Literary Renewing in Dutch Literature', paper presented at the conference on Convergences and Interferences, University of Antwerp, 6–8 April.

Moore, H. (1999), 'Anthropological Theory at the Turn of the Century', in H. Moore (ed.), *Anthropological Theory Today*, Cambridge, Polity Press.

Ong, W.J. (1982), *Orality and Literacy*, London and New York, Methuen.

Ortner, S.B. (1991), 'Reading America: Preliminary Notes on Class and Culture', in R. Fox (ed.), *Recapturing Anthropology*, Santa Fe, Mexico, School of American Research Press.

Paasman, B. (1999), 'Een klein aardrijkje op zichzelf, de multiculturele samen-leving en de etnische literatuur', *Literatuur*, 6(16): 324–34.

Parker, A., Russo, M., Sommer, D. and Yaeger, P. (1992), *Nationalisms and Sexualities*, London, New York, Routledge.

Rabinaw, P. (1988), 'Beyond Ethnography: Anthropology as Nominalism', *Cultural Anthropology*, 3(3): 335–64.

Rimmon-Kenan, S. (1989), *Narrative Fiction*, London, New York, Routledge.

Rinner, F. (1998), 'La Théorie des Polysistemes', in J. Chabot (ed.), *Après le Structuralisme, Journées de l'Ecole Doctorale Lettres et Sciences Humaines, Février 1995*, Aix-en-Provence Publications de l'Université de Provence.

Rosaldo, R. (1989), *Culture and Truth: The Remaking of Social Analysis*, Boston, Beacon Press.

Sahar, H. (1995), *Hoezo Bloedmooi* (What Stunning Beauty), Amsterdam, Antwerpen, De Arbeiderspers.

Sahar, H. (1996), *Zo veel liefde* (So Much Love), Amsterdam, Antwerpen, De Arbeiderspers.

Said, E. (1979), *Orientalism*, New York, Vintage Books.

Said, E. (1984), *The World, the Text and the Critic*, New York, Vintage Books, 1991 (first edition) London, Faber & Faber.

Spivak, G.C. (1990), 'The Post-Colonial Critic: Interviews, Strategies, Dialogues', in S. Harasym (ed.), *The Post-Colonial Critic*, London and New York, Routledge.

Stitou, M. (1994), *Mijn vormen* (*My Forms*), Amsterdam, Vassallucci.

Stitou, M. (1998), *Mijn gedichten* (*My Poems*), Amsterdam, Vassallucci.

Straver, H. (1999), 'Tussen orale cultuur en literatuur', *Literatuur*, 99–6(16): 343–9.

Tedlock, D. (1983), *The Spoken Word and the Work of Interpretation*, Philadelphia, University of Pennsylvania Press.

Thomas, N. (1999), 'Becoming Undisciplined: Anthropology and Cultural Studies', in H. Moore (ed.), *Anthropological Theory Today*, Cambridge, Polity Press.

Wilford, R. and Miller, R.L. (eds) (1998), *Women, Ethnicity and Nationalism*, London, New York.

Zima, P.V. (1981), *Semiotics and Dialectics*, Amsterdam, John Benjamin.

Zima, P.V. (1985), *Manuel de Sociocritique*, Paris, Picard.

Notes

1. I would like to thank Dr Deborah Bryceson for her editorial work. I am grateful for the comments of colleagues present at the conference 'Migrant Families and Human Capital Formation in Europe: Home Areas and Economic Vistas' and Frans Willem Korsten.
2. There is indeed a plurality of definitions depending on different points of view and research interests.
3. Gramsci's observations on hegemony, subordination and resistance in language and society have been particularly influential, although often indirectly, on the studies concerned with the relationships between literature and society.
4. See Bhabha (1990), Braidotti (1994), Gilroy (1993), Haraway (1991), Hargreaves (1997), Jameson (1986), Spivak (1990).
5. See for example the plays by Amhali, plays by the young theatre group Stichting Amazigh (i.s.m. Stout Jeugdtheater) under the direction of Massaoudi, and the theatre pieces by writers such as Al Houbach, Bouazza, and Benali. Several Moroccan semi-professional bands are also active in the Netherlands.
6. Authors such as Benali, Bouazza, El Bezaz, El Barakat, and Sahar who experienced social marginality.
7. See Mustafa Stitou and Mohammed Chacha who writes poems and short stories in Berber.
8. Hafid Bouazza won the Belgian E. Du Perron Prize in 1996 for his collection of short stories *De voeten van Abdullah* (*Abdullah's Feet*). Abdelkader Benali

won the Geertjan Lubberhuizen Prize in 1997 for this novel *Bruiloft aan zee* (*Wedding by the Sea*). Naima El-Bezaz (1996) won the International Board of Books for Young People prize for her *De weg naar het noorden* (*The Way to the North*) and recently Aziza El Barakat won the El Hizira Prize for 1999 for her story 'Acht zakken meel' (in *Smurfen en shadada*) and Rachid Novaire's collection of short stories *Reigers in Cairo* was shortlisted for the NPS Prize in 2000. The works by other authors such as Hans Sahar (1995, 1996), the poet Mustafa Stitou (1994, 1998), the journalist and writer Malika Al Houbach (1996), and Said El Haji (2000) have also been well received by the public and critics alike.

9. It can also be debated whether this position can be related to the social and cultural position of the writers: Benali and Bouazza are university graduates and work at highly specialized professional levels in the artistic circuit, but also in university institutions and in the media.

10. 'I am forced to think about my Moroccan origin and how far it is a source of inspiration for me' (*De Roskam* 31 January 1997).

11. 'Classic' Dutch literature also includes the diary of Anne Frank who was from a German Jewish immigrant family, the works by Conrad Busken Huet (1826–86) who was born into a family of French refugees, the works by Isaac da Costa (1798–1860) from an old Portuguese Jewish family, and by Jan Janszoon Starter (1594–1626) who was born in London, lived in Amsterdam and Friesland, and died in Hungary. Even the works by a 'father' of Dutch literature, Joost van de Vondel (1587–1679), could paradoxically be considered as written by an 'allochthone' as he was born in Keulen, although his family came from Brabant, and he lived and worked in Amsterdam.

12. On migration, literary trends and criticism in the Dutch language, see articles by different authors in *Literatuur*, November and December 1999.

13. My translation agrees with the English translation by I. Rilke in H. Bouazza, *Abdullah's Feet*, London, *Review*, 2000.

14. 'I wanted to believe that I could turn back into the underworld of my youth and decide whether the salty pillars of my disobedience were not worth more than the reward for absolute submission. I was young and thought a mythic injection could give meaning to my life.' (p.124)

15. By 'external narrator' I refer to what is defined as a third-person narration in classic literary terminology. 'Character-bound narrator' refers to the 'I' character who narrates the story. As to these terms and their differences in classic literary terminology, see Bal 1985, Rimmon-Kenan 1989.

16. 'Lamarat was thinking that he was the illiterate one of the family and indeed he was at the moment' (p. 90).

17. 'In this town Lamarat's father . . . had ordered a house to be built, a house with five pillars and a water pipe that soon became clogged up with cockroaches and crumbling mortar' (p. 86). 'The whole thing was eroding, crumbling at high-speed' (p. 6).

Part III

Life-Cycle Uncertainties

6

Reconceptualizing Motherhood: Experiences of Migrant Women from Turkey Living in Germany

Umut Erel

Migrant women from Turkey are generally perceived in an Orientalist manner as backward, oppressed and passive. The family unit is seen as the main site of their sexist oppression and their social identity and agency is viewed as limited to the family. This chapter addresses the ways in which migrant women from Turkey challenge their ethnocized and gendered subject positions in relation to their society of residence and its ethnic community.[1] The focus is on the experiences of mothering and family relations, particularly from the daughters' perspective, based on research findings from a project about subjectivity and agency in life stories of women of Turkish background living in Germany.[2]

Certain aspects of the image of migrant mothers from Turkey are deconstructed. The notion of mothering used here is broadly that of caring for and educating children. Mothering is bound up with the concept of biological motherhood and the notion that the mother is the primary point of reference for her children. The ethnocentric (and class-specific) assumptions underlying such narrow notions of motherhood are critically examined. Secondly, mothering is an essential aspect of producing and reproducing the ethnic and national collectivity, both biologically, culturally and socially (Anthias and Yuval-Davis 1992). Images of and discourses about mothers therefore feature prominently in ethnic and national projects. Accounts of migration and motherhood are used to question the notion of the family as a culturally unified cornerstone of an ethnic or national group.

In the first section, public discourses on 'the Turkish family' in Germany are sketched and the dichotomy of 'modern German' versus 'traditional Turkish' gender and family relations are critically evaluated. The role of the overbearing, caring mother that has been ascribed to migrant women of Turkish background does not take into account the ways in which women have actively adapted their mothering to the migration experience. This is exemplified with reference to women's negotiation of temporary single motherhood in Turkey and with reference to women who migrated leaving their families behind. For many mothers, migration leads to a separation from their children. This throws into question the naturalization of emotional and geographical closeness between biological mothers and children. Children's accounts of separation and rejoining their mothers are examined to show the importance of others, besides the biological mother, in fulfilling the mothering role. Socialization and acculturation into an ethnic or national group are important aspects of the mothering role. The different experiences of siblings within one family may be used to question the ethnic homogeneity of the family unit. Finally, the ways in which migration can put women in a difficult position to fulfil external and internal notions of 'good mothering' are discussed.

Public Discourses on 'The Turkish Family'

Ethnic minority families from so-called Muslim countries are often conceptualized as embodying a close-knit and traditional family. In this view, the main site of oppression of women is the family, which is backward and patriarchal (Lutz undated, Otyakmaz 1995, Waltz 1996). This view on the traditional structure of families of Turkish background can be evaluated in various ways. While New Right ideologies may perceive a traditional family model as ideal for the dominant ethnic group, they may at the same time see the perceived strength of ethnic minority family ties as a threat to the apparently weaker, more vulnerable social structure of the country of immigration and of the majority population. Outspoken racists may see the higher birth rates of families of Turkish origin as a threat to the national identity of Germany, given the decline in the German birth rate. In a contrasting position, instrumentalist racist[3] policymakers argue the need for controlled and regulated immigration and integration of the existing ethnic minority population in order to safeguard the social security system and in particular the pension schemes which depend on the contributions of younger working people. To this end, the higher birth rates of Turkish families can be seen to be in the German national interest.[4]

Thus, discourses on the Turkish family in Germany are contradictory, complex and multifaceted. However they mostly converge around a racialized dichotomy of modernity versus tradition (Bhatt 1997, Appiah 1990). Germany is seen as a modern society, characterized by individual-ization, the fragmentation of stable relationships and forms of belonging, increasingly rapid change and the pluralization of cultural options as well as a sharpening of social inequalities and a decline in economic opportunity (cf. Heitmeyer et al. 1997). The nuclear family is one of the central social institutions challenged by modernization (Beck and Beck-Gernsheim 1995). However, these challenges can also be seen to have positive aspects such as an increasing realization of democratic and egalitarian family relations (Giddens 1992). Within such discussions of the modernization of family relations, migrant families' experiences are not considered and are tacitly assumed as residues of tradition (cf. Klesse 2000). Families of Turkish background are contrasted with the modern German family as the embodiment of tradition in the sense of patriarchal gender relations, continuity, and stability.[5]

My main concern here is to point out the inadequacies of such a view. Bhabha (1990) argues that the effectiveness of a stereotype results from its power to fix certain groups to an image. The stereotype is not a simplification of reality because it is false but because it fixes a singular reality. Stereotypes often contain empirically verifiable facts. However, the meaning attached to these facts exceeds the empirical level, generating ambivalent emotions ranging from love and desire to hatred and disgust. The stereotype of the Turkish family as an embodiment of tradition can be seen to exert ambivalent responses of longing and envy for stability as well as disdain for a presumably archaic and sexist institution.

However the life stories of women of Turkish background alert us to evidence that diverges from the stereotype. The truth of these life story accounts should also be seen as situated and partial. They serve to construct a notion of self that is in dialogue, negotiation and at times in open resistance to other public German or Turkish accounts, especially those emanating from a tradition-modernity dichotomy. This points to the need to critically question dominant representations of migration and motherhood while showing their impact on the lives of migrant families.

The process of migration may be a reaction to changing family relations. Thus, some of my interviewees migrated from Turkey because they were divorced and faced social and familial pressures that they tried to avoid through migration. Others migrated because they found it impossible to support their children on their own wages as single mothers. In fact, the process of migration itself puts into question stable family relations and changes in familial relations. These changes may be initiated by women, although the choices they make are often severely restricted by factors

over which they have limited or no control such as immigration legislation, childcare provision, economic necessity, and power structures
within the family.

Trajectories of Migration

The process of migration often does not take place at the same time for
the whole family. The question as to who constitutes 'the whole family'
is not unequivocal. Although the nuclear family is the only family type
recognized for purposes of immigration, extended family networks are
frequently instrumental in enabling the migration process by providing
support in terms of childcare and other resources (cf. Krüger and Potts
1995). This points to the problematic logic of immigration legislation
where the country of immigration's interests are paramount in defining
who has the right to enter. Thus the reproductive labour of child raising
is 'outsourced' to Turkey. However this indirect, unpaid or underpaid
contribution to the smooth running of the German economy does not
entitle these (mainly) women to make any claims on the German state.

Many of my second-generation interviewees recounted that their fathers
had migrated first. This male migration turned many women temporarily
into single mothers. Many women in Turkey suffered from being left
behind, often living with their husband's families. There has been some
interest in Turkey in the problems of these 'migration widows'. There
was concern over the loss of status these women experienced while living
with their in-law families, and their lack of protection from exploitation
by in-laws. Vivid descriptions of how the husbands turned to 'Western
ways' and often to Western women, abandoning their families in Turkey,
are part of this repertoire of discourses. From my interviews, such a picture
does not emerge. This may be because the stories relating to this stage of
migration were related to me by daughters, rather than by their mothers,
who may have a different perspective.

> *Lale*:[6]   We had a house and we grew tobacco. And there were four of us [I
> had two sisters] and I had a brother. And we always had labourers
> during the day because we would not have managed [the workload]
> on our own. And at first my father was in the military, then he was in
> Holland, and then in A-town. And later he fetched us. But I cannot
> remember my father very well because he was always away, you see.
> And when he came we always hoped for presents, I remember that.
> (*Laughs.*)
>
> *Umut*:   (*Laughs.*)

Lale: But it was my mother who managed everything, all of it. And I think
she found that great. She was very independent. And then she came to
Germany and she didn't know the language, she didn't know how to
read and write. At the time there weren't so many migrants here, yet.
There weren't any Turkish shops either. Therefore she could hardly
go shopping. I think that was horrible for her, not to be able to defend
herself. All of a sudden to give up her independence and to live day
in, day out with this man who after all she had not seen for years. He
hadn't had any say in things anymore. And then she started working
[at a department store] as a cleaning woman, ten hours a day.

This extract, contrary to many stories about the migrant-widows in
Turkey, shows that Lale's mother gained independence through her
husband's absence. It is a narrative that constructs a familial tradition –
albeit and interrupted one – of female independence. For Lale's mother,
migration to Germany meant a loss of independence. The skills she had
as a farmer were not relevant in the big city, and her illiteracy and inability
to speak German made her even more dependent on her husband, turning
the relationship between the spouses upside down. Her estranged husband
was now the person on whom she had to depend. In her working life, she
experienced a decisive deskilling, from managing a farm and employing
labourers to an unskilled low-paid and low-prestige job with long hours.
This experience runs counter to a familiar argument in the migration
literature that sees migration and paid employment as factors facilitating
emancipatory processes (Zentrum für Türkeistudien 1995; for a critique
cf. Räthzel and Sarica 1994).

It was not always the men who migrated first. In fact during certain
periods of guest-worker recruitment women were preferred when workers
were needed for so-called women's jobs in the electronic, textile and
clothing industries as well as in the service sector (Eryilmaz 1998). One
interviewee recounts that her mother took the decision to go to Germany
first.

Meral: And it seems my mother also had problems paying the rent, and some
time ago my sister told me that for example there were situations in
which we had to share an egg between the four of us, you know.
Umut: Hmm.
Meral: And because of this my mother at one point said to herself – she listened
to the radio a lot then and she heard on the radio that one could go to
Germany to work and that many had done so already. Then she just
thought 'I can try that, too'. She filled in a form and got a letter and
then she went back to school for a year in order to – one had to have
at least a middle-upper school-

Umut: Middle school?

Meral: Well, five years of schooling, she caught up on [her last year of schooling]. Me, my grandmother and her went to the X-school, where I went later on. [That is the school] where my mother took her exams ... She was in N [a German town] for three months, and then she brought my father over and they stayed for a year in N. My uncle had been in Germany since he was 17 or 18, and he helped them to move to A-Town. And then they fetched us.

This instance challenges the traditional role of the father as the breadwinner: the inadequacy of the father's income in Turkey led to the mother taking over the role of breadwinner more successfully, even if only for a limited period. However, the reversal of economic roles between the spouses does not necessarily lead to a reversal in power relations or to a change in the domestic division of labour.

Separations of Mothers and Children

Many mothers who migrated left their children behind temporarily. This is an experience that has shaped the familial relationships of migrant families in important ways. The separation of mothers and children runs counter to hegemonic discourses on the mother as the primary carer of her children, and the emotional, physical and thus geographical closeness that is claimed and naturalized by such discourses (cf. Tizard 1991, Phoenix and Woollett 1991). In much of the research on migrant women from so-called Muslim countries, the women are constructed as embodying traditional gender roles, including that of the self-sacrificing, overbearing mother (Schmidt-Koddenberg 1989). This image holds in balance the other pole of the dichotomized construction: the modern, emancipated Western woman who enjoys gender equality, including choices about mothering roles. Such dichotomies are highly problematic and preclude a closer look at migrant women's self-definition and their actual practices of gendering.

There is a proliferation of discourses around mothering, and women's mothering practices are a focal point of regulatory interest. Although these discourses vary, one can identify the question of physical/geographical closeness of mother and child as a key issue. This is mainly discussed with respect to the issue of the mothers' employment. The argument most often put forward concerns the special attachment of biological mothers and children. It is argued that the child's attachment to its mother is crucial for developing a sense of trust. This is seen as a precondition for a healthy development throughout later stages in life. The success of the initial attachment to the mother is seen as influencing children's later social adaptation or delinquency, their educational success or failure, their ability to build a 'normal family life' and so forth (cf. Tizard 1991, Young 1994). The mother-child dyad is thus constructed as the relationship most crucial to a child's development. Other carers are seen only as substitutes. This has the effect of exercising pressure on mothers and holding them singularly responsible for their child's development. Other persons, such as fathers, are thus exonerated from responsibility for child development, and other social influences such as schooling, peer groups, media, and poverty are discounted as significant factors for child development. Moreover, kindergartens and after-school clubs are not seen as adequate alternatives so the improvement of such facilities is not discussed.

These discourses reinforce the model of heterosexual, white, middle-class, nuclear families. The mother as the primary carer is a class-specific ethnocentric construction. Thus, neither working-class women who have to work even in their children's infancy nor rich women who have the opportunity to rely on nannies for childcare conform to this ideal. Furthermore, this notion is far from ethnically universal. In rural Turkey, where women participate in agricultural work, the raising of children is the collective labour of mothers, older siblings and grandmothers. In urban areas, even if the mothers do not take part in paid employment, housework and childcare often take place in a wider social context of extended-family members and neighbours.

The issue of mother-child attachment that is disturbed by the mothers' employment is brought into even sharper conflict for mothers who migrate and are separated for long periods of time from their children. In my sample of eight second-generation women, five had experienced periods of separation from their mothers. All of them had been left in the care of close relatives, mostly grandparents or aunts. Some were also separated from some of their siblings and from their fathers. Their life stories show that the process of migration was not linear, either for the individual or for the family unit. Difficulties in organizing childcare and schooling were often solved by relying on transnational family networks. The following extracts illustrate this:

Deniz: Well, I was born in Istanbul and lived there until I was four years old. And when I was two years old or so, yes, when I was two years old, my father came here to Germany. And then, two years later we, the three of us, my mother, my sister and me, we followed. We lived for two years in S-town, which is where my parents still live. And when I got to the age to go to school, at six years old, two years later, my parents said that we should go to school in Turkey. Because they anyway did not want to stay here for long (*laughs*), like all the others. And they knew some things about this from others who had older children, that they had to – well, they started school in Germany and were then sent to Turkey, a constant to and fro. And then they saw that this was really quite bad for the children. And then my sister, she is two years younger than I am, we went to my grandparents, my mother's parents.

Umut: In Istanbul?

Deniz: No, they lived in B . . . We lived in a village there. And that is where I went to school for the first two years. That was beautiful. My childhood was actually very beautiful. I like to remember my childhood. Well, and then my mother was here, and then we went to Istanbul. That is where all my other relatives are and my paternal grandparents. And then we continued school in Istanbul, and lived with my mother with her in-laws. Well, and then my mother and my sister – well we came here [to Germany] in the school holidays and my sister and my mother stayed here and I went back because I had only one year of primary school left to finish, the fifth grade. [In Turkey] primary school finishes after the fifth grade. Then I went back and stayed with my grandparents and they lived in the same street as my three maternal aunts . . . Well I lived with them and also with my paternal grandparents

Umut: Hmm.

Deniz: Yes, and then I came here.

Deniz's process of migration thus included two stays in Germany and also migrations within Turkey to different parts of the family. The pattern was related to her family's hope to spare her and her sister difficulties in adapting to a different society, language and education system. As it turns out, Deniz still had to adapt to two different education systems and languages because the family stayed on longer than originally intended. When her parents brought her to Germany permanently, it was motivated by their wish to alleviate the grandparents' caring responsibilities. There are a variety of reasons involved in selecting the children's place of residence, which may not always be obvious, either to the children themselves or to outsiders. From other interviews it emerges that factors considered important by mothers were the availability of affordable childcare that suited their needs as single mothers, the price of childcare and the reliability of the carers. Thus, it was often considered a better solution to separate from the children in order to have a trusted member of the family care for the child than to have to rely on the care of strangers.

Deniz does not recount any negative feelings regarding the separation from her mother. She in fact 'did not want to come [to Germany] at all . . .

I had my friends and felt happy there, I wanted to stay.' However, she conceded that her grandparents were too old to look after her, although she actually enjoyed the greater freedom her grandparents' relaxed attitude allowed her in contrast to her mother's stricter adherence to rules.

In my sample of second-generation women, Meral was the only one who indicated that the separation from her mother was traumatic. She was left behind in Turkey in the care of her paternal grandmother who was extremely strict. She is also the only second-generation interviewee who vividly remembers the moment of separation from her mother.

Meral: Well, and then my parents brought the three of us to Germany.

Umut: They were here already?

Meral: My mother went to Germany first. It was very tough when she said goodbye. She gave us five Lira. I saw that she put something in my brother's hand and in my sister's hand. And then my brother and sister quarrelled. I was the youngest . . . Something was going on, but I was too young to understand what it was. But it was something grisly, something frightening, something that would probably hurt me. I felt that it was a parting. And then I realized that my mother was crying. And something happened to my sister and brother, I noticed them just marginally. And then she approached me to say goodbye. She was crying, and because she cried I started crying. And I did not know what was going on. I cried and realized something bad was happening. I did not want her to go. And then she gave me five Lira, which was worth a lot at the time, like ten Deutsch Marks today. When does a child get ten Deutsch Marks?

Umut: Hmm. Yes, yes.

Meral: And then I looked at my mother and thought it must be something important that she has to go. I looked at her. Somehow I did not want to let her go. On the other hand I thought that if she gives me so much money, it must be something damned important. All right, Meral, stop crying. Even if you do not really want the money and feel bad about it. Don't make your mother sad, so that she can go. I stopped crying and then she left.

Meral became very emotional during the interview when recounting this experience. Her lack of comprehension as a five year old of the significance of her mother's absence clearly comes out in this extract. This lack of comprehension actually compounded her feelings of fear because she could not understand the meaning of the event. Moreover, in her memory she went through this experience on her own, her older brother and sister did not comfort her, and her father seems absent from this memory. Despite the pain and sadness of the separation, Meral also remembers the efforts to show love and affection that she and her mother exchanged across the physical distance:

> *Meral*: And at school I started to write. And then I began to write a letter to my mother. She sent us chocolate-flavoured chewing gum. Those green ones, Wrigley's Spearmint Gum (laughs). She always put one or sometimes three, for each of us into the letter. I was always looking forward to this chewing gum. That was my greatest happiness – chocolate-flavoured chewing gum, real chocolate, they were slightly brown in colour . . . This chewing gum was so thin it fit into a letter. These were the smallest signs of love, but for me they were worth as much as – I don't know. It was as if my mother was a bit closer.

Meral's experience seems to give validity to the thesis that young children experience separation from the mother traumatically. However, Tizard (1991) argues that the separation of a mother and her child does not necessarily traumatize the child. A separation from the mother is traumatic only when the child does not have good care or a trusting relationship with her carers. This argument seems to be borne out by the life stories of my interviewees. Left behind in Turkey, they had good relationships with those looking after them and they did not feel abandoned by their parents. Meral is the only one who articulates the separation from her mother as a painful experience. This may be due to the fact that she was left in the care of her very strict grandmother. Although she does not openly criticize her grandmother's attitudes, she clearly suffered:

> *Meral*: But then my grandmother was a bit funny. I was not allowed to go outside. We had a balcony, and I looked down from the balcony and watched the children playing. I was a child myself. And I would have liked to go and play outside with them. Somehow I was not allowed. In the afternoons, after school I had to clean the house.
>
> *Umut*: Hmm.
>
> *Meral*: Really, just like a grown-up I had to clean the stairs and stuff, at that age. And I had to do other domestic work. And my playmates were my brother and my sister and my uncle who was 14 or 15 at the time. And we used to play great games with him . . . But still I missed the fact that I could not go out.
>
> *Umut*: Were the others allowed out?
>
> *Meral*: My brother was allowed out. I didn't know why I wasn't allowed out. But I was too young to enquire further into this. For the time being I accepted it in order to understand at one point the reason for this.
>
> *Umut*: Hmm.
>
> *Meral*: And one day, the girl from across played ball outside and I was watching her, and at one point she looked up at me and asked whether

I fancied playing ball with her. I said I am not allowed out. Then she said 'I'll throw the ball up to you'. (*Laughs.*)

Umut: (Laughs.)

Meral: . . . And then we had some fun together. And then my granny saw it and fetched me inside. 'Come on in.' I did not know why I was not allowed but well that was it . . .

Meral: And then at school it was a problem for me that I was not allowed to play with others. It was like a law that forbade me, Meral, to play with other children . . . although my granny was not there.

While she stayed with her grandmother Meral was isolated from other children. She could not understand the reasons for this. She was treated very differently from her brother who was allowed to play outside and did not have to do housework. Thus, it seemed to Meral like a personal punishment. While she was living with her mother, Meral was allowed to play in the garden and her mother also played with her. Thus, she did not only experience a separation from her mother but also a harsh change in upbringing styles. She does not mention any positive experiences with her grandmother. At one point Meral did not want to go back to school anymore. When her sister took her to school despite her refusal, Meral blocked out a whole year from her memory.

Despite the traumatic experience of separation, Meral's relationship with her mother remains very close, although problematic. She feels she is still in the process of finding her emotional independence from her mother.

Nilgün's experiences of separation from her mother were different. Her primary relationship with her grandparents during her early childhood was more positive. Nilgün lived with her sister Saniye, who was two years younger, and with her paternal grandparents in a village in Turkey. Her parents migrated to Germany when she was five years old:

Nilgün: Somehow I was a happy child, I would say until the age of ten. And I didn't have that with my parents that I was lonely or felt left alone or abandoned. I didn't have such feelings, and for me it was rather frightening to think of the future where at one point I had to go to my parents because they were strangers to me. [I felt my actual] parents were my granny and gramps to whom I was very attached and who treated us very lovingly. But I was not there on my own, my sister [Saniye] was also there. And at one point the day came when they came to fetch us, that was when I was ten years old . . . And, the separation was rather tough actually for me. For my grandparents it was very tough because they were very much attached to us . . . Well, and when I got here I was feeling very bad.

This illustrates how social mothering and biological mothering cannot be equated. Nilgün's grandparents fulfilled the parenting role. She did not feel her parents' absence as abandonment, contradicting the normative assumption that mother-child separations are necessarily traumatic for children.

In fact, the memory of separation is most vivid with regard to her grandparents. An important factor of continuity was the presence of her younger sister, Saniye, with whom she shared the same parenting and migratory trajectory. Nilgün refers to Saniye to explain that she 'was not alone'.

Sibling Relationships

While mothering is my focus in this chapter, it cannot be seen in isolation from other familial and caring relationships. In fact, consideration of variations in mothering experiences with regard to different siblings in the same family may help to deconstruct the naturalization of assumptions around mothering. Moreover, by considering the caring roles of others besides the biological mother, discourses on the primacy and naturalness of the mother-child dyad are placed in perspective.

The separation of family members can, in fact, lead to diverse experiences of migration and related issues such as language acquisition and education. Nilgün recounts her initial problems when she joined her parents in Germany.

> *Nilgün*: Well, I had really big difficulties, because I had to look after my younger siblings, and then I slowly realized 'this is a new family' that I did not know at all. I only knew my younger sister [Saniye]. I did not know Ülkü and Cemile [the two youngest sisters] at all at the time. I had seen Cemile, she had stayed in the village for eight months, and Ülkü was with foster-parents, with a German family. She did not know any Turkish at all. I did not know any German, and Saniye neither. And nobody understood Cemile, because she stayed with a German family for one year as a child, then my parents brought her to A-town. She was somewhere in [the suburbs]. And they lived in the same house with a Kurdish family. At the time it was quite common that labour migrants did not have a flat of their own . . . then she spoke a bit of Kurdish with the neighbours, then she spoke a bit of Turkish with my parents Then she was sent to the village for eight months and nobody could understand her, apart from one aunt who always translated for her. Probably [this aunt] could put herself in [Cemile's] place so she translated for her.

Siblings can fulfil certain roles usually ascribed to mothering, such as providing a continuous point of (mutual) emotional reference (cf. Tizard 1991). Nilgün's relationship with her two other younger siblings, in contrast, was difficult. Although she was expected to look after them, she was not able to communicate with them verbally. If language acquisition is seen as a central part of bringing up children, and the mother's role is to transmit the mother tongue, this multiplicity of languages spoken by the children is itself an indicator of the existence of diverse other mothers.

The transmission of the mother tongue is considered a part of mothering vital to the construction of ethnic communities. Deutsch (1966) claims that the ability to communicate more easily with members of the national collectivity is central in explaining the attachment of individuals to the national collectivity. Anderson (1993) argues that the language commonality achieved through the print media, education systems, and so forth, is a precondition for constructing a shared imagination of the national community. At the same time, he compares the emotional attachment of the individual *vis-à-vis* the national community to the emotional attachment that the individual feels towards his or her family. This metaphorical substitution of family and nation is problematic on several counts, but it remains powerful (McClintock 1993). Nilgün's family's multi-linguality stems from the fact that both parents were working outside the home and therefore had to rely on others to bring up their young children. The example of Nilgün's family shows how the actual practice of migrant families may undermine theories that rely on the family as a linguistically and culturally uniform unit. Migration may in fact undermine not only the primacy of the mother in caring for and educating her biological children, but also the transmission of ethnically specific cultural resources such as language through mothers.[7]

In my sample, grandmothers, aunts, neighbours, paid child minders and also foster-parents provided primary-caring responsibilities for varying periods because of the mother's migration and her paid work outside the home. Nilgün also recounts taking on the mothering role in relation to her younger siblings particularly concerning her youngest siblings who were born after she came to Germany. When Nilgün was 23 and decided to leave the family home and live in a flat with her sister Saniye, the most difficult thing was not her parents' disapproval but the separation from her younger siblings.

Nilgün: It was very hard, because we were very attached to the children, me in particular . . . I was there when they were born. It was the first time that I have experienced my siblings from when they were little, the two youngest ones . . . When the fifth one, Döndü, was born there was a crisis at home, because she was a girl. Actually, my mother wanted a boy, or my father and my mother did. And I had the impression that she was being excluded. And I was – then I was always there for the child. When she cried I was at her side before my mother. Actually I cared for her totally because I had the feeling that she is an excluded child. And I had a very close relation with her. That made it so difficult to move out before. I certainly would have moved out earlier, when I was 18 or so [if it were not for this attachment]. The reason that I delayed moving out was always the children, the younger siblings. Because I felt I was letting them down. We always stuck together against my parents and I was . . . their point of reference. They could talk to me. I was simply the person to whom they related most closely. Then there was the responsibility. On the one hand towards my own struggle, on the other hand this familial attachment. I did not have a problem [leaving] my parents . . . But with my siblings it was difficult . . .

Nilgün: That was the toughest thing, when they threatened us with [breaking off contact with the children]. Then [the parents] said 'you won't be allowed to see the children anymore', you know. Because they knew exactly that that would make us insecure. But then we made ourselves leave home, anyway.

Nilgün identifies herself as the person her siblings related to most closely. This may be because her parents worked in shifts, and thus not being able to spend much time with the children. Nilgün's view is naturally partial and cannot be taken to mean that her parents did not fulfil any parental roles or responsibilities. They provided financially for their children, and also fulfilled emotional and physical caring roles for them. Nevertheless, certain aspects of Nilgün's relationship with her younger siblings can be described as social mothering which was apparent in the conflict between Nilgün and her parents about her departure from home. Her parents used her maternal feelings to put pressure on her to stay. This is a constellation that is usually found between spouses, where the children are used as arguments for or against continuing the relationship.

Migration and the Pressures of 'Good Mothering'

Mothering is a highly regulated social role. There are many normative expectations and rules about good mothering. These vary within and across different societies and may even be contradictory within the same society. In Turkish official discourses, the role of the mother is highly valued. There is a proliferation of proverbs about the value and uniqueness of a mother (Fritsche et al. 1992), and the official Kemalist state doctrine also relies on and promotes positive images of mothers (Delaney 1995). These discourses are not necessarily reflected in praxis. Single and divorced mothers are not included in these positive images of the mother. The mother is identified with an immediate caring role, and going abroad or out of the home and leaving the children to provide for them financially is not part of that positive image. These discursive factors may contribute to the difficulties migrant women experience when leaving their children.

The experience of separation can be very painful, not only for the children but for the mothers as well. Some of my interviewees mentioned this, however they did not always elaborate on it. This may be because such feelings are still difficult to cope with. One compounding factor is that the mothers may experience intense feelings of guilt. Ayla, one of my first-generation interviewees separated from her husband in England and moved to Sweden. Because of her job, she had to travel on a regular basis and found it very difficult to organize childcare for her son who was four years old at the time. For this reason she decided to send him to Turkey where her parents looked after him until the age of 11. In the meantime, she had migrated to Germany, where her son finally joined her after finishing primary school.

Umut: So how did you feel about sending your son to Turkey, was that fine, did you feel well – him being cared for there or . . .

Ayla: No, well I think I trusted that he was taken care of that was not – but it was also emotionally very difficult for me. On the one hand the separation from him, I missed him a lot and I was also thinking what am I doing – I felt very guilty. What am I doing to this guy, I took him away from his father and now I am sending him away from me. So that was a very bad feeling.

Umut: Did you feel people were reproaching you or . . .

Ayla: No, it was never openly, nobody ever said anything but it was my own feeling, I didn't feel good about it.

Such feelings of guilt can last for a long time and may be brought up much later during conflicts. Thus, Nilgün recounts that in the conflict that ensued when she and her sister left the parental home, her mother brought up these issues.

Nilgün: Well, my mother could not cope at all [with our leaving home]. She felt betrayed because she had worked hard for us all her life, and sacrificed all her life for the relationship because of her children.

Umut: Her relationship with your father?

Nilgün: Yes, exactly, yes. Her relationship with her husband.

Umut: Is that how she put it?

Nilgün: Yes she said that. And she also worked very hard. She felt very frustrated, and she could not play the role of a mother according to her own feelings. And the children were scattered, and at one point they came. And she had very big problems with this, she had huge complexes, actually. Everyone was alone in the family. Well, that is a whole issue in itself. She was very embittered.

Nilgün's mother revealed deep regrets about her mothering role. She had worked very hard all her life and felt she had stayed with her husband for the children's sake. Moreover, she had not been able to fulfil her own expectations of mothering. Nilgün does not spell out these expectations. However, it may have been to spend more time with her children. While the children were young they did not live with her. Even when they came to live with her, she was working from noon till midnight so that she had very limited time with them. Interviews with other migrant mothers suggest that migration had effects on the relationships between mothers and children, that mothers found it difficult to cope and could not always easily reconcile themselves with their own ideas of good mothering. Their own experiences of being mothered may have played a role here too. Family networks become disjointed in the process of migration so that mothers do not have on-site help with childcare. Thus, the pressure on the individual woman to be a 'good mother' is intensified.

Conclusion

The self-representations of migrant women of Turkish background give a more complex view of mothering relations and migration than the stereotyped fixation on tradition. In this chapter, I have discussed aspects of the mothering relationship that may be altered by the migration process.

The status of women in Turkey as migration-widows may include aspects of loss of status and protection due to a lack of male financial and social support. On the other hand, women may attain more autonomy by being able to make household and economic decisions on their own and migration to Germany will constitute a subsequent loss of this social status and autonomy.

Some married women who first migrated on their own may have taken on the role of main breadwinners, thus reversing the gendered division of labour. The migration process has often led to the separation of mothers and their children for long periods of time. This is an event that does not fit in with traditional expectations, either in German or in Turkish hegemonic conceptualizations of mothering. Family members in Turkey have temporarily taken on the mothering role for these children. Although such experiences may have painful effects on both mothers and children, it cannot be automatically assumed that such separations are traumatic for the children if the primary care-giving relationship is positive and stable. In this context, relationships between siblings can also be seen as a source of stability and support.

The process of migration may differentially affect siblings within the same family. This challenges theoretical assumptions about the unified nature of the family as well as the national collectivity. The family is often used as a metaphor for the emotional closeness and linguistic and cultural homogeneity of the national or ethnic group. The notion of homogeneity of the nation or ethnic group has been deconstructed before (cf., for example, Anthias and Yuval-Davis 1992, Balibar 1997, Yuval-Davis 1997), but the significance of linguistic and cultural differentiation within family units has not been sufficiently documented. As the experiences of my interviewees show, mothering roles are not limited to biological mothers. A geographically and ethnically diverse range of persons can take on aspects of this role.

The theorization of mothering roles needs to take into account inter-ethnic and transnational networks of education and care. Migrant family relations cannot be understood wholly through the framework of tradit-ional patriarchal family units. On the other hand, their linguistic and cultural diversity should be interpreted as a challenge to primordialist familist metaphors and theories. It can show that even in these so-called traditional families, closeness, responsibility and caring do not entirely depend on ties of shared blood, language or culture. The experiences and self-representations of my interviewees testify to their agency and resourcefulness despite difficult circumstances and painful experiences. In the process, motherhood, gender relations and ethnic and national projects are shaped that bear little or no resemblance to migrant stereo-types. Finally, good mothering and the personal sacrifices so often associated with the term may be manifested in what could be interpreted as the ultimate sacrifice of any mother: long-term physical separation from her children.

References

Anderson, B. (1993), *Die Erfindung der Nation: Zur Karriere eines folgenreichen Konzepts*, Frankfurt, Campus.

Anthias, F. and Yuval-Davis, N. (1992), *Racialised Boundaries*, London, Routledge.

Auernheimer, G. (1988), *Der sogenannte Kulturkonflikt*, Frankfurt, Campus.

Appiah, K.A. (1990), 'Racisms', in D.T. Goldberg (ed.), *Anatomy of Racism*, Minneapolis, University of Minnesota Press.

Balibar, E. (1997), 'La Forme Nation: Histoire et Idéologie', in E. Balibar and I. Wallerstein, *Race, Nation, Classe: Les Identités Ambiguées*, Paris, La Découverte.

Beck, U. and Beck-Gernsheim, E. (1995), *The Normal Chaos of Love*, Cambridge, Polity Press.

Bhabha, H.K. (1900), 'The Other Question: Difference, Discrimination and the Discourse of Colonialism', in R. Ferguson, M. Gover, T. Minh-ha, and C. West (eds), *Out There: Marginalization and Contemporary Cultures*, New York, New Museum of Contemporary Art.

Bhatt, C. (1997), *Liberation and Purity: Race, New Religious Movements and the Ethics of Postmodernity*, London and Bristol, Pennsylvania, UCL Press.

Delaney, C. (1995), 'Father State, Motherland, and the Birth of Modern Turkey', in S. Yanagisako and C. Delaney (eds), *Naturalizing Power: Essays in Feminist Cultural Analysis*, London, Routledge.

Denzin, N., *Interpretive Biography*, London, Sage, 1987

Deutsch, K.W. (1966), *Nationalism and Social Communications: An Enquiry into the Foundations of Nationality*, Cambridge MA, MIT Press.

Eryilmaz, A. (1998), 'Die Ehre der Türkei. Türkiye'nin namusu!', in A. Eryilmaz and M. Jamin (eds), *Fremde Heimat. Die Geschichte der Einwanderung aus der Türkei. Yaban Silan Olur. Türkiye'den Almanya'ya Göçün Tarihi*, Essen, Klartext Verlag.

Fritsche, M., Ege, M. and Yekin, M. (1992), 'Das Paradies liegt unter den Füssen der Mutter', *Hessische Blätter für Volkskunde*, 29: 83–94.

Giddens, A. (1992), *The Transformation of Intimacy: Sexuality, Love and Eroticism in Modern Societies*, Cambridge, Polity Press.

Heitmeyer, W., Müller, J. and Schröder, J. (1997), *Verlockender Fundamentalismus*, Frankfurt, Suhrkamp.

Klesse, C. (2000), 'Lesbians and Gay Men as the Vanguard of Modernisation? Sex, Relationships, and the Transformation of Intimacy', unpublished manuscript.

Krüger, D. and Potts, L. (1995) 'Aspekte generativen Wandels in der Migration: Bildung, Beruf und Familie aus der Sicht türkischer Migrantinnen der ersten Generation', *Zeitschrift für Frauenforschung*, 13(1 and 2).

Leiprecht, R. (1994), *Rassismus und Ethnozentrismus bei Jugendlichen*, Duisberg, DISS.

Lutz, H. (undated), 'Migrant Women from so-called Muslim countries' University of Amsterdam, Occasional Papers, Institute of Social Science.

McClintock, A. (1993), 'Family Feuds', *Feminist Review*, vol 44, 61–80.

Otyakmaz, B.Ö. (1995), *Auf allen Stühlen: Das Selbstverständnis junger türkischer Migrantinnen in Deutschland*, Köln, ISP Verlag.

Phoenix, A. and Woollett, A. (1991), 'Motherhood: Social Construction, Politics and Psychology', in A. Phoenix, A. Woollett and E. Lloyd (eds) (1991), *Motherhood: Meaning, Practices and Ideologies*, London, Sage.

Räthzel, N. and Sarica, Ü. (1994), *Migration und Diskriminierung in der Arbeit: Das Beispiel Hamburg*, Berlin, Argument-Verlag.

Schmidt-Koddenberg, A. (1989), *Akkulturation von Migrantinnen: Eine Studie zur Bedeutsamkeit sozialer Vergleichsprozesse zwischenTuerkinnen und deutschen Frauen*, Opladen, Leske and Budrich.

Tizard, B. (1991), 'Employed Mothers and the Care of Young Children', in A. Phoenix, A. Woollett and E. Lloyd (eds), *Motherhood: Meaning, Practices and Ideologies*, London, Sage.

Waltz, V. (1996), 'Toleranz fängt beim Kopftuch erst an. Zur Verhinderung von Chancengleichheit durch gesellschaftliche Verhältnisse', in W. Heitmeyer and R. Dollase (eds), *Die bedrängte Toleranz*, Frankfurt, Suhrkamp.

Young, I.M. (1994), 'Making Single Motherhood Normal', *Dissent*, 94: 88–94.

Yuval-Davis, N. (1997), *Gender and Nation*, London, Sage.

Zentrum für Türkeistudien (ed.) (1995), *Migration und Emanzipation. Türkische Frauen in Nordrhein-Westphalen*, Opladen, Leske and Budrich.

Notes

1. I would like to thank the editors of this volume, the Gender, Ethnicity and Social Research Discussion Group in London, Richard Johnson, Eleonore Kofman, Tijen Uguris and Nira Yuval-Davis for their helpful comments on drafts of this chapter.

2. The sample consisted of 15 highly educated or professional women of Turkish background living in a large German city with whom I conducted topical life-story interviews (Denzin 1987). Nine interviews were conducted in 1996 and six interviews in 1999. The interviews lasted from two to six hours. The age of the interviewees ranged from 26 to 60 at the time of the interview. Seven of my interviewees migrated to Germany as adults, and eight either migrated as children or were born in Germany. Seven of the interviewees were mothers, the ages of their children at the time of interview ranged from seven to mid-twenties. Nine of the interviewees were divorced; the rest had never married, among them three had been in love relationships with women, one of which was explicitly identified as lesbian. The interviewees were all identified as ethnically Turkish, although their families were not all homogeneous. One interviewee's parents were second-generation Macedonian immigrants to Turkey, one interviewee was of Kurdish and Turkish parentage, and one was a member of the religious minority of Aleviis. Throughout the chapter, I use the term 'of Turkish background' to indicate the ethnic diversity of Turkey's population, but also to account for diverse identifications of migrants as hybrid, non-national or 'migrant'.

3. Leiprecht (1994: 37) uses the term 'instrumental racism', which I refer to here. Instrumental racism reduces migrants and other racialized people to their functionality for the needs of the dominant society. Often instrumentalist racist discourses are used to legitimize the presence of migrants, thus appearing to be 'friendly to foreigners' rather than openly racist.

4. Although not focusing on Turkish migrants, these arguments are presented in the current debate on the green card, and the oppositional slogan of 'Kinder statt Inder' – 'children instead of Indians' (the green card aims at recruiting people with information technology expertise internationally).

5. The only instance of instability of the family structure is identified as originating from the so-called culture conflict between parents and children (for a critique cf. Auernheimer 1988, Otyakmaz 1995), with the parents upholding Turkish values while the children rebel against these and try to incorporate German values. This conflict may destabilize the second generation and lead to them entering criminal, drug and other 'deviant' subcultures.

6. The interviews are anonymised. All quotations are my translation from German or Turkish. '[ ]' signifies my explanatory insertions, and '. . .' signifies my shortening of the extract through omission.

7. The material and symbolic resources for mothering are also class specific. Thus, for example, Ayla's financial resources and her social networks enabled her to bring a live-in child minder from Turkey to look after her son. This helped to transmit the Turkish language to him, although Ayla was in paid employment and her husband was not Turkish. However, after her divorce and another migration Ayla's circumstances changed so that she had to find alternative childcare. The transmission of ethnic resources does not only take place within the family, of course. Turkish schools, organized by the consulate, peer groups, and social and political organizations were mentioned by my second-generation interviewees as influencing their interest to learn the Turkish language, read literature, listen to music, learn folklore dancing, and so forth, or learn about social and political issues in Turkey.

7

Righteous or Rebellious? Social Trajectory of Sahelian Youth in France[1]

Mahamet Timera

The concept of second generation migrants is controversial. There is ambiguity in the way young people of African parentage are defined principally as descendants of immigrant families even though they were born and brought up in France and represent an autochthonous population. Are they going to be indefinitely associated with their foreign roots, making it impossible to extricate themselves from this heritage, perceived by some as a social burden and by others as cultural richness?

This chapter focuses on adolescents of Sahelian descent growing up in France. This encompasses youth who can trace their descent from the Senegal River valley and other regions and towns in Mali, Mauritania and Senegal as well as from Niger, Burkina Faso, Guinea and Côte d'Ivoire. Their migrant parents originally came from both rural and urban areas. For more than a decade, and in the wake of primarily male labour migration to France, family reunion has taken place. This migration increasingly has formed communities demographically balanced in terms of gender and age even though there is still a large number of Sahelian men living together in hostels for single men.

Recent migrants remain relatively tied to their country of origin and for some, especially those from the Senegal River valley, deeply committed to the collective development and transformation of their home villages (Kane, Chapter 13). Their associational ties are structured either on a village or an intra-village basis for those of rural origin or on a neighbourhood or town basis for urban dwellers. Religious and national identities also serve to rally collective effort. Local community life is spearheaded principally by women reunited with their husbands. Alongside the communal feelings of migrants based on home areas is a more open and cosmopolitan association based on residential locality and structured by Sahelian Islam, but no section of the Islamic faith constitutes the basis for regrouping or association.

Perceived as an enclave of migrants, this ghettoization, far from constituting the only reality of their lives, is differentially experienced within the communities. For the parental generation powerful mechanisms of ghettoization are relayed through communal dynamics. Young people are far less engaged in these dynamics, nonetheless in French sociological literature they more often form the object of the sociology of migration than the sociology of French youth (Noiriel 1984 and 1996).

The sociology of immigration has constructed its object of study as a separate world without questioning, or only belatedly and hesitantly questioning, migrants' experience of discrimination and segregation. Its focus is primarily on the sociology of being different, a world apart, a people apart. What is interesting to them is difference itself, its exoticism, rather than a community identity grounded in social practices. This portrayal of essential difference attaches an irreducibility to the status of being a migrant. It is akin to old-style colonial ethnology that puts the researcher in a superior position *vis-à-vis* the subjects he or she is studying.

In this vein, migrants' children, in spite of themselves, are seen to mirror the process of immigration. They become indices of assimilation or integration *vis-à-vis* their parents' lack of integration and assimilation. The migrants' future therefore lies in their children. This is a discourse revived from an earlier time of migrations to France from Eastern Europe.

Certainly the incorporation of migrants past and present into the French melting pot is an undeniable and tangible fact. What is contestable is the idyllic and peaceful character postulated by many commentators. Noiriel (1984) has unveiled the ideological constructions that surround this rewriting of history and the violent character of the integration process attested to by the historical facts of Poles, Italians, and other migrants' settlement in France. Their French-born and educated children know of the immigrant's suffering as that of 'foreigners'.

The literature's obsession with migrants' assimilation into French society, especially amongst youth, detracts from a clear understanding of the critical arena of migrant family home life and the intergenerational and gender struggles that occur there. This chapter attempts to redress this oversight.

At Odds: Socialization within Families and within French Society

Unlike their children, migrant parents have been primarily socialized in the country of their birth and arrive in France with a relatively well-constructed identity. Indeed this identity transforms itself, but through another logic, namely adaptation and acculturization.

For the children of migrants, a contradictory process of socialization begins within the family. In their early years, children are plunged into a specific cultural space. From dietary habits through to religious practices and ways of dressing, language and body language, hygiene standards, and values and social norms, this is the apprenticeship of life in a familial cell and in the framework of their parents' migrant community. At school, the child realizes his or her foreignness in terms of differences between his familial environment and the dominant society. Here the notion of 'us' and 'them' is instilled. He realizes that his way of doing things is at odds with what constitutes mainstream French society. It dawns on the child that 'his country' – in other words i.e. his parents' country – is elsewhere, that the food he eats is different at home from that of the wider society, and names, language, holiday celebrations, table manners, prayers and religious beliefs are different. He discovers that there are French people around him as opposed to 'others', which can be interpreted as Africans, blacks, Muslims, or immigrants. Clearly he is an 'other'.

Parents speak of their native country with romantic sentiment. For them it is a paradise lost but it becomes purgatory for their children who deviate from its norms and who therefore 'turn out bad'. Parents are not consciously opposing French society by imposing a 'non-French' code of behaviour on their children. They simply transmit who they are and what they believe, in accordance with their historical and cultural contexts. Thus, it is in the family setting that the child first discovers the conflictural nature of otherness. The reality of this status and the realization of difference can be more, or less, harsh depending on the context, the period and the actors.

School reinforces young people's awareness of difference. At school, the child confronts the norms of mainstream French society. Children discover that their family norms are not upheld at school. In some cases they are devalued and in the process the child experiences a sense of stigma and marginalization. Most adapt by keeping silent in the classroom about domestic matters. This silence is defended at a price. Feelings of 'cultural strangeness' and the need for pride in one's familial identity are submerged. Efforts are made to hide difference, refuse distinctions, to avoid prejudice. School is the place where youth first experience the forcefulness of French cultural domination. They must acquiesce to a greater or lesser extent.

The influence of the school on the ideological and cultural development of youth is enormous. By advancing French norms, language, and national culture, it dramatizes the divergence of young people's familial culture on a daily basis. Schools are vectors of French culture with the object of culturally assimilating the young people. Migrant parents adhere to the direction of the school, not seeing it as anything more than an institution with the task of teaching reading, writing and mathematics, and preparing children for a future job. They ignore the role the school has in the cultural development of French citizens.

French schools promote the majority culture, integrating other cultures to the point of eradicating difference. They largely succeed in this role within the institutional parameters of the schools themselves. Even if the process is painful, even if 'their roots have been murdered' (Noiriel 1984), the assimilation of these French-born young people and their auto-chthonous status is achieved at school. However, French-born children of immigrant parents return to their homes where identity crises often ensue. The management of intergenerational conflicts and the remoteness of young people from their parents does not occur in the same way nor with the same stakes for boys and girls.

Girls beyond Familial Law and Boys beyond Public Law

Recent legal cases have been brought forward by young girls of African descent against members of their own community and indirectly against their parents concerning female circumcision and 'forced' or arranged marriages. The number and frequency of calls for help from social workers and teachers by these same girls, and conflicts with their parents translate into specific quandaries within the family and community *vis-à-vis* the French state.

Unlike these young girls, many of their brothers seem, despite contra-dictions with their parents, to conform willingly to the values of the community. However, they often develop antagonistic, deviant or violent attitudes in the public sphere of French society. Differences in the socialization of girls and boys are believed to underly these modalities, inscribed in the heart of French society: in the street, the neighbourhood, the educational system and the workplace.

Together with Catherine Quiminal, I recently studied the position of young women in their families and traced their life trajectories in educational matters, career selection, choice of a husband, and various aspects of their emancipation from family control, notably when and how they leave their parental homes. Our study reveals that relations with the community of origin were experienced differently by boys and girls. Girls express a sense of ease in the wider society; they have easier recourse to French institutions. Their problems are concentrated on conflicts with their parents. By contrast, boys admit to finding it less easy to talk about their role in the wider society. They seem to be more conformist at home and to make fewer demands on institutional mediation concerning domestic problems. Boys sometimes express their opinions about family difficulties but more indirectly. They tend to be more tolerant and understanding towards their parents and more inclined to compromise. This is confirmed by the research of Barou and Mauger (1999) who studied a group of adolescents aged between 12 and 25 years of age:

> Les jeunes sont peu diserts au sujet des problèmes familiaux. Ils ne les évoquent que de façon très indirecte . . . Les souffrances que l'on pressent chez eux du fait des embrouillaminis familiaux qui les entourent ne sont jamais exprimées. (Barou and Mauger 1999: 2)[2]

The differentiated position of boys and girls within familial and community space indirectly condition their public space. Both discover a sense of being different, of 'foreignness' through contrasting contact with their parents, on one hand, and contact with the dominant society via social institutions like schools and the media on the other. Both perceive their allocation to an inferior social, political and cultural position within French society, whereby their group's status is more or less stigmatised. However, this consciousness of otherness is lived differently by boys and girls. Noiriel (1984) accounts for these gender differences in terms of contradictory forms of socialization at a decisive age. This attitude relates to the fewer constraints and greater leniency that boys experience within their families compared with girls.

At the heart of familial space, social roles and positions are relatively differentiated in households of Sahelian Muslim origin. In comparison with boys, girls occupy a secondary position and are expected to receive an education that prepares them to be good mothers and wives, rather than preparing them for individual fulfilment through the pursuit of work opportunities. Girls are expected to submit to marriage to a member of the local community whereas boys are allowed to choose their partner from outside the local Muslim community. There are no sanctions against marrying 'white French' girls if they so desire.

Boys tend to leave school and enter the labour force at an early age. Girls, on the other hand, are obliged to live in their parental home until marriage. Somewhat paradoxically, their duty to reside in the parental home and the extended 'parental hospitality' that they experience relative to their brothers seems to contribute to their higher levels of scholastic achievement. Unlike boys, they are not subjected to parents' pressing questions about their future in the labour force. Girls perform better at school due to less distractions and longer attendance.

Thus, migrant parents are a decisive influence on the social trajectories of their male and female offspring. The social position of girls within their families and local communities induces an ambivalence. They are inadvertently afforded superior educational opportunities to boys, but community expectations circumscribe their realization. In this paradoxical situation, girls develop a form of feminist consciousness at odds with familial and community norms. They are seen to be betraying the honour of their families in the process. Thus, girls are rebels within their families and communities, righteously upholding French cultural norms in their demands for decision-making power as young women.

By contrast boys are rebels against French public order, in opposition to the law of mainstream society while seeming to be at peace with parental authority. Facing anti-social, deviant male youth, a number of voices within French society at large have spoken out, blaming migrant parents for their lack of control over their sons. In fact, many parents do not believe that their male children are capable of the wrongdoings of which they are being accused given their exemplary behaviour at home.

Parental Responsibility and Public Furore

This perplexing duality of male youthful behaviour has sparked debate on the issue of the role of the migrant father in domestic space. Public criticism is levelled at 'the absence and silence of fathers'. Usually this absence and silence is delinked from its historical context namely that migrant workers, whose arrival in France preceded that of their wives and children, often established their own identity principally around their work function. Work legally justified their presence in France. Yet the work itself was degrading unskilled manual labour at the bottom of the professional ladder, synonymous with self-effacement as citizens in the public domain. Under these circumstances, the migrant was absent as a citizen in the French public domain, as well as being physically absent from his family and circumscribed in his role as a father. There was a double negation of Sahelian male migrants' social status in both public and private spheres.

As Sahelian families began to be reunited in France and set up domestic family units, migrant men experienced rehabilitation in the private sphere. They were masters at home in their role as fathers. They laid down family law, which their sons were compelled to respect. Boys' outlet for rebellion became the wider society as they inherited their fathers' lowly status in the French labour market.

The public debate about male youth rebellion has spin-offs for girls' rebellion within the home. French society is widely in sympathy with these young girls' assertions within familial space, and in some cases the media manipulates public sympathy in ethnocentric even racist directions. The current media attention surrounding phenomena such as the forced marriage of young Muslim girls from black Africa raises many questions. Arranged marriages and polygamy are commonplace phenomena and have always been associated with Muslim migrants from places such as the Magreb and Turkey. The press, however, now sensationalizes polygamy and female circumcision, portraying them as Sahelian cultural imports and exposing the way immigration is seen in the French collective imagination.

Never have arranged marriages excited so much interest not only among the general public, parents, student associations, and so forth, but also among French government ministers and African presidents. A new public attitude is surfacing that extends beyond the boundaries of the black African community. Sahelian girls are seen as youthful victims of an unjust internal system of domination within their own culture. Are these marriage practices even more intolerable to the public now that they are committed by black Africans within French society? Or is this debate merely an extension of the French assimilation programme, the *civilisateur* quest and the elimination of cultural difference.

At issue in this debate are the frontiers of identity and cultural difference and the invention of the image of the stranger in a specific phase of French history. Modes of perception, of assimilation and of stigmatization of migrants are being contested. Cultural boundaries are moving and the actors are changing, constantly being redrawn while opening up and enlarging spaces for identity formulation, but also by closure of certain spaces. These frontiers, despite their apparent objectification in pseudo-scientific ideas regarding race, religious, or country of origin are ideological constructions. As Wieviorka (1992) remarks, racism and xenophobia do not have to have different objectives to exist. They continually generate themselves in struggles for political power and cultural supremacy.

Conclusion

In this analysis, I have shown how children discover cultural differences between the norms of their family and wider French society at school. In the process of being socialized to accept society's dominant norms, they are relegated to a position of social inferiority. Socialization and assimilation almost always succeed amongst the offspring of migrant parents, whereas their social destiny sometimes introduces enormous differences and imprisons them in the *entre-soi* of the parental community of origin or local residential community. Identity crises ensue that are particularly acute for girls. Having embraced values of individual equality espoused by the dominant society, they are seen by their families to be betraying family values and social expectations for their fulfilment of family roles as women.

I have juxtaposed male and female dynamics of young migrants from the Sahel. They cannot be taken as unique or exclusive examples in defining girls on one hand as rebels *vis-à-vis* family and community law and boys as rebels challenging French state law. But they are nonetheless two significant tendencies.

Neither skin colour nor physical traits produce in themselves more difficulties in assimilation making integration impossible. These physical characteristics are less reasons for cultural difference and more objects for constructing or manipulating ideological images. The struggles of Sahelian youth within their families and within society are real, but an understanding of these struggles must go beyond the ideological constructions of public debate and embedded notions of ethnic and cultural superiority and inferiority.

References

Barou, J. and Mauger, A. (1999), 'Modes de vie et intégration des enfants et adolescents issus de familles africaines subsahariennes', *Migrations Etudes* 88.
Elias, N. and Scotson, J.-L. (1992), *'Les Logiques de l'Exclusion'*, Paris, Fayard.
Noiriel, G. (1984), *Longwy. Immigres et Proletaires,* 1880–1980, Paris, PUF.
Noiriel, G., Laforcade, G. de and Tilly, C. (1996), *The French Melting Pot,* Paris, University of Minnesota Press.
Wieviorka, M. (1992), 'Preface', in Elias, N. and Scotson, J.-L. (eds), *Les Logiques de l'Exclusion*, Paris, Fayard.

Notes

1. This article has been translated into English by Ann Reeves with advice from Patricia Paravano.
2. Translated: 'Young people are not very forthcoming regarding family problems and only refer to them indirectly. The difficulties that one can imagine they encounter at home due to family tensions are never openly discussed.'

8

Breaking the Chain of the Generational Contract? Japanese Migration and Old-Age Care in Britain

Misa Izuhara and *Hiroshi Shibata*

A new pattern of global movements involving Japanese goods, capital, and people (both labour and tourism) started in the post-war period. In traditional migration theory, the role of women was often obscured by assumptions concerning their inferior labour-market status and the consensual household decision-making processes in which they were involved (Ackers 1998). In addition, migration is frequently thought to be a collective action of labourers in a global economic and political system (Castles and Miller 1998). Although both theories are applicable to the case of organized labour migration of Japanese people to the American continents in the pre- and inter-war periods,[1] women also moved independently and of their own free will. Using a qualitative approach, this chapter considers the experiences of female Japanese migrants who moved to post-war Britain. Due to the 'individual' nature of the migration, these migrants tended to become well integrated, and thus occupy a less visible position as a group in the host society, compared with established communities of other ethnic minorities such as South Asians or Afro-Caribbeans. Combined with the difficulty in locationally mapping this population, there has been little recognized research on their experiences in British society to date. There is also a gap in the availability of qualitative data on women migrants in general (Ackers 1998, Campani 1995, Pedraza 1991).

As women grow older in a foreign society, care issues come to the fore. This chapter analyses the life-cycle advancement of Japanese migrant women living in Britain with special focus on their ties with family relations and reliance on kin in old age. Even within post-war Japanese society, urban migration and the accompanying social change have created

155

a geographic distance between generations of the family which has impacted upon traditional living arrangements, transforming intergenerational relations and making family support exchange more problematic in old age (Izuhara 2000, Kendig 1989, Ogawa 1992). Changes that have taken place within a 'localized' society over time and over generations are likely to become more exaggerated when family members cross national and cultural boundaries. Linking migratory movements to issues of family relations and old age, this chapter explores how migration has affected traditional norms and practices of old-age support for Japanese migrants in Britain. The individual informants are referred to by the age they were when interviewed in 1999.

Processes of Migration

Motivations and processes of migration differ amongst individuals even in a small select group such as this sample of 25 Japanese women aged between 50 and 65 years of age who moved to Britain in the post-war period, mainly between the late 1950s and the early 1970s. Four of the women had never married, four others were either divorced or widowed and the rest were currently married. Eighteen were married, or had been married to a British partner and three to a Japanese partner. Eight of the women did not have any children. Their employment history was also examined as well as their socio-economic status including the issue of home ownership.

People's decisions to migrate are often motivated by a complex assemblage of inter-related factors. Indeed, post-war transnational migration is not necessarily exclusively economic. Social, institutional, political, personal and even environmental factors may also be influential (Ackers 1998, Bogue 1977). In fact, the female migration to Britain tended not to be driven by economic factors. Their motivations were primarily social and personal.

Educational benefit was the most frequently mentioned reason given for migration by the women. The vast majority of the informants initially left Japan to further their education, including short-term language education. Although not everyone was necessarily planning a major career step up after their studies, many women came to enhance their life chances.

> I worked in an office for a few years, but Japanese companies did not let women do any interesting jobs. So, I quit my OL [office lady] job and came to England to study English for one year. [53 years old, arrived in Britain in 1972]

Various institutional and personal constraints led the women to want to leave Japan. The country's post-war social system rested on male-dominated families and labour markets (Osawa 1993, Izuhara 1999a). Women felt pressurized to conform to family norms involving prescriptive behaviour based on their gender and age. Marriage rates[2] were high and in accordance with the notion of appropriate ages for men and women to marry. Indeed, some of the women interviewed mentioned that the breakdown of their proposed marriage prompted their decision to seek an alternative lifestyle outside Japan.

As Lewis (1992) notes, once women marry in a society adhering to the male-breadwinner family model, gender roles are likely to be enforced in conformity with the model. Japanese women were discouraged from seeking employment opportunities and faced heavy discrimination in the workplace. Gender inequalities in salary, promotion, and hiring processes continue in defiance of the Equal Employment Opportunity Act 1986. By moving to Britain, the women hoped to escape the stresses and frustrations of the Japanese workplace and gain more social equality.

My first marriage in Japan broke up after three months . . . At that time [in the late 1960s], unmarried people were looked on as though they had some sort of disability. Equally, I did not want to remarry a divorcee with children [which seemed the only option regarding remarriage for women in her position] . . . I was a qualified pharmacist. But, even with such qualifications, it was impossible for us women to make a living. From the start, our pay was so low compared to that of our male counterparts. Even among pharmacists [professionals], women were expected to marry and leave their job within three years or so. That's why I thought, if I could speak English, combined with my qualification, I would be able to survive. That's why I came to study English for six months. [She subsequently married an Englishman.] [54 years old, arrived in Britain in 1971]

When I broke up with my boyfriend, my parents tried to arrange my marriage. I was so fed up with everything that I wanted to get out wherever I could . . . At my workplace, all the girls were staying to find their future husbands. If I tried to work hard, people made me uncomfortable. My male colleagues used to say, 'Miss . . . are you still here? We are bored with looking at your face.' I was not satisfied to stay as an assistant forever! [She originally signed a two-year contact to work in London and stayed in the job for four years.] When I went back, I felt as though there was no place for me in Japan. I was 30 years old, and my parents hassled me to marry as soon as possible. I could not relax there. So I worked a little and saved money to come back here. [She later married a British partner.] [56 years old, arrived in Britain in 1968]

Barring those who had already married a British national before migrating, the women's initial intention was to move only temporarily to Britain. However, most married host nationals and settled permanently in the UK.[3] Only a few women mentioned employment opportunities, such as being assigned to a fixed-term position to work in Britain, as the reason for their initial migration.

In the post-1973 period, Japan's economic fortune led to a dramatic increase in Japanese overseas business investment and increased tourism. As a result, by the early 1990s, Britain had become home to one of the biggest expatriate Japanese communities in the world (*The Japan Times*, 11 April 1992: 3). Even for those who came to Britain with a different intention, newly emerging work opportunities in branches of Japanese companies or Japan-related businesses offered single women different life chances, which led to their subsequent stay in Britain.

> I came to learn English shorthand but instead got employed as a typist in a Japanese company on my third day after arrival. In those days, Japanese companies were doing very well, and the pay was good as well. I switched to take an evening course to learn the language. [After that, she worked for various Japanese companies in London for over 20 years.] [60 years old, arrived in Britain in 1976]

Work opportunities abroad provided residential choices between Japan and Britain but did not necessarily bring upward social mobility. However, the women were migrating from a highly industrialized society and the achievement of economic betterment was not their main objective. Many were from relatively privileged backgrounds and could afford to pay the relocation costs themselves. Some managed to improve their socio-economic position through participation in the boom of Japanese business expansion in the UK. Others were marginalized in the mainstream labour market in Britain. In the latter case, the women experienced constraints caused by their initial lack of language competency, insufficient skills or qualification levels. Contrasting outcomes are evident in the following work histories:

> Because I could speak English fairly well from the beginning, I took up a job as a translator. Work opportunities and income are a lot to do with the timing [of entry to the labour market]. Japanese business happened to be expanding in the 1980s and brought me many opportunities. [56 years old, arrived in Britain in 1974]
>
> Perhaps none of them was a proper job, but I have always worked to earn pocket money. A cleaning job was good because it did not constrain me from taking

my children to work. I saved the money from cleaning twice a week to go to Japan. I also did knitting for Japanese expatriates' wives and accounting for a Japanese restaurant. [60 years old, arrived in Britain in 1969]

Better living conditions in the form of more spacious housing provided an incentive for some women to remain in Britain. The cross-national difference was especially apparent in the case of single women. All single informants had succeeded in becoming homeowners in Britain thanks to their employment and to mortgages that were less discriminatory than those in Japan. Asset accumulation tended to influence their residential choices in later life and whether they planned to return to Japan.

Most of the women were relatively well educated, and migrated to the host society early in their economically active years. In welfare terms, the majority were financially secure by virtue of their own or their partner's income and assets, and had drawn little upon statutory welfare services or benefits. However, particular concerns and the universal needs of old age inevitably arise in the process of ageing.

Migration, Family Relations and Old Age

Migrating from Japan in their youth, care issues in later life would have been of little concern to the women interviewed. As their parents began to require old-age support, and subsequently as the women themselves approached retirement age, such life-cycle perspectives in relation to family support have started to pose a challenge for the cohort.

As far as intergenerational relations within families are concerned, it is commonly assumed that the informal contract between generations is determined by norms of reciprocity and affection (Bengston et al. 1991). Traditional Japanese culture, however, provides more scope for structuring predictable and fair exchanges between parents and children than is generally found in many Western societies with long-established values of individualism (Kendig 1989). In Japan, the debt children feel towards their parents for having sacrificed throughout their upbringing has to be reciprocated and repaid by caring for their parents in old age (Hashimoto and Kendig 1992). Although such traditional 'contracts' have become less explicit in the process of post-war socio-economic and legal change, older people still receive high levels of support from their adult children. This pattern typifies Japanese intergenerational relations.

However, over the past 50 years, increased geographic mobility in Japan has separated the generations in many families and has started to create more generationally autonomous family relations. International migration has compounded this social force. The insertion of different cultural contexts and ways of raising children have generated inevitable cultural gaps between different generations. Traditional culture, norms and day-to-day practicalities clash with newly emerging family norms and practices.

The interview evidence suggests that family reciprocity between the women and their parents in Japan is certainly constrained by the distance created by transnational migration. Although geographical distance affects the opportunities for family support, it does not necessarily weaken support (Finch 1989). Particular responsibilities in the realms of emotional, financial and practical support may not be restricted by distance. Financial support can easily be maintained over large distances and sending money back to relatives greatly strengthens support mechanisms (Finch 1989). None of the interviewed women were, however, involved in financial support exchange with their families in Japan. This was perhaps due to the nature of the sending and receiving countries, two highly industrialized societies with developed welfare systems.

Moreover, in recent years, 'intimacy at a distance' with family in Japan can be achieved due to shortened travel times, discounted airfares, telephone calls, and e-mails. The situation that prevailed in the 1990s was, therefore, very different from their initial experiences of isolation in Britain in the early 1970s. Psychological distances have indeed been shortened as a result of globalization. Many women, however, mentioned that distance is still crucial in the event of a family emergency. Their common regret was not being able to see their parents spontaneously, at times of serious illness, or before they passed away.

Japanese family relations traditionally involved generationally structured co-residency to facilitate old-age care. If the meaning of 'structural support' is strictly defined as accommodation or extended-family living arrangements, migration has indeed led to a breakdown in such aspects of family relations. In some circumstances, however, migration can facilitate other structures of support. 'Chain migration' is one example in which family linkages provide both the financial and cultural capital to facilitate the gradual movement of family members over time, resulting in eventual 'family reunion' (Castles and Miller 1998, Finch 1989). In this scenario, family networks may help to provide shelter, work, assistance in coping with new environments and bureaucratic procedures, or support in personal difficulties. This form of structural rapport was not prevalent amongst the surveyed migrants.

Instead of the migrating women facilitating structures of support, their parents in Japan have tended to provide a structural base, usually in the form of a family residence that the women could visit or even return to in the future. This has a practical and psychological significance. The women's ties with Japanese society remained strong as long as their parents were still alive and able to provide a home base, but they diminished or ceased with the death of their parents, especially their mother's death. For women without children or those who never married, having a family residence and their mother living in Japan seemed to be a strong pull-factor for their visits and possible return migration in the future.

> Since I have been abroad almost all my adult life, it was as though I was a kite and my mother was somehow holding the string of the kite. I was able to float around freely in the sky while my mother held the string tightly. When my mother died, it was as though the string had suddenly been cut. [60 years old, arrived in Britain in 1971]

Having siblings in Japan did not necessarily help a woman retain the same strength and quality of ties with her original family and society. In this context, the conventional structure of Japanese family becomes significant. In some societies, such as those of Hispanic or South Asian origin, the extended family includes both horizontal and vertical relationships. It is, therefore, not unusual that 'joint families' with two kin-related nuclear families of a horizontal relationship live in the same household (Garcia 1993). On the other hand, in Japan, co-residency means almost always an 'intergenerational' living arrangement – a traditional patriarchal stem family. Once the siblings marry and have children, a new family is formed separate from the original family. Some women mentioned that their siblings with their own family interests and commitments may not be very different from 'other' people (non-blood relations). Their existence was, therefore, not likely to provide an intimate environment (or support structure) to attract expatriate women back to Japanese society in later life. The meaning of the family home also changes at this point with respect to inheritance. In extended-family living arrangements, when the generational transfer of the household head passes from the parents to their sibling family (traditionally the eldest son), the relationship of a woman with her family home may also be transferred.

> Since my parents have already passed away, I describe my trip to Japan as a 'visit to Japan' rather than 'going home' . . . Although I have siblings, they are all married. Since my older sister took over my parents' house, I always stay with her family when I visit Japan. But after she had the house rebuilt due to the [Kobe] earthquake, I became more reserved about staying in her house.

It's *her* house now, no longer *my family home*. So, I have some reservations about staying in her house for four weeks or so as I used to do. These days, I stay in a hotel for half of the time when I visit Japan. [61 years old, arrived in Britain in 1965]

On the other hand, unmarried family members, especially female members like sisters and aunts, associated with the women differently. Female family members tend to provide more support and companionship for each other in general and a stronger family tie is likely to remain between them (Finch 1989, Finch and Mason 1993). This was certainly the case between single women, perhaps because they did not face competing commitments from their own families. Such blood relationships may leave some women with the possibility of return migration in their old age.

After retirement, I would like to live between Japan and Britain. Since I will retire in the same year as my unmarried sister, we are talking about spending time together. [60 years old, arrived in Britain in 1976]

One of my widowed aunts wants me to come back. If she will provide me with a house, it's possible. Since she has a divorced daughter, 'three single women can live together,' she says....I'm not so desperate to go back to Japan since I have a much nicer life here. But when I reach 80 and realise that without any relatives Britain is just a foreign county, it will be too late to return. [63 years old, arrived in Britain in 1972]

Having been away from Japan, the majority of the women were excused from their traditional duties as a daughter, in terms of functional support in providing old-age care for their parents. In the situation of a British marriage, the role and responsibility of daughters-in-law is not structurally or functionally determined as they would have been had the women remained in Japan. Thus, the burden of old-age care for their parents and parents in law was significantly lessened for the surveyed women as a result of migration. Some women, however, strategically provided their parents with old-age care by visiting whenever possible or necessary.

Two women in the research, being the only children in their respective families, had brought their widowed mothers over to Britain to provide support through co-residency. Notwithstanding their desire to be with their daughters, the older parents may have been normatively and institutionally constrained from seeking alternative support to that provided by their own children. Underdeveloped welfare services in Japan, especially in the area of personal care, as well as the stigma attached to receiving public services may have driven them to the drastic step of migrating to Britain in old age.

My mother had been totally dependant on my father, and [after his death] I was the only person she could rely on . . . Since my mother was quite frail, all my relatives said, 'If you leave her behind, we can not be responsible to look after her since we are also getting old.' . . . Since she did not have many friends, it did not make any difference where she resided....My mother was lucky to have me, but I wonder what will happen to me when I get older. [She and her British partner had no children.] [56 years old, arrived in Britain in 1979]

Bringing their mothers to Britain, where more extensive and widely available statutory social services were offered, created a different scenario for the women compared with the burden of care-giving in Japan. In contrast to the pressures many women face when forced to choose between paid work and care-giving responsibilities in Japan, one informant in Britain was able to continue her full-time job even after her co-resident mother started suffering from slight dementia.

After an assessment, housing adaptation was made and some goods such as a portable toilet were offered free of charge. The social worker also arranged a carer to come twice a day to wash and feed her. A Japanese volunteer comes once a week for a friendly chat . . . These are much more advanced services than those you could receive in Japan. If my mother gets worse, needs more intensive help and feels lonely, I do not mind being with her at home. But, I like my job and I have responsibilities. If she cannot eat at all without full assistance, that could be a problem. [56 years old, arrived in Britain in 1979]

For the majority of Japanese migrants resident in Britain who were unable to provide care for their parents, the 'unfulfilled' feelings of some women may reinforce their own attitudes towards receiving support from their own children. This suggests that the generational contract of family reciprocity is a continuous chain of obligations over generations rather than one particular parent-child relationship.

A few years ago, my daughter said, 'Mom, I'll look after you when you get older'. 'Oh, please do not say that,' I said, 'My biggest regret in life is the fact that I did not look after my mother.' My mother and I were very close. Although I promised her I would look after in her old age, I left home [to marry a British partner]. I still regret it [even though my mother was looked after by my sister]. That's why I tell my daughter not to make such a promise. She may regret it if she can not keep it. [61 years old, arrived in Britain in 1965]

Most of the women with children raised and born in Britain did not expect to receive old-age support from them. For many women, especially those who were still in their early fifties, care issues were not yet a pressing matter. However, the majority explicitly stated that their children would not be the major resource for financial or practical support in their old age.

Their children were often brought up with some influence from Japanese social and cultural values. Partly due to the limited facilities and services available to assist with Japanese education, including language support, the second generation of the research cohort could hardly speak any Japanese. Lack of Japanese language competency and the Westernized upbringing of their children may alter their expectations of receiving old-age care from them. A similar situation was found even among children of Japanese couples. The following comments typify the women's expectations:

> My daughter thinks she is white and British with a Japanese mother and a British father. Except for occasionally eating Japanese food, she has nothing to do with Japan....Since I did not raise my child speaking Japanese, if I become ill and my daughter tries to nurse me, we cannot communicate in Japanese.... [Compared with parent-child relationships in Japan] the level of affection may be the same, but practicality can be different. She does not understand unless I explain to her in detail. Even when I am tired, she won't do anything unless I tell her exactly what she should do for me. (56 years old, arrived in Britain in 1974)

The women themselves tend to have developed individualist values, seeking to live independent lives, much as their children do. Their collective view was one of not wishing to become a burden to their children, which resembled the views of older women in Japan in the late 1990s (Izuhara 2000). Overall, family reciprocity in a traditional Japanese sense did not seem to be expected by either side.

> When I need old-age care, I'll sell this house if financially necessary, and move to a nursing home. Although I want to leave the house to my children, they may also suggest that I sell it. My son's partner said, 'Don't worry about your sons. They both have a job. Just look after yourself.' Even between parents and children, we need to respect each other. Old-age care is hard work even for professional nurses, not to mention ordinary individuals . . . Even if I have to sell this house, I would hire a professional helper. [60 years old, arrived in Britain in 1958]

The majority expressed a preference for a Western independent lifestyle as opposed to the Japanese tradition of co-residency. Only one widowed informant suggested the possibility of receiving family support in an extended-family living arrangement in the future when she becomes older. Despite the availability of such support in the future, however, she also expressed a reluctance to give up her own independent lifestyle.

When my daughter's family decided to move, we bought a house together. I own two rooms, a bedroom and a living room, in their house. At the moment, when I visit them, I cannot avoid babysitting their small children. But, in the future, perhaps, I would move there to live with them. There are not many people who live with their parents in this country. In general, older parents do not want to be looked after by their children. In my case, I did not ask for it, but my children decided it's the best option for me . . . But, as long as I'm healthy, I would like to live on my own. I have a lot of friends, and since this house is located close to London it enables me to visit various places. Even though I bought the house with my daughter, if I get ill and need intensive care, I do not mind moving to a home. [65 years old, arrived in Britain in 1957]

In the absence of family care, the women's coping strategies for growing older in a foreign society focused on alternative support provision. Access to welfare services was sought more positively by Japanese migrant women. Compared with their age cohort resident in Japan, these women seemed to be less constrained normatively or institutionally about making use of alternative support provided by other welfare sectors. Although many women were aware of decreasing levels of statutory welfare provision in Britain at the end of the 1990s, independent living assisted by a variety of service suppliers was their preferred option.

However, many women seemed to have rediscovered Japanese ethnic or cultural needs during the ageing process. Some expressed particular needs, such as diet, language or companionship, which were not fulfilled by existing services and facilities in Britain. Some needs are currently met through the individual allocation of tailor-made services, notably home visits by Japanese informal carers or Japanese-speaking social groups organized by local authorities and volunteers to offer companionship in their own language. The need for 'Japanese carers' was keenly felt by some women who cited cases of older Japanese people losing their ability to speak English after suffering a stroke or developing dementia. This need would emerge if they became unable to communicate with their children who only speak English. Their preference for their original culture may also limit their choice to live in residential homes for predominantly older British people. Some women voiced a reluctance to move into a British nursing home due to the type of food served. Not having shared experiences of being brought up in British society, some informants thought that they would find it painful to listen repeatedly to co-residents' experiences, to which they would be unlikely to relate.

> When I think about my old age, networks with fellow Japanese seem important. My father-in-law who is suffering from Alzheimer's was lucky to move into a nice nursing home. Although the building is big and wonderful, the food is unbearable to me. It's OK for him being an ordinary Yorkshire man, but I cannot stand having such meals three times a day . . . I don't like pudding with lots of custard, for example. I cannot eat sandwiches all the time either. [61 years old, arrived in Britain in 1971]

Some women emphasized the importance and necessity of companionship and support networks among fellow Japanese migrants for their wellbeing in later life. In response to unfulfilled needs of this particular migrant cohort, collective interest in the theme of 'welfare for old age' acted as a magnet for the formation of a sub-group within a Japanese residents' association.[4] Their purposes included developing semi-formal support and information networks among themselves, and providing mutual help in many welfare areas. Although still a far-off dream due to limited financial resources, the group is seeking to operate its own group home.

> I had never noticed any adverts by Japanese clubs in the paper before. When my husband got sick, I suddenly started thinking of my own old age . . . If something happens to our husbands, we cannot go back to Japan anymore. That's why we need to help each other. Our previous generation [of Japanese women who married British partners] had no choice but lived an isolated life or completely adapted to a foreign way of living [but we are a different generation with more collective power]. [56 years old, arrived in Britain in 1968]

> I joined the group because I agreed with their purpose of considering our welfare in old age, and also because I do not have any children. [61 years old, arrived in Britain in 1971]

However, membership in a formal Japanese association was the desire of only a few. Other women had already established support networks with friends, neighbours and the family, and were happy to retain their existing networks rather than participate in an ethnic club. They were more convinced that friendships, and thus social networks, need time to be cultivated and having the same cultural background did not always provide a good basis for friendship. One of the motivations for many women to migrate out of their original society was their resistance to the 'group consciousness and orientation' of Japanese people (Izuhara 1999b). Therefore, joining a group of Japanese residents was the least desirable option for these women.

Conclusion

This chapter has explored the choices and expectations of female Japanese migrants in Britain, highlighting their enhanced life chances emanating from migration. Removed from Japanese society, many women appreciated the reduced pressure on them to conform to Japanese social norms, and their escape from the restricted opportunities of the Japanese labour market and the male-breadwinner family model. In the case of single women, access to better employment in Britain has helped them achieve home ownership, which offers security in later life. In terms of the provision of family support, care duties for their parents(-in-law) seemed significantly less onerous as a result of migration.

However, social costs were also involved. For instance, they had lost strong or intimate social ties with Japanese society. The initial intention of many women was to migrate temporarily, the possibility of return migration had remained in the minds of many women. Often with the death of their parents, however, the possibility for return migration tended to have become an increasingly unrealistic option socially and financially.

Migration tends to undermine the conventional support structures of Japanese families. The experience of their parent's lifestyle, followed by that of the women themselves, brought to the fore how transnational migration made reciprocity between successive generations of a family problematic. The majority of the women could not fulfil their traditional role as a daughter by providing old-age care for parents in Japan. Combined with a shift in their values towards independent living, guilt and 'unfulfilled' feelings regarding care for their ageing parents were likely to influence the women's expectations of old-age support from their own children when they themselves become older. Many women believed that their children would not be their main source of care. Instead they would seek alternative support services provided by the welfare services of their host society. Some women, however, stressed the constraints they faced as they grew older in a foreign society. For the first cohort of Japanese migrants reaching retirement age in visible numbers there are few facilities catering exclusively for the particular needs of Japanese migrants. Some initiatives have recently begun to emerge at the end of the twentieth century that might provide a good basis for these ageing Japanese migrants.

References

Ackers, L. (1998), *Shifting Spaces: Women, Citizenship and Migration within the European Union*, Bristol, Policy Press.

Bengston, V.L., Marti, G. and Roberts, R.E.L. (1991), 'Age Group Relations: Generational Equity and Inequity', in K. Pillemer and K. McCartney (eds), *Parent-Child Relations Across the Lifespan*, Hillsdale, NJ, Lawrence Erlbaum.

Bogue, D.J. (1977), 'A Migrant's-eye View of the Costs and Benefits of Migration to a Metropolis', in A.A. Brown and E. Neuberger (eds), *Internal Migration: A Comparative Perspective*, London, Academic Press.

Campani, G. (1995), 'Women Migrants: From Marginal Subjects to Social Actors', in R. Cohen (ed.), *The Cambridge Survey of World Migration*, Cambridge, Cambridge University Press.

Castles, S. and Miller, M.J. (1998), *The Age of Migration: International Population Movements in the Modern World*, London, Macmillan.

Finch, J. (1989), *Family Obligations and Social Change*, Cambridge, Polity Press.

Finch, J. and Mason, J. (1993), *Negotiating Family Responsibilities*, London, Routledge.

Garcia, C. (1993), 'What Do We Mean by Extended Family? A Closer Look at Hispanic Multigenerational Families', *Journal of Cross-Cultural Gerontology*, 8: 137–46.

Hashimoto, A. and Kendig, H.L. (1992), 'Aging in International Perspective', in H. Kendig, A. Hashimoto and L.C. Coppard (eds), *Family Support for the Elderly: The International Experience*, Oxford, Oxford University Press.

Izuhara, M. (1999a), 'Women in the Development of the Japanese Welfare State', in United Nations International Research and Training Institute for the Advancement of Women (INSTRAW) (ed.), *Ageing in a Gendered World: Women's Issues and Identities*, Santo Domingo, INSTRAW.

Izuhara, M. (1999b), 'Migration and Old Age: Japanese Women Growing Older in British Society', paper given at International Sociological Association XXXVIth CFR seminar, Berlin, June.

Izuhara, M. (2000), *Family Change and Housing in Post-War Japanese Society: The Experiences of Older Women*, Aldershot, Ashgate.

Kendig, H. (1989), *Social Change and Family Dependency in Old Age: Perceptions of Japanese Women in Middle Age*, Tokyo, Nihon University, Population Research Institute.

Kudo, M. (1983), *Shakonzuma (Picture Brides)*, Tokyo, Domesu Shuppan.

Lewis, J. (1992), 'Gender and the Development of Welfare Regimes', *Journal of European Social Policy*, 2(3): 159–73.

Management and Co-ordination Agency, Japan, (1980/1995) *Kokusei Chousa (Population Census of Japan)*, Tokyo, Bureau of Statistics, Volume 3.

Ogawa, N. (1992), 'Resources for the Elderly in Economic Development', in H. Kendig, A. Hashimoto and L.C. Coppard (eds), *Family Support for the Elderly: The International Experience*, Oxford, Oxford University Press.

Osawa, M. (1993), *Kigyo Chuushin Shakai wo Koete: Gendai Nihon wo Gender de Yomu (Beyond the Firm-Oriented Society: Examine Modern Japan with Gender Studies)*, Tokyo, Jiji Press.

Pedraza, S. (1991), 'Women and Migration: The Social Consequences of Gender', *Annual Review of Sociology*, 17: 303–25.

Shimpo, M. (1995), 'Indentured Migrants from Japan', in R. Cohen (ed.), *The Cambridge Survey of World Migration*, Cambridge, Cambridge University Press.

Notes

1. From the late nineteenth century up to the end of the Second World War, tens of thousands of 'indentured migrants' left Japan to work on the plantation farms of the American continents. These migrants were usually young single males, and subsequently acquired their Japanese brides by an arrangement through an exchange of photographs (Kudo 1983, Shimpo 1995).

2. Up to 1960, only 1 per cent of the population under the age of 50 had never been married. By 1980, although the rates had increased, they still remained low: 4.5 per cent of females and 2.6 per cent of males in the same age groups never married. The rates increased to 5.1 per cent for females and 8.9 per cent for males by 1995 (Management and Co-ordination Agency 1980, 1995).

3. According to the 1997 statistics by the Consulates-General of Japan in Britain, of 54,649 registered Japanese, 6,872 (1,768 males and 5,104 females with a Japanese passport) have settled in the UK (*The Nichi-Ei Times*, 5 March 1998, p. 1). The numbers are, however, inevitably under-estimated as the data exclude those Japanese who have not registered or who have become naturalized.

4. The sub-group was established within a Japanese Residents' Association in London in January 1998. The total JRA membership is currently around 130. The majority of the membership are women (approximately 85 per cent). The largest age cohort is of females in their fifties.

Part IV

Transnational Family Consolidation through Religion

9

Religion, Reciprocity and Restructuring Family Responsibility in the Ghanaian Pentecostal Diaspora

Rijk van Dijk

The recent literature on the African diaspora devotes considerable attention to processes of identity formation, to representation of the community and to the logic of movement (Gilroy 1993, Holloway 1994, Akyeampong 2000). Similar studies in the anthropology of migration and globalization have begun to emphasize a transnational and multi-local perspective (Appadurai 1995, Glick Schiller et al. 1992, Basch et al. 1994, Clifford 1994, Shami 1995). These studies investigate how identities are formed in situations where, as a result of migration, diasporic flows and modern state formation, communities and neighbourhoods arise that seem neither to have a firm geographical anchorage nor to furnish the means for the production of the individual as a local subject: 'Actors who properly belong to a situated community of kin, neighbours, friends and enemies' (Appadurai 1995: 205). In modern processes of state formation in Africa and the West, the (labour) migrant, the refugee, the tourist and the traveller form indeterminate categories and localities. In one sense they may still belong to a particular nation state or society, but from another they remain uncaptured. Appadurai proposes that indeterminate communities of this nature should be termed 'trans-localities', and he calls for an anthropology that can deal with all such deterritorialized processes of identity formation (Appadurai 1995: 204, 213).

This perspective clearly moves away from the type of migration studies common in the 1970s and 1980s, which were dominated by what Rouse (1995) has called 'bipolar approaches'. They held that people moved between places that were fundamentally distinct in social, cultural, economic and political terms, that maintaining meaningful relations across such distinctions was a difficulty every migrant faced and that therefore two models of adaptation usually developed during the process of migration. One was circular with the migrant remaining attached to the place of origin; identification with the place of destination remained limited and the migrant returned sooner or later. The other was linear and the migrant became reoriented to the place of destination, sought permanent settlement and realised a change in identity.

This bipolarity has been largely amended by current studies that seek to understand the multifaceted networks and translocal spaces that migrants in present-day interactions appear to create through modern forms of communication, movement and information. Through continued movement back and forth and the increased circulation of money, goods, services and information, a compression of time and space has occurred leading to new kinds of social spaces which can be called multi-local sites. This notion, however, only slowly percolates into conventional migration studies, as Baker and Aina (1995) show.

This chapter examines one of the newly emerging, transnational, social sites that has developed in the process of intercontinental migration of Ghanaians abroad. The social space concerned is that of Ghanaian Pentecostalism, which in recent decades has developed both in Ghana and in migrant communities of Ghanaians in the West. This rapidly growing form of Christianity appeals predominantly to an urban and mobile population because of the international linkages and branches it has established outside Ghana, the entrepreneurial style of its leadership, and its emphasis on Western-oriented consumption styles and social relations. Likewise, in the migrant communities abroad, many Pentecostal Churches continue to propagate and support the multifaceted international (religious) networks through which they communicate with Pentecostals either in Ghana or in the West. They are members of a larger transnational community and identify with a multi-local frame of reference.

In its project of delocalizing its subject, Pentecostalism restructures kinship relations and obligations. This chapter argues that its appeal is based on the opportunities it provides for bringing kinship obligations under the supervision of its individual members. It confronts the ancestral past of family authority, pursues a replacement of the authority of family heads, and seeks to implant conjugal relations, which it promotes as being part of a modern identity. Pentecostalism reformulates the hierarchical and obligatory gift-giving system upon which kinship relations are based. It subjects reciprocity to moral supervision while making it thoroughly multi-local. This is of particular significance in the diaspora where many migrants see themselves faced with the obligation to send money to relatives living at home and elsewhere. In restructuring such obligations, the Ghanaian Pentecostal Church located in Ghanaian migrant communities seems to be taking on surrogate family responsibilities, thereby communicating the message that a religious and moral control of such relations is at stake.

Pentecostalism at Home and Abroad: Its Transnational Dimensions

Pentecostalism has become the most popular form of Christianity in Ghana over the last 20 years. Between 1987 and 1992 the number of Pentecostal churches grew by as much as 43 per cent (Ghana Evangelism Committee 1993). Although there are many different forms of Pentecostalism, and not all are gaining popularity at the same rate; recent figures show a marked increase in the spread of Pentecostalism throughout rural and urban Ghana. The Church of Pentecost is one of the oldest Pentecostal denominations. According to the National Church Survey, it has now become the largest single Church with a steady adult membership of nearly 260,000 people belonging to just under 3,600 congregations. By comparison, the Presbyterian Church has a steady membership of about 180,000 divided across 1,900 assemblies (Ghana Evangelism Committee 1993).

Pentecostalism in Ghana has also been institutionalized through the founding of an umbrella organisation called the Ghana Pentecostal Council that serves more than 120 Pentecostal churches. Many of these churches belong to what became known as the 'second Pentecostal wave' that has swept across Africa since the 1970s, and has led to the emergence, particularly in the urban areas, of a newer, charismatic type of Pentecostalism. These Churches, such as Dr Mensa Otabil's International Central Gospel Church and Bishop Duncan Williams' Christian Action Faith Ministries founded in the late 1970s, attracted many members from the young and urban middle class who are seeking success and prosperity in life (Gifford 1994, 1998, Van Dijk 1997, 1999).

This popular second wave of Pentecostalism followed and continued a process that can be described as the indigenization of earlier mission-based Pentecostalism (Meyer 1995, Larbi 1995). Missionary Pentecostalism was introduced to Ghana during the first three decades of the twentieth century, and took root with the founding of Churches such as the Assemblies of God and the Apostolic Church, from England and the United States. Though sometimes viewed as belonging to the category of so-called spirit-healing Churches that emerged at roughly the same time (Wyllie 1980), important differences in terms of ritual discourse and practices meant that eventually Pentecostalism took a different path to these other independent Churches.

In terms of the various forms of Christianity, the Pentecostal Churches have engaged in a cultural dialectic on two fronts. They have challenged mainstream Christianity on the perception of evil, on the diabolization of key elements of African cosmology and on ways of counteracting witchcraft and evil spirits. Mainstream Christianity (Presbyterianism, Catholicism, Methodism and Anglicism) has preferred to deny the existence of witchcraft (*bayie*) and has rejected the power of spirits (*adze*), amulets (*asuman*) and traditional healing practices as being mere superstition (Debrunner 1959). It has refused to accommodate or absorb any of the elements of African cosmology to save the pure faith from being contaminated by devilish and occult forces. The development of independent African Christianity and its diverse forms of spirit healing Churches can be interpreted as a process of coming to terms with the powers that mainstream Christianity denied and ignored, and as a way of providing individual members with healing and protection. Churches like the Nazarene Healing Church and the Musama Disco Christo Church included Christian doctrines and provided healing through a range of objects and substances that originated from ritual practices rooted in the veneration of *abosom* (family and ancestral spirits) and their worship through the shrine priests (*okomfoo*). The use of herbs, candles, oils, baths, concoctions, magical rings and the like were very much a part of this world and were included in the spirit-healing Churches' symbolic repertoires.

However, the Pentecostal Churches engaged in a second dialectic as they could not accept practices that would signal the continuation of a cultural past and make the Church vulnerable to attacks from the Devil and his many demons. Ancestral spirits, witches and ritual practices that related to veneration and protection were classified as demonic and were diabolized (Meyer 1992). A rigid dichotomy was developed distinguishing benevolent from malevolent powers and spiritual forces leaving no middle terrain for ambiguity. Whereas ancestral deities (*honhom ananom*) can either work for good or bad in the community or particularly in the family, in Pentecostalism, not denying their existence, their influence is equivocally brandished as malevolent. Healing and deliverance from such powers can only take place through the 'blood of Christ', the laying-on of hands and ecstatic prayer sessions in which the benevolent presence of the Holy Spirit is manifest through speaking in tongues (in Twi *kasa foforoo,* literally 'speaking the new language'). Objects and substances relating to a cultural past are not allowed within its ritual practice and discourse. In Pentecostal practice a great deal of attention is focused on fasting which is perceived as a way of arriving at a spiritual control and inspection of the 'belly' (*yam*) as the place where the ancestral spirits make their presence felt and influence the reproduction of society.

When the mission Pentecostal Churches started to Africanize around 1950 in terms of leadership and forms of worship, the importance of their own distinctive ways of dealing with evil forces in society grew. This approach was in stark contrast to mainstream Christianity which denied the efficacy of these forces and opposed the spirit-healing Churches' demonic practices. While the Pentecostal Churches were growing in strength, the spirit-healing churches became weaker, less appealing and increasingly less able to adjust to the changing fortunes of Ghanaian society as it entered a global system.

Although the older Pentecostal Churches were represented in Ghana's urban areas and could claim international links through their overseas branches, the new type of charismatic Pentecostal Churches made internationalism their hallmark (van Dijk 1997; Gifford 1998). In Accra and Kumasi, Churches were adding terms such as 'international', 'global' and 'world' to their names, thus promising religiously inspired access to transnationalism.[1] Furthermore, this new Pentecostalism appears to have been strongly inspired by Pentecostal developments in America. Firmly located in the prosperity gospel, it propounds the notion of the individual's combined spiritual and socio-economic success. Leaders exude charismatic power and demonstrate their acumen in business relationships.

Another salient feature from the mid-1980s onwards has been these Churches' international self-presentation. The 'global claim' has become a prominent feature. It shows that, unlike most spirit-healing Churches, they can extend beyond Ghana, and Ghanaian and West African culture. Consequently, they have sought to enter other cultural contexts and have ascribed to them a place in their ideology, organization and subsequent religious experience. The claim is not simply that Ghana is 'too small a place for our message', but that entering other cultural contexts deepens, enriches and essentializes the religious experiences of Pentecostal communities. Operating from Accra or Kumasi, these Churches began setting up branches outside Ghana, particularly in Western Europe and the US. Pentecostalism has connected with the new African diaspora through its message for a mobile urban population eager to participate in transnational movement. Over the last decade migrating to the West has become increasingly difficult due to stiff measures taken by many governments to curtail immigration from Africa. As Europe became a fortress, large numbers of Ghanaian Pentecostal Churches were establishing themselves in the continent's major cities, adding to Pentecostalism's international image and promise of success.

An estimated 12 per cent of the Ghanaian population is presently living abroad (Peil 1995) and the ambition of many young urbanites is to join the intercontinental labour migration. Pentecostalism in Ghana feeds into notions that many young people harbour about the affluence and desirability of living in the West. Major communities of Ghanaians can be found in the US, the UK, and in other Western European countries such as Germany and the Netherlands (Nimako 1993, Ter Haar 1994, 1998, Attah-Poku 1996, Van Dijk 1997). These communities tend to maintain close links with Ghana and relatives living in Ghana, but also with one another as members of one family can often be found living in a number of Western countries as well.

Movement between these various communities is an important part of the new Pentecostal Churches. The Churches have connections with international Pentecostal circles that create an extensive exchange of people and materials both to and from Ghana. Conversely, some of the Pentecostal churches founded in the Ghanaian diaspora have evangelized their way back to Ghana. In other words, alongside Ghanaian-based Pentecostal Churches that have been set up among Ghanaian communities in Amsterdam, London or Hamburg, full-fledged diaspora Pentecostal Churches have originated with no formal links with Ghana. Pentecostalism has become a transnational phenomenon that, in its modern form, is locally expressed through a highly accelerated circulation of goods, ideas and people. It has formed a moral and physical geography whose domain is one of transnational cultural interpenetration created and recreated through travel and encounter.

There are approximately twenty-five Ghanaian Pentecostal Churches in the Netherlands where sizeable Ghanaian migrant communities exist, centred on Amsterdam, the Hague and Rotterdam (Ter Haar 1998). They vary in membership from 50 to 600 adults and include both legal and illegal migrants. In the Hague, which is the location of one half of my multi-sited research (the other being in Accra), eight Pentecostal Churches are currently operating in a community of (officially) 2,000 adults.[2] They hold an influential position in the community and function as a *de facto* moral authority over a wide range of matters pertaining to births, marriage, funerals and other rituals and arrangements. Three of these Churches have direct links with Churches in Accra while the other three were founded in the Hague during the late 1980s. Styles of ritual practice, worship, the elements of personalism and international linkage refer to what can be observed in the Accra Churches and therefore a deep sense of transnational continuity, global unity and exchange, and direct accessibility is created for the Ghanaian migrant. The fact that so many Ghanaian migrants adopt more than nominal membership in these Churches signals the profound relationship between the one and the other. In effect, Pentecostalism produces its own specific politics of identity – an identity separate and distinct from that of the host society. Furthermore, Pentecostalism expounds a moral supervision over one of the most immediate social circles for the production of a person's identity: the family.

Family Relations, Migration and the Pentecostal Ideology

Many families in Ghana perceive migration to the West of one or more of its members as a secure strategy for economic success and survival. This strategy is a departure from earlier colonial and post-colonial movements of labour migration in and out of the country. Much of twentieth-century Ghanaian history can be described as highly mobile. In the colonial period which lasted until the mid-1950s a great deal of internal migration occurred from northern groups moving to southern and central regions in search of wage employment in the emerging sectors of cocoa production, mining and urban industries. Large migrant quarters arose near cities such as Accra and Kumasi where the northern labour migrants settled and from there contributed to the growth of the urban areas and their economic success. Experiencing an economic boom during the 1960s, independent Ghana witnessed an influx of labour migrants of a more regional nature as labour migration, by Nigerians in particular, became unprecedented (Peil 1979, Sudarkasa 1979). During the 1970s, however, Ghana's economy, especially cocoa production and similar export-oriented activities, was hit hard by deteriorating world-market commodity prices. Massive outward movement began of Ghanaian labour migrants seeking their fortune regionally. Nigeria, by then a new, booming economy attracted and absorbed large numbers of Ghanaian migrants until 1983. However, during Nigeria's rapid decline in the mid-1980s, the country's rulers developed a new and violent policy of mass deportation of labour migrants. Hundreds of thousands of Ghanaian labour migrants were faced with expulsion from Nigeria but a return to Ghana with its weak economy was no viable option for them (Aluko 1985, Yeboah 1986). It was at this time that massive intercontinental migration began, leading to the establishment of Ghanaian migrants in New York and in European cities such as Hamburg, London and Amsterdam. Ter Haar (1998) shows that by 1996 the Ghanaian migrant population had become the largest group among all the officially recorded migratory movements from Sub-Sahara Africa to Europe.

Among young men, the desire to participate in the migration wave became, and still is, all consuming. Almost everyone has some short or long-term plan to become *woyayie* (the one who 'has arrived' and has made it in life). Many undertake an assortment of odd jobs, try to borrow money from relatives and seek help anywhere they can in their efforts to migrate. The investments are enormous in terms of the money required for a ticket, for the necessary documents, and for the bribes that are usually involved in 'making the papers'. A young man or woman's departure is received with joy and excitement in spite of the serious hardships they are likely to face upon arrival in the West, especially in the case of illegal travellers. After a certain period of time, remittances are expected back home. Usually the recipients are not informed of the circumstances in which the income was generated in the West. Commonly a veil of disinformation is created to hide the fact that, after arrival in the West, life is indeed hard. Jobs are menial, and violence, intimidation and disrespect are the migrant's fate. Remittances are squeezed from only very meagre savings.

Failure to travel to the West, deportation, or lack of success in finding some sort of income once in the West, are all considered disasters. Deportation back to Ghana means the loss of the investment made towards the goal of seeking one's fortune in the West. In addition, there is a tremendous loss of social esteem, a perceived weakness in one's entrepreneurial skills, and a burden on the shoulders of one's family. The causes of failure are not only interpreted by Ghanaian migrants in terms of Western policies, practices and institutions, but are predominantly explained in terms of weaknesses in personal, spiritual and protective power. Somehow and somewhere other forces have been able to take hold of such a person's life. Often witchcraft originating from within one's own family is suspected. The family is the domain of both primary attachment and primary fear. Its powers ambiguously work for good and for evil. Pentecostal groups everywhere relate to these ambiguities and offer spiritual ways of dealing with them.

Many aspiring migrants in Ghana eagerly visit so-called Pentecostal prayer camps that specialize in removing the 'spiritual blockage' to success. Dozens of these camps exist throughout the country, each regularly visited by hundreds of people seeking redress for difficult situations such as illness, infertility, unemployment, and travel, visa and passport problems. The largest is the one at Edumfa, led by the

70-year-old prophetess Grace Mensah Adu, and which was visited by more than 75,000 people in 1997. Commonly, the camp leaders and their assistants investigate the person's past history and location in his or her family (Meyer 1998; van Dijk 1997). Evil powers may reside in the family, based on its ancestral past and ancestral veneration, which haunt the person into the present and 'pull him down'. Pentecostalism has gained a tremendous appeal in Ghana due, among other factors, to the so-called deliverance rituals it offers to spiritually break (*obubu*) ancestral bondage (Atiemo 1994, Meyer 1998, Van Dijk 1997). The hope and belief is that after spiritual breaking the road will be open for the person to acquire the necessary documents to travel to the West. Through prayer and fasting under the guidance of leaders at the Pentecostal prayer camps, the stranglehold of evil powers will be broken and success and prosperity can be restored. Most prayer camps take a residential form. People stay for a number of days until they feel their personal power has returned. Many Pentecostal believers do not seek help from the family shrine priest (*akomfo*) who is responsible for the veneration of family deities. Instead, the spiritual help they obtain at Pentecostal camps offers disentanglement from such a priest and the strengthening of family relations in the spiritual world that he would prescribe.

Beside the desire to travel, find healing and protection, Ghanaians in Ghana and in the diaspora are attracted to Pentecostal Churches and their leaders for deliverance from two major family concerns. These include 'crisis rituals' that take place within the family in relation to marriages, births and deaths, and the exercise of moral control over reciprocal obligations towards the wider extended family (in Twi: *abusua*). Both have clear-cut transnational and transcultural implications and ramifications.

With respect to the first, the Pentecostal leaders seem particularly concerned with the creation of monogamous, conjugal but not necessarily equal relations between husbands and wives. This concern with marriage relations should be placed in the context of developments that have been affecting kinship systems as a whole, particularly those of the Ashanti, Ghana's largest ethnic unit (54 per cent of the entire population) and the one that also holds a dominant position in migrant communities. Developments in what is largely considered a matrilineal kinship system have been the subject of rigorous anthropological analysis for a long time (McCaskie 1995). Most studies are interested in the dynamism of the matrilineal kinship system including marriage relations that allow for considerable flexibility and individual freedom that render them highly adjustable to all sorts of changing circumstances (McCaskie 1995, Clark 1999). The institution of marriage in the matrilineal system of the Asante was of less importance than the place of the woman in her lineage. A woman and her children are the smallest unit (*fie* or *oyafunu koro*) that belongs to the matrilineage and is therefore subject to the authority of the matrilineal elders. Men would have little say in the affairs of the *fie* of their wives and this has been one of the greatest issues of concern, negotiation and conflict over past decades. The twentieth century saw substantial changes in what were once considered by anthropology the systemic characteristics of Asante kinship and marriage relations, due to intermarriage with other ethnic groups and the breakdown of the authority of family elders in the process of urbanisation, missionisation and colonisation.

Pentecostal ideology, in broad terms, proceeds along this trajectory of engaging with kinship relations and customary (marriage) practices and articulates a modernist discourse on these persisting issues. For most Churches and their leaders marriage relations form a domain of contestation with the family and the authority vested in the elders (*abusua panyin*) in what they see as a fight against backwardness and ignorance. Theirs is a modern faith that critically examines tradition and often portrays culture as blocking progress and prosperity. Pentecostal marriage rituals are therefore fully copied from the West, with the bride often wearing an expensive white wedding dress. Pentecostal leaders concern themselves with the minute details of the contractual arrangements that precede the official marriage, thereby assuming a great deal of the authority that customarily rests with the family elders. Pentecostal members are supposed to marry in a Pentecostal manner which offsets a great deal of customary ritual and subsequently has the effect of curtailing the dominance of the family, its ancestry and forms of ancestral veneration. For instance, although it is common to serve alcoholic drinks at wedding ceremonies to all guests, and alcohol is used to pour libation to the ancestors, in Pentecostal wedding rituals this is unacceptable. Whereas the traditional coming together of the families to exchange gifts marks the official status of the marriage, in Pentecostal Churches this exchange is called the 'engagement' and implies that the marriage is not yet complete and still has to be officiated some time later in Church. Pentecostal leaders are involved with the bride-payment, make enquiries about the marriage partners independent of the family heads who traditionally hold that right, and assume the authority to accept or refuse to officiate at a marriage. In other words Pentecostal leaders have appropriated and at the same time replaced a great deal of the authority for their members that otherwise would have rested with the family elders and that other, mainstream Churches often still fully respect.

This contestative replacement is even stronger when the marriage is transnational and one partner lives in Ghana and the other in the Netherlands or in some other country. Pentecostal leaders use their international links within the global Pentecostal network to make enquiries about prospective marriage partners (whether they have been previously married, have children, their residence status and so forth). Through modern means of communication and their international branches they are often in a much better position to make such enquiries than the family elders of both marriage partners would ever be able to do. For these reasons, marrying in a Pentecostal Church in Ghana and in the diaspora has become a status symbol, a mark of genuineness and trustworthiness and, above all, a mark of modern personhood, a modern identity underlined by expensive, Western-oriented consumption styles. This identity is further strengthened by the fact that marrying in a Pentecostal Church signals a certain distance from family obligations, ritual and authority. It exemplifies a kind of appealing independence that has become highly valued by the younger generation.

Once the marriage has taken place, most Pentecostal Churches continue to engage with the couple by stressing the kind of conjugal relationships that keep the backward family obligations at bay. One aspect of this ideology relates to the investments that the man and wife will make for their old age. The Pentecostal Churches tend to stress that true Pentecostal couples should make no secrets about each other's income, and that savings and investments from these incomes should be for the benefit of both partners and their children. This ideology follows some of the laws that the Ghana government implemented in the 1980s decade affecting customary family inheritance rules. These laws, generally known as the Intestate and Succession Laws, were passed by Parliament in 1985 and validate rules of inheritance that prevent the matrilineage from taking hold of the man's property when he dies (Awusabo-Asare 1990). In Ghana's predominantly Asante matrilineal family system, inheritance would follow the line of the mother's brother. Ego would inherit from his mother's brother and not from his own father. The new laws, however, have put in place a defence for any man to ensure that his own children and not the nieces and nephews from his sister's side will inherit his property. In other words, these laws strengthen the conjugal relationship against the interest of the wider extended family. Pentecostalism has taken up this issue and carried it much further as an ideology to the control of family expenditure. Each conjugal unit is expected to spend one tenth of its net income on the Church (the so-called Biblical law of tithing). All other expenses are considered subservient to this. Only when tithing has been closely adhered to can the Pentecostal believer be assured that gifts to his wider family are sanctioned. In the following section I will explain how and why gifting is considered morally and spiritually hazardous by most Ghanaian migrants.

In addition to responsibilities towards the wider family, most couples also have other financial commitments. Usually each makes investments in plots and houses separately (Van der Geest 1997, 1998). In this way if a marriage breaks down, the partners will have their own investments to fall back on and their own means to accommodate and help other family members and their own provision for old age. While, in this sense, this is a guarantee which is highly common in Ghanaian society, Pentecostal leaders and Churches argue against these practices. Such independence in their view encourages divorce and other marriage problems. (In the Hague many consider marital affairs as one of the most pressing problems of migrant community life.) Women are considered by leaders (often men) as the weaker members of the conjugal couple spiritually, the most easily deceived by Satan, and the most vulnerable to occult attacks emanating from within the family. According to Pentecostal ideology, the man's position as head of the household should entail having access to, and control over, his wife's possessions and investments, which runs against the grain of a matrilineal family system. In the migrant community of the Hague, men feel especially dependent on their wives, not because of a transnational transposition of the matrilineal kinship system but because in many cases their permit allowing them to reside and work legally in the Netherlands is dependent on that of their wives.[3] In this context, Pentecostalism recompenses men for what they perceive as a loss of power brought about by the Dutch legal system.

Another way of understanding the Pentecostal emphasis on conjugal relations concerns gifting relations to the extended family. Whereas much of the power of the matrilineage and its elders appears to have been diminishing in past decades, the notion of living under the obligation to give (especially money) to one's close relatives persists remarkably. To a great extent, kinship relations and a person's connection to a family are dictated by reciprocal relations, much more so than in any other domain of life. Almost by definition, family means the people one maintains reciprocal relations with. Structuring of family relationships and family obligations along money lines developed as part of the monetization of important aspects of Ghanaian social and ritual life in the late colonial and present post-colonial situation (Arhin 1995, Manuh 1995, Mikell 1995, Van der Geest 1997, 1998, Senah 1997). One of the important reasons for money becoming the marker of family relationships is its deterritorialized quality. Paying respect to the family elders and the ancestors traditionally was, and still is, a highly territorial act marked by pouring libation on the ground or on a specifically designated spot, money can be sent from any part of the world as a sign of paying homage to those that deserve respect (Van der Geest 1997). Money (*sika*) may intentionally and above all work as a conduit for the powers that emanate from within the family: *sika ye mogya*. This is borne out by the saying 'money is one's blood'.

Through tightening conjugal relations, Pentecostal leaders hope to delimit reciprocity. Conjugal relations help to control and supervise gifting, not only in material terms but also, and more importantly, in spiritual terms as I argue in the following section.

Dangers of the Gift

One of the most important concerns of Pentecostal Churches and their members in the diaspora is the obligation to give, to remit money back home usually to one's mother and sisters. This section focuses on how this positions the Pentecostal believer within the gift economy of the Church, and within Dutch society.

The development of intricate gift systems in migrant communities is certainly not a unique phenomenon; nonetheless the cultural, moral and situational features of the Ghanaian Pentecostal discourse and practice warrant analysis in their own right. Through fasting, ecstatic prayer sessions, deliverance rituals and home cell meetings, an agency is constructed that, in ideal terms, should be able to control, supervise and inspect the gift-giving relations with the family back home. At first glance the aim of Pentecostal ritual practice appears to be the creation of individuality by cutting ties with the family, by controlling the 'belly' (*yam*) such that the influence of the ancestors is curtailed, and by organizing funerals, weddings and birthing ceremonies that replace traditional practices and reduce the influence of family elders. The roots of this concern and how it relates to gifting can be traced by looking more closely at practices of the charismatic Pentecostal Churches in Accra and their concepts of the gift and subjectivity. In one of these Churches the following event happened:

> On a Sunday in November 1996, Pastor E. of the International Bible Worship Centre (IBWC) at Kokomlemle in Accra explained to me that he had received a lady for prayers who asked to be cured of her infertility. She had been unable

to conceive and she suspected that the problem was caused by panties that had been given to her by her mother-in-law. Pastor E. explained that this lady had given testimony to a congregation of more than 500 members at the central Sunday meeting in which she recalled the fact that her newly wedded husband was supposed to give money to his mother (her mother-in-law) and that the mother fornicated spiritually with her son. The son was therefore unable to refuse giving to his mother despite trying to stop redirecting his attention fully to his wife, in accordance with Pentecostal ideology. In laying-on of hands the pastor revealed that there was a spirit of envy (*bayie*) included in the gift of the panties which the lady initially wore without a second thought. On advice and after being prayed for by Pastor E., she returned the gift to her mother-in-law, unmistakably a daring and highly confrontational act, and with it the evil spirit of envy went. She is now expecting a baby.

This short story encapsulates in a nutshell the complexities of gift giving, desire, morality and family relations. It is typical of many that are told in the narrative form of testimonies, chronicling how difficult it is to become a modern individual no longer subverted to the powers that govern the family, the house or *fie*. Manifestly, this story refers to the importance of the gift in terms of capital formation and distribution within the confines of the family. The family, specifically its smallest unit, the *fie*, is tested on the basis of the efficacy of the gift. The father's and husband's responsibility is largely determined by giving money to his wife and children for clothes, school fees, medical care and so forth while the maternal part of that care exists in the reciprocity of food production, cooking and the selling of agricultural produce (and with regard to her husband, the reciprocal rendering of sexual pleasure).

As Clark (1999) shows, since independence and with the mounting costs of such expenses and particularly that of food, the husband's income has gradually become a gift of 'chop money' required to meet the basic needs of the family but from which his wife could no longer hope to save and accumulate for all other types of expenses. This rising inflexibility became critical during the late 1970s and the early 1980s just prior to the implementation of economic reform policies and structural adjustment programmes. Wives increasingly became direct rivals of their mothers-in-law and their husbands' sisters to whom they were supposed to entertain gift-giving relations while facing decreasing financial resources of their own.

Gift obligations towards both the nuclear family and the extended family therefore have become a widely shared and hotly debated issue in Ghanaian society as interests of different matrilineages constantly collide. A husband's responsibilities towards his wife and his biological children run counter to his responsibilities as a *wofa* (maternal uncle) with regard to his sister's children who all belong to his mother's lineage. As Clark shows, these conflicts, negotiations and imbalances have been exacerbated by men's current inclination to invest in the *fie* of their wives rather than in their sister's children. Family elders have heightened their pressure in retaliation and women are caught in between. The strengthening of conjugal ties implies that they are obliged to give financial assistance to the husbands' mother as well, something that, under customary kinship notions, would have been out of the question.

Pentecostal leaders address these issues and the ambiguities of being entangled in inseverable obligations towards the extended family (*abusua* as distinct from *fie*) through deliverance rituals. Deliverance rituals heighten members' awareness of the notion that real progress in life can only be made when one has the audacity to sever ties binding them to the family and its past. A person's past is interrogated and investigated and a complete break with the past is promoted as a safe route for escaping bonds with an ancestral past (Meyer 1998, Van Dijk 1998, 1999). People are often asked to fill out extensive written questionnaires dealing with a variety of aspects of their past lives, particularly events which symbolically mark their position in the family and its family history. For example, a person can be given certain statues, god objects, markings and incisions on the body, certain concoctions to drink, baths to take or medicines to take with their food. Gifts may signal the presence not only of kinship obligations but at a deeper level the ties that bind people to their ancestral past.

It is through the ancestral past, kept alive by rituals of veneration by the family shrine priests (*akomfoo*), that curses (*nnomee*) become manifest in the present. Certain gifts, such as eggs, are signifiers of that ancestral past and ancestral curses. They are considered food for the ancestral deities, which should be broken and poured to invoke their presence 'and make them eat'. Ancestral spirits and the curses that may have been concocted in the past through their interference usually manifest themselves through or in the belly (*yam*), the metaphoric place of metabolism and reproduction of the extended family, somewhat like an egg. In the story cited above, what was manifested was the evil spirit of *bayie*, loosely translated as witchcraft but in essence a force that precludes individuality and disentanglement from the family and its belly. Infertility resulted but the deliverance from the gift in the hands of the Pentecostal leader restored the desired individuality and a breaking (*obubu*) of those ties. The gift was brought back under the control of the person instead of the other way round.

Deliverance forms the most essential ritual in Pentecostal practice (Meyer 1998; van Dijk 1997, 1998, 1999). Many Pentecostal Churches such as the IBWC have special deliverance teams, deliverance hours and produce special magazines in which deliverance testimonies are recorded. Gifts, giving and receiving play a substantial role in these narratives of ordinary people, members or clients of Pentecostal healers. In these stories one notices that there is a sudden realization that the gift is not free, not empty but imbued with intentions, messages and obligations, all of which the person would not have discovered if he or she had not been a Pentecostalist. The Pentecostal ideology, therefore, informs people of the ambiguities of the gift, exposes its history, its intentions and messages and prepares it for alienation so that it can be returned, disposed of or destroyed,[4] which is often seen as an act of contestation.

Among Pentecostal members in the diasporic Churches, many hours are devoted to instructions by the Pentecostal leaders on how to give, when and how much, whom to trust in remitting money and, above all, how to combat the curses that may be part of these politics of the gift. Living in the West means that many feel especially vulnerable to witchcraft attacks from jealous kin and therefore in need of the special charismatic powers that Pentecostal leaders may wield over their lives. Couples take their advice and hours of counselling to heart. One such couple in the Hague for instance explained that for this reason they started 'cross-giving'. Whenever the financial situation allowed it, the husband would send €50 to his wife's mother and she would do the same for his so that devotion and attention are shared in the hope that jealousy and envy, always the source of witchcraft, would not arise from either of the two mothers and their families.

However, in addition to inspection and moral supervision of the reciprocal relations and the remitting of money, Pentecostalism seeks direct replacement when gifting relates to capital accumulation within the family. Paradoxically, although Pentecostalism appears to display a type of individualistic ideology for its members, by stressing conjugal relations and with supervision of reciprocal relations, in certain circumstances the interest of the family still prevails. The prime moment of family interest in any Ghanaian migrant's life is when death occurs among his or her immediate kin. Death is not only a social and emotional catastrophe but is also the single most important moment for the elaboration of the gift economy as a major form of capital accumulation (Arhin 1994: 312, Manuh 1995). The family's representatives living in the West take on a crucial position. They have the formidable responsibility of turning the funeral celebrations into a profit-generating operation. This is a responsibility that even the most confirmed Pentecostal member has great difficulty denying or ignoring.

Generally when a relative dies either in Ghana or elsewhere, kin living in the West are expected to organise funeral parties on behalf of the family in Ghana to contribute towards the costs, debts and financial obligations they have to meet. Usually some time after the actual burial a lavish party is organized with dancing and highlife music to which members of the migrant community are invited. In the Hague, often hundreds if not thousands of Ghanaian migrants, not only from the Netherlands but from other European countries, show up dressed in their finest clothes to pay their respects to bereaved family members and enjoy the social occasion. The party takes the form of a gift-giving event whereby everyone is supposed to donate substantial amounts of money to the family. Organized in the form of a type of contest, amounts donated by individuals may vary between €25 and €2,500. Money is the symbol of status and power, and the names of money givers are proclaimed together with the amounts donated. These gifts are a way of showing one's relationship to the family of the deceased and one's standing in the community as a whole. The expectation is that reciprocal relations are established or entertained so that when death occurs in one's own family a time of cashing in on the 'seed-money' can be held. Arhin describes the present-day situation in urban Ghana of these prospective reciprocal relations:

> Donations . . . compel reciprocal donations; habitual failure to attend funeral gatherings and make donations evokes its own punishment in the boycott of one's funeral performance by the community. (Arhin 1994: 313)

This compelling function of the gift-economy is well recognized by the migrant community. Such gift parties go on throughout the night and often end with donated amounts ranging from Euro 25,000 to 50,000. Having deducted their expenses, the remainder is then sent to Ghana: free profit without any taxation makes the gift-economy a royal road to capital accumulation. At other locations in the West the same will also be repeated so that the family among whom death has occurred is able to raise substantial funds, which are then largely controlled by the matrilineal family head (*abusua panyin*).

The Pentecostal Churches in the diaspora, particularly the Churches located in the Hague, have, however, all been active in creating their own morally supervised domain for such funeral exchanges. For members in whose families death has occurred these Churches have taken on the task of organizing funeral parties. Visited by hundreds of members of Ghanaian

communities in the Netherlands and abroad, and irrespective of membership of the church, donations are equally impressive and contribute
substantially to the family's wealth back home.

There are, nevertheless, a number of major differences with the secular
version of this important family ritual and its economy. During the secular
celebrations alcohol is served (the 'Schnapps' as they are called which
preferably consist of Schiedam jenever) and it is used to pour libation in
honour of the ancestors of the family. Through pouring of libation the
ancestors are invited to 'come and drink' (*nsa*) so as to include the
deceased in their spiritual realm. Pentecostal Churches have ostensibly
moved away from this practice. If a funeral party is organized by a
Pentecostal in and through the Church there will be dancing and music
but no alcohol will be served, and above all no pouring of libation will
take place. Its message is clear: reciprocity is crucial for social relations,
for the building of a social safety net and for the survival of the family in
Ghana, but it requires safeguarding against malevolent influences that
the ancestral past of any family may harbour.

An advantage of organizing the celebration in a Pentecostal way is that
it reduces costs and expenditures for the people responsible for its
organization. The fact that no alcoholic drinks are served leads to higher
expectations of profit.

During the Pentecostal funeral celebration the donated money is
constantly prayed over by the Pentecostal leaders thereby purifying (Twi:
nteho) whatever may come along in terms of evil powers in such gifts.
In other words, Pentecostalism debates the ambiguities of such gift-giving
events and makes its members aware of the hidden dangers that lie in
receiving and passing on such donations. The Pentecostal believer is
expected to control the donation morally so that the inverse will not occur
imbuing the donation with powers that control the believer.

When a person dies while living in the West, those travelling home
carry fingernail and haircuttings of the deceased, which will be buried at
the place of birth as a sign of homecoming. The charismatic powers of
the Pentecostal leader are expected to grant spiritual protection to those
who are the bearers of bad news and to provide protection against
witchcraft attacks from the family they need to visit.

Hence Pentecostal funeral ritual replaces the funeral rituals commonly
organized by family elders and therefore grants its members the opportunity to accumulate through the gift-giving economy in a way that is
beyond the control of these elders. Although the purpose of Pentecostal
funeral ritual is the same, namely capital accumulation within the family
at a time of crisis, the spiritual sanctioning of who is in control, who is

supervising the establishment of reciprocal relations and who is inspecting the powers that may be imbued in its functioning are very different. The Pentecostal leader becomes a mediator and a true ritual broker who is usually engaged on behalf of his followers challenging the authority of the family elders. In other words, theirs is a discourse that acutely makes its members aware of the relationship between religion, reciprocity and the restructuring of family responsibilities in the Ghanaian diaspora.

Conclusion

There is a profound spiritual side to the migration of Ghanaians to the West, which so far has been little explored (Van Dijk 1997, 1998, 1999). The relationship between Pentecostalism and intercontinental migration is broad and multifaceted. Charismatic powers provide protection, success, wealth and prestige. Despite increasingly inhospitable immigration procedures and identity politics generated by many Western states, a great number of Pentecostal Churches display their success in being able to become established in the West and adeptly negotiate their way back and forth in transnational flows of people and capital. The relation between religion and mobility is, however, far from new and Pentecostalism, in a way, appears to build on much older Ghanaian (or perhaps Akan) tradit-ions of travel protection and security cults (Werbner 1989). In other words, the Pentecostal ideology of breaking away from family tradition and bondage as a way of liberating the individual and making him or her fit for travel should in itself be historicized as belonging to a much wider cultural pattern. One of religion's major functions, to put it boldly, is after all the growth of personal power, the *tumi* as it is called, that is sought to achieve success, prosperity and social esteem in life; a desire widely displayed by many in present-day Ghana. Travelling to the West requires religious strength; *tumi* is of central concern.

What Pentecostalism, however, has done is to replace all kinds of medicines, potions, baths, statues and incisions with an emphasis on prayer and fasting as a strategy of spiritual inspection and introspection. Pentecostalism appears to continue a cultural pattern in which the migrant is included in a protective religious domain. Interestingly, however, Pentecostalism in the diaspora does not construe this domain as a contin-uation of Ghanaian or Ashanti culture *per se*, but as a means of affording a critical distance from it. Social science may see continuities, most Pentecostal leaders, however, emphasize discontinuities. The Churches' identity politics are not those of custodians of Ghanaian cultural traditions in the West. Indeed the opposite is true as modern personhood is stressed, sanctioning the pursuit of wealth and prosperity in the West without submissiveness to family obligations that cultural traditions prescribe.

At the same time, and perhaps somewhat paradoxically, family relations still play a dominant role in most migrants' lives. There is a constant moving back and forth *vis-à-vis* one's family, and the pressure of family obligations is felt strongly. Pentecostalism addresses the ambiguities that arise from this: on the one hand the breaking away from the family's ancestral past, while on the other hand still feeling responsible for family survival and doing the best one can as a migrant to remit money back home. Despite their ancestral past, for many Pentecostal believers, the family remains an important source of social security in the long term, even for those in the Netherlands, who on the basis of a legal residence permit may have access to state social security schemes. This notion of the family in terms of social security is even stronger for those residing illegally in the country.

Opposition to the family's ancestral past and the dangers that therefore reciprocity may entail should be interpreted as a discourse and a deliberate strategy towards Christianizing the family. Through Pentecostalism, Christianity appears as a new religious domain of superior power, more forceful than any of the other religious forms that provide security, protection and success (see Field 1960, Fortes 1975, McLeod 1975). This implies a thorough delocalization of identity, that is an identity that is no longer grounded in a specific, circumscribed locality of the family. Whereas the pouring of libation in honour of the ancestors literally takes place by pouring 'schnapps' on the ground, or by breaking an egg on the floor, Pentecostalism offers a much wider transnational frame of identification. For its healing and protective rituals it does not rely on herbs, plants, water, concoctions, baths and so forth, which other religious forms employ in the fabrication of their security 'medicines' and which all stress the notion of the individual being tied to a specific context, locality or even territory. Pentecostalism claims that healing and protection take place through prayers and fasting, activities that do not require a specific attachment to place and locality.

The relationship between Pentecostalism and migration can be best understood in terms of the internal strangerhood that is created. Other protective and security rituals emphasize the fact that a person, through migration, leaves a certain circumscribed locality where the benevolent influence of the family ancestors reigns and therefore must face the unprotected status of being a stranger elsewhere. Transnational Pentecostalism is appealing to many because it creates the notion that, although a migrant may travel abroad and take up residence in another cultural domain, the true believer still remains within its wider protective circle. Leaders of Pentecostal Churches, particularly in the diaspora, are often spoken of in terms of *abusua panyin* (head of the family), and clear signs of attachment to the leader are deemed necessary like small gifts, tithing, and consultation. As was discussed in the context of marriages, the leader is consulted on a range of issues by many migrants, sometimes even taking decisions on their behalf, settling family disputes, assisting in arranging funerals, and dealing with the authorities when necessary and asked to do so. He takes on what, in ideal terms, could be expected from a Christianized family, leaving all propensities to jealousy and envy towards his wealth and prestige behind so that witchcraft, the ultimate power of individuality, will have no place.

As Amin (1995) indicates, most migration studies *a priori* perceive of the migrant as an individual, an ordered person who takes decisions, makes choices and possesses an identity. This chapter has demonstrated the process of construction and fabrication of individuality that the Ghanaian migrants are involved in. Individuality, particularly in terms of attachment or detachment from the family and its obligations, rests only in the making and therefore needs to be problematized. Individuality cannot be assumed but is constantly being articulated and negotiated, and its contradictions are played out within the context of the Pentecostal churches. *Vis-à-vis* the family, the need for greater individuality is stressed and an enticing picture of modern personhood is presented that clearly evokes the imagery of a Western-styled person. At the same time, in the diaspora, the very same Pentecostal Churches create new domains and strategies of attachment so as not to become entirely engulfed in Western lifestyles. After all, the West remains a rough place where immorality in terms of sexual permissiveness, violence, hostile identity politics and criminality runs high. Pentecostal internal strangerhood is a project aimed at creating a critical distance both from Ghanaian culture and its powers, and from a Western world where one's personal powers again may easily run short of protection and security.

References

Akyeampong, E. (2000), 'Africans in the Diaspora: The Diaspora and Africa', *African Affairs,* 99(395): 183–215.

Aluko, O. (1985), 'The Expulsion of Illegal Aliens from Nigeria: A Study in Nigeria's Decision-making', *African Affairs,* 84(337): 539–60.

Amin, S. (1995), 'Migration in Contemporary Africa. A Retrospective View', in J. Baker and T.A. Aina (eds), *The Migration Experience in Africa,* Uppsala, Nordiska Afrikainstitutet.

Appadurai, A. (1995), 'The Production of Locality', in R. Fardon (ed.), *Counterworks: Managing the Diversity of Knowledge*, London, Routledge.

Arhin, K. (1994), 'The Economic Implications of Transformations in Akan Funeral Rites', *Africa*, 64(3): 307–22.

Arhin, K. (1995), 'Monetization and the Asante State', in J. Guyer (ed.), *Money Matters: Instability, Values and Social Payments in the Modern History of West African Communities*, London, James Currey.

Atiemo, A. (1994), 'Deliverance in the Charismatic Churches in Ghana', *Trinity Journal of Church and Theology*, 4(2): 39–41

Attah-Poku, A. (1996), *The Socio-Cultural Adjustment Question: The Role of Ghanaian Immigrant Ethnic Associations in America*, Aldershot, Avebury.

Awusabo-Asare, K. (1990), 'Matriliny and the New Intestate Succession Law', *Canadian Journal of African Studies*, 24(3): 1–16.

Baker, J. and Aina, T.A. (eds) (1995), *The Migration Experience in Africa*, Uppsala, Nordiska Afrikainstitutet.

Basch, L., Glick Schiller, N. and Szanton Blanc, C. (1994), *Nations Unbound: Transnational Projects, Postcolonial Predicaments and Deterritorialized Nation-States*, Reading, Gordon & Breach.

Clark, G. (1999), 'Negotiating Asante Family Survival in Kumasi, Ghana', *Africa*, 69(1): 66–85.

Clifford, J. (1994), 'Diasporas', *Cultural Anthropology*, 9(3) 302–38.

Debrunner, H. (1959), Witchcraft *in Ghana*, Kumasi, Presbyterian Book Press.

Field, M.J. (1960), *Search for Security: An Ethnopsychiatric Study of Rural Ghana*. London, Faber and Faber.

Fortes, M. (1975), 'Strangers', in M. Fortes and S. Patterson (eds), *Studies in African Social Anthropology*, London, Academic Press.

Ghana Evangelism Committee, (1993) *National Church Survey*, Accra, A.G. Literature Centre.

Gifford, P. (1994), 'Ghana's Charismatic Churches', *Journal of Religion in Africa*, 24(3) 241–65.

Gifford, P. (1998), *African Christianity: Its Public Role*, London, Hurst & Company.

Gilroy, P. (1993), *The Black Atlantic: Modernity and Double Consciousness*, London, Verso.

Glick Schiller, N., Basch, L. and Blanc-Szanton, C. (1992) *Towards a Transnational Perspective on Migration: Race, Class, Ethnicity and Nationalism Reconsidered*, New York, New York Academy Series.

Holloway, J.E. (1994), 'Time in the African Diaspora: The Gullah Experience', in J.K. Adjaye (ed.), *Time in the Black Experience*, London, Greenwood Press.

Larbi, K. (1995), 'The Development of Ghanaian Pentecostalism: A Study of the Appropriations of the Christian Gospel in Twentieth Century Ghana Setting', unpublished PhD thesis, Edinburgh, University of Edinburgh.

Manuh, T. (1995), 'Changes in Marriage and Funeral Exchanges in Asante: A Case Study from Kona, Afigya-Kwabre', in J. Guyer (ed.), *Money Matters*.

Instability, Values and Social Payments in the Modern History of West African Communities, London, James Currey.

McCaskie, T.C. (1995), *State and Society in Pre-Colonial Asante*, Cambridge. Cambridge University Press.

McLeod, M., (1975), 'On the Spread of Anti-Witchcraft Cults in Modern Ashanti', in J. Goody (ed.), *Changing Social Structure in Ghana*, London, International African Institute.

Meyer, B. (1992), '"If You Are a Devil You Are a Witch and If You Are a Witch You Are a Devil": The Integration of "Pagan" Ideas into the Conceptual Universe of Ewe Christians in Southeastern Ghana', *Journal of Religion in Africa*, 22(2) 98–132.

Meyer, B. (1995), 'Translating the Devil. An African Appropriation of Pietist Protestantism: The Case of the Peki Ewe in Southeastern Ghana, 1847–1992', unpublished PhD dissertation, University of Amsterdam.

Meyer, B. (1998), '"Make a Complete Break with the Past", Time and Modernity in Ghanaian Pentecostalist Discourse', in R.P. Werbner (ed.), *Memory and the Postcolony*, London, Zed Books, Postcolonial Identities Series.

Mikell, G. (1995), 'The State, the Courts, and Value: Caught Between Matrilineages in Ghana', in J. Guyer (ed.), *Money Matters. Instability, Values and Social Payments in the Modern History of West African Communities*, London, James Currey.

Nimako, K. (1993), 'Nieuwkomers in een gevestigde samenleving: Een analyse van de Ghanese gemeenschap in Zuidoost (Amsterdam). Gemeente Amsterdam', Report to Stadsdeel Zuidoost.

Peil, M. (1979), 'Host Reactions: Aliens in Ghana', in W.A. Shack and E.P. Skinner (eds), *Strangers in African Societies*, Berkeley, University of California Press.

Peil, M. (1995), 'Ghanaians Abroad', *African Affairs*, 94(376): 345–67.

Rouse, R. (1995), 'Questions of Identity. Personhood and Collectivity in Transnational Migration to the United States', *Critique of Anthropology*, 15(4) 351–80.

Senah, K. (1997), *Money Be Man*, Amsterdam, Het Spinhuis.

Shami, S. (1997), 'Transnationalism and Refugee Studies: Rethinking Forced Migration and Identity in the Middle East', paper for the Elizabeth Colson Lecture, Oxford University.

Sudarkasa, N. (1997), 'From Stranger to Alien: The Socio-political History of the Nigerian Yoruba in Ghana, 1900–1970', in W.A. Shack and E.P. Skinner (eds), *Strangers in African Societies*, Berkeley, University of California Press.

Ter Haar, G. (1994), 'Standing up for Jesus: A Survey of New Developments in Christianity in Ghana', *Exchange*, 23(3) 221–40.

Ter Haar, G. (1998), *Halfway to Paradise: African Christians in Europe*, Cardiff, Cardiff Academic Press.

van der Geest, S. (1997), 'Money and Respect: The Changing Value of Old Age in Rural Ghana', *Africa*, 67(4) 534–59.

van der Geest, S. (1998), '*Yebisa Wo Fie*: Growing Old and Building a House in the Akan Culture of Ghana', *Journal of Cross-cultural Gerontology*, 13: 333–59.

van Dijk, R. (1997), 'From Camp to Encompassment: Discourses of Trans-subjectivity in the Ghanaian Pentecostal Diaspora', *Journal of Religion in Africa*, 27(2): 135–60.

van Dijk, R. (1998), 'Pentecostalism, Cultural Memory and the State: Contested Representations of Time in Postcolonial Malawi', in R.P. Werbner (ed.), *Memory and the Postcolony*, London, Zed Books, Postcolonial Identities Series.

van Dijk, R. (1999), 'The Pentecostal Gift: Ghanaian Charismatic Churches and the Moral Innocence of the Global Economy', in R. Fardon, W. van Binsbergen and R. van Dijk (eds), *Modernity on a Shoestring: Dimensions of Globalization, Consumption and Development in Africa and Beyond*, Leiden, African Studies Centre, London School of Oriental and African Studies.

Werbner, R.P. (1989), *Ritual Passage, Sacred Journey. The Process and Organization of Religious Movement.*, Washington, Smithsonian.

Wyllie, R.W. (1980), *Spiritism in Ghana: A Study of New Religious Movements*, AAR Studies in Religion, no. 21, Missoula, Scholars Press.

Yeboah, Y.F. (1986), 'The Crisis of International Migration in an Integrating West Africa: A Case Study of Nigeria and Ghana', *Africa and Development/Afrique et Développement*, 11(4), 217–56.

Notes

1. Examples include the well-known International Central Gospel Church, the Global Revival Outreach Ministry, the Harvest Ministries International and the World Miracle Church. In some of these churches, their international approach is represented symbolically by placing near the pulpit the flags of each country in which branches have been established.

2. This is probably a conservative estimate of the total population. There is no way to obtain an accurate figure.

3. It appears that it has been and still is much easier for women than for men to move out of illegality and achieve a legal status of residence. This is because the illegal system of contract marriage has been more accessible for women than men. Women marry Dutch nationals legally, paying their husbands a fee for their willingness to enter a marriage contract. After a woman has fulfilled the requirements for permanent residence, she divorces her husband and can then remarry, this time a Ghanaian man, or she can bring her husband over from Ghana. Further details of this strategy are beyond the scope of this chapter.

4. A pastor of the IWBC explained to Birgit Meyer that upon receiving a basket full of eggs, precious food during the prevailing economic crisis, he asked his wife to go down to the beach and destroy all the eggs at once.

10

Religion, Migration and Wealth Creation in the Swaminarayan Movement[1]

Rohit Barot

Although changes in the traditional nuclear forms of family are wide-spread in modern European societies, they are not necessarily universal or unilinear. In contrast to narratives on fragmentation and breakdown typically associated with modern family living, this chapter seeks to show how Indians retain an ideology of family in the context of migration in their adopted homes in the diaspora, increasingly forming transnational and globalized networks. One of the key factors that this chapter attempts to highlight is that the family cannot be treated in isolation from other social and cultural institutions.

To explain the relative stability and the persistence of the South Asian family as an institution, it is necessary to examine the family in relation to two different levels of community formation. Although they may conflate in practice, social community based on caste or *jati* can be distinguished from a religious and sectarian community. Both at the level of caste or *jati* and at the level of shared faith, group formation is corporate and exerts considerable influence on those who, through their family, are embedded in a community of multiple affiliations.

As the traditional nuclear family has given way to a whole range of different family forms from single parent to gay and lesbian families in European societies, it is useful to outline briefly the meaning that Indians attach to the word 'family'. In Indian languages that derive from Sanskrit, the words *kutumb* and *parivar* refer to an extended family consisting of a three-generation residential unit or a joint family typically consisting of a man, his wife and married sons. A nuclear family may be formed by a husband, wife and children sharing a common residence. The most important part of *kutumb* and *parivar* is the universe of kinship and affinity that gives a more corporate expression to a caste or *jati* collectivity. The

197

embodiment of such a social community in a religious organization creates long-lasting social ties. It is the relationship or *sabandh* or *rishta* through which families create a community which, due to a shared belief system, leads to both a social and a religious community. This type of group formation is the focus of this chapter.

Such caste and *jati*-based religious groups described here belong to the Swaminarayan movement. The caste and sectarian groups within this movement have become a part of the social structure of the Gujarat state and of Gujarati communities in their diasporic destinations including those in the UK (Barot 1980). To explain the way in which religious organization has made an impact on both migration and settlement it is necessary to trace the origin of these groups and their transformation into a movement consisting of a number of sectarian communities. The formation of the Swaminarayan sect and its gradual formation into different communities indicate a complex process that marks a social change that is typical of the colonial and post-colonial period. Changes in stratification open up venues for mobility. They also create unease between groups struggling for better opportunities and higher status.

The tension generated in this process shows that evolving stratification systems are in flux and that contested and contradictory expectations are likely to develop in the family, between men and women and between different generations. The distance between parents, children and grandchildren is marked by tension as cultural differences grow between the primary and secondary generations who are experiencing less conventional Indian socialization. When such cultural differences manifest themselves within the family, they can create a communication hiatus and misunderstanding. Such changes can create solidarity for the achievement of goals but they can also create tensions that threaten the unity of the family. Needless to say, most Swaminarayan families contain elements of unity and division over a period of time.

To highlight the significance of social cohesion and divisions in the Swaminarayan movement, it is important to situate its genesis in historical changes. This perspective shows that the initial Swaminarayan community is going through a process of segmentation and change that is common for a transnational religious movement. The migration of individuals and families within the Swaminarayan movement to East and Central Africa, the UK, the US and Canada and their economic success is conceptually related to divisions within the movement.

In terms of this argument, this exposition illustrates that the families in the Swaminarayan movement have deployed their socio-cultural and economic resources to better the quality of their life in Britain where they have settled on a permanent basis. The interface of tradition and modernity is something that these families face as a critical challenge in relation to maintaining their religion, language and culture in their adopted country. This chapter focuses on the diffusion and segmentation process and assesses the impact of modernity and transnationalism on the formation of different Swaminarayan groups. Changes in gender and inter-generational relations are highlighted.

The Historical Origin of the Movement

In the eighteenth and nineteenth centuries, the Mogul Empire declined as Europeans competed for power and influence in India. From the beginning of the nineteenth century, the British emerged as the dominant power and introduced elements of Westernization to India, creating social change that brought tradition and modernity into a dynamic interrelationship (Srinivas 1966). One particular consequence was the movement of population. Throughout the nineteenth and twentieth centuries, Indians were on the move in the British Empire – a movement that created Indian communities in many parts of the world (Tinker 1974, 1976, 1977, Clarke, Peach and Vertovec 1990).

The economic and political turmoil involved in India's transition from Mogul to British rule created uncertainties and insecurities, providing the backdrop for the development of the Swaminarayan movement. The Vaishnavite tradition of devotional worship, *bhakti*, had already emerged as a dominant religion amongst Gujarati Hindu merchant groups in Western India. Within this tradition, the Pushtimarg of Vallabhacharya[2] was a well-established sect (Barz 1976). Sociologists and anthropologists often associate the rise of a religious movement with a charismatic leader (Eisenstadt 1968). Hindu tradition is rich with stories of leaders with special qualities that appeal to followers, leading them to take whatever course of action may be prescribed. A traditional belief is that divine beings such as Rama, the hero of the epic Ramayan, or Krishna, a main character in Mahabharat, appear in human form when religious values decline. In the endless struggle between good and evil, it is their mission to restore moral values.

The founder of the Swaminarayan movement, Sahajananda Swami, is often viewed in this way. Scholars such as Williams (1882) have suggested that the Swaminarayan movement developed as a puritanical reaction to moral decline associated with the practices of the Pushtimarg leaders. It is most likely is that people from a wide range of castes were attracted to

Sahajananda Swami's puritanical charisma. However, nineteenth-century socio-economic changes created a whole set of new opportunities for groups at the lower end of the caste scale. Their success as landlords, farmers and merchants created social conditions under which they wanted to undergo what the Indian social anthropologist Srinivas (1966: 1–45) describes as 'sanskritization'. Srinivas identified this change as having an ideological element combined with political mobilisation and economic success. In this process, the aspiring lower caste groups emulated the behaviour of Brahmins or other dominant groups. As in other parts of India, in their desire to conform with the dominant groups and their ideology, many lower groups embraced the Swaminarayan movement, which initially ignored ascribed differences between individuals and families from different caste groups.

Sahajananda Swami, a Brahmin from Utter Pradesh, arrived in Gujarat in 1800 (Fuchs 1965, Dave 1974). According to tradition, he completed his ascetic spiritual journeys and began building up a following in Gujarat. Many middle-ranking and lower-ranking groups joined Sahajananda Swami to receive salvation as well as to improve their ritual and social status in local communities.

The sect and its organization expanded rapidly throughout Gujarat. Before his death in 1830, Sahajananda Swami declared that he was the supreme Swaminarayan, the highest deity for his supporters. By then his following had crystallized into a distinctive organization with jurisdiction divided into northern and southern regions at Ahmedabad and Vadtal respectively (Williams 1984). Sahajananda Swami adopted the sons of his two brothers and appointed them as hereditary heads, the *acharya* of the two regional seats. The *acharya* headed both the lay members as well as the male renouncers who preached salvation and took little interest in the material affairs of the sect. However, the accumulation of assets and their management, or mismanagement, as some were to allege, created differences resulting in disputes and court cases involving litigation about particular *acharyas*. In addition, according to the primary tradition of the sect, since Sahjanand Swami had declared himself to be the supreme Swaminarayan, it was this divinity who was the source of ultimate salvation.

A number of leading renouncers began to claim that they also possessed divine charisma and were equally capable of granting final salvation. When these differences surfaced in public, the factions that broke away from the two main seats formed separate sectarian organizations. A unitary sect changed into multiple sects. For the purpose of distinguishing the original sect of Sahajananda Swami, it is useful to identify it as the primary sect and to distinguish the schismatic sects as secondary organizations. Those who follow the primary Swaminarayan sect of Sahajananda Swami view all the breakaway organizations as heretical or *vimukh*, an expression which literally means 'against the source'. They argue that members of the heretical organizations do not follow the sectarian precepts as laid down by Sahjanand Swami and therefore cannot legitimately use the designation Swaminarayan. However, the sects that have come into existence since their separation from the main body refuse to accept this and offer their own grounds for self-legitimation. The perception of differences between the primary sect and secondary organizations is sharp and forms an important part of sectarian self-consciousness.[3] The identity of each sectarian group has become a highly contested issue.

Segmentation has given rise to a number of different Swaminarayan sects all of which are now represented in Britain. Opposition to the Ahmedabad *acharya* led to three splits: the Shree Swaminarayan Siddhanta Sajivan Mandal based in Maningar near Ahmedabad, the cult of Abji Bapa based in Kutch, and a dissident *acharya* who was excluded from hereditary succession and established his own independent seat at in Saurashtra.

The *acharya* Vadtal also experienced splintering. Swami Yagnapurushdasji separated from the jurisdiction of the *acharya* in 1906 to establish Shree Akshar Purshottam Sanstha. The affiliation of women to a Swaminarayan sect was usually through the family. Women were expected to live within the sectarian jurisdiction as a consequence of desertion or widowhood. They pursued a path of ascetic devotion and were known as *sankhyayoginis*. When a layman within Shree Akshar Purshottam Sanstha recruited and initiated women as renouncers, his views were opposed by the established sects. He thus broke away and established the Yogi Divine Society concerned with the spiritual welfare of women. The society further divided along gender lines: Gunatit Jyot was established for women renouncers and the Anoopam Mission was set up to initiate men.

Several renouncers from the Vadtal seat of the primary sect have also branched out on their own. Using the model of traditional Hindu schools called *gurukul*, they have established their own independent schools for children from Swaminarayan and non-Swaminarayan Hindu families. Although they do not formally identify themselves as a sect, as they have not established their own separate forms of worship and temples, they have a loyal band of followers. They accept the supremacy of Swaminarayan in the tradition of the primary sect.

Migration and Transformation of the Swaminarayan Sect

Sanskritization is frequently linked to changes in the socio-economic positions of groups as demonstrated in Indian anthropological literature.

Land ownership, prosperity through cash crops, and the development of trade were sources of wealth creation for established groups. By the mid-nineteenth century, Gujarati merchants had created trading links with the Gulf and the East African coast, mainly in Zanzibar (Pearson 1976). Besides the seasonal migration of merchants within the Indian Ocean region, male heads of families who found themselves facing poverty and marginality often chose to leave their rural communities for urban settlements like Ahmedabad and Bombay from where they migrated to other areas of the British Empire, particularly East Africa.

Gujaratis who settled in the Indo-Pacific zone from Fiji to East and Central Africa played an important part in the development of colonial economies. Their prosperity supported religious causes and sectarian institutions. In Saurashtra, a renouncer explained to me that the wealth that the East African Gujaratis created went into supporting the sect and building prestigious and magnificent temples in Gujarat and in East Africa. Settlement in East Africa played a vital part in the transnational consolidation of the Swaminarayan movement. As East Africa's Gujarati shopkeepers, buyers of primary produce and wholesalers proliferated and prospered, they formed temple-based sectarian communities. It could be argued that migration and the socio-economic advancement it created was a necessary condition for the elaborate and complex development of Swaminarayan sects within both East Africa and India. This argument is not economic reductionism but rather highlights the fact that economic advancement was necessary for the followers of the Swaminarayan to invest their resources in the religious sphere. The dynamic connection between economic and religious goals has intertwined serving to consolidate both the social and economic organization of sects within the movement.

The story of East African Indian migration to Britain is sufficiently well known in the literature to require no detailed amplification (O'Brien 1972, Tandon 1973, Mamdani 1973, Humphry and Ward 1974, Twaddle 1975, Kuepper, Lackey and Swinerton 1975). However, the framework that takes into account facts of colonization and decolonization and the status of East African Asians as British citizens is crucial for grasping their further migration to the UK. In addition, some of the salient features of colonial stratification show that minorities like Indians were insufficiently integrated into wider British society to legitimate their claims for moral citizenship although they had legal citizenship.

Although the Indians were a part of a colonial three-tiered black, brown and white racial pyramid in which they faced severe racial discrimination at the hands of British colonial officials, they tended to identify more with the dominant white rulers than with the Africans. The colonial stratification and the kind of separation it created between groups failed to provide a basis for multi-ethnic communities to develop in independent Africa (Morris 1968, Dotson and Dotson 1968, Ghai and Ghai 1970). Decolonization in the 1960s created uncertain conditions for Indians who saw that they were going to be unable to protect their privileges based on the colonial social structure. Political changes and the policy of Africanization that gave greater prominence to African aspirations adversely affected Indians. Many began leaving East Africa and followers of Swaminarayan sects came to Britain from this period onwards. As migrants they were not isolated individuals who had decided to settle in the UK. They departed from East Africa as families, relatives and friends with common settlement objectives. Their vision was not merely personal settlement but the settlement of their kin and the re-establishment of their religious organization, only this time in the UK. It should be noted that these families did not see themselves as victims of xenophobia, racism or exclusion in East Africa or the UK. Such a simplistic victim's perspective masks the kind of energy and human resources which families utilise to improve their social and material conditions in an unwelcoming environment. They were intent on turning adverse conditions to their advantage.

In contrast to the single male migration of the 1950s from India and Pakistan, the East African Asian migration generally tended to be family migration. The politics of decolonization demanded that the families leave together, as was particularly the case with the expulsion of the Asians from Uganda in 1972–4. When Swaminarayan families came to Britain in the 1960s and 1970s, a shortage of housing compelled many to live in lodging houses either singly or with other families in the short term. They did not desire public sector housing, even if it had been possible. It would have made it almost impossible for them to recreate their residential sectarian communities. Although private sector housing was never free from discriminatory practices and market constraints, members of various sects were able to recreate quite rapidly residential communities familiar to them from their time in India and East Africa (Modood 1997).

For example the Leva Kanbi Patels of Kutch, with whom the author spent two years in London in the 1970s, lived in their own Swaminarayan neighbourhood. This pattern applies not only to other caste and sectarian communities but also to other Indian groups such as Sikhs who live in close-knit communities ensuring daily face-to-face contact. The lodging house and the system of tenants, which were typical of the early years of settlement, have nearly disappeared and most families now own their own homes.

When they first came to Britain, members of a sect would set up a small Swaminarayan shrine for personal and collective worship. In time, they moved from worshipping in a small room to a terraced house and finally to a large hall or an old church building converted into a temple. Construction of a proper temple in the traditional Indian style is the final step in the consolidation of such religious communities. From the late 1980s, the movement for the construction of temples has gathered pace in Swaminarayan sects. The followers of the primary Swaminarayan sect of Tejendraprasadji funded and supported the construction of a *sikharbandhi mandir*, a temple with traditional domes in Willsden in 1989. This was an important expression of their sectarian identity in spatial terms. In the 1990s, the followers of Shree Akshar Purshottam Sanstha brought about the most effective and successful mobilization of resources for the construction of a magnificent marble Swaminarayan temple in traditional style in the Neasden district of London. The followers of transnational links embracing Europe, Africa and North America formed a vital factor in creating the resources for this temple, which is one of the most impressive and imposing Hindu temples in the Western hemisphere. The fact that the followers as well as the wider British society view this temple as a Hindu temple (as distinct from a temple of a particular Hindu sect) has important implications for identification and identity.

Census data on the ethnic minority population in Britain only provide statistical information about individuals born in each of the Commonwealth countries. Information about the number of people and the size of a religious community is a matter of informed guesswork. Knott and Toon (1981–4) estimate that there were 307,000 Hindus out of about 840,000 Indians living in Britain in the mid-1980s. Based on the British survey of ethnic minorities, Modood (1997) estimates that there may be nearly 325,000 to 350,000 Hindus living in Britain, the majority of whom are probably Gujarati Hindus. Fifty thousand men, women and children in the Swaminarayan movement is a realistic guess. In the US, Williams (1984) estimates there are 10,000 families or 35,000 people in the Shree Akshar Purshottam Sanstha and 10,000 in the Ahmedabad-based primary Swaminarayan sect. It is possible that there are more than a million Hindus belonging to this dynamic movement in Gujarat in India, the UK and the US.

As Indian migration has spread geographically, the Swaminarayan movement has expanded since the mid-1970s both in the UK as well as in the US.[4] There are at least 15 or 16 Swaminarayan temples representing different sects within the movement. Now there are also extensions in Sweden and Portugal where small numbers of Gujarati Hindus have settled permanently. It is worth noting that now there are more than a million Indian Americans living in the US (*Migration News* 2000 and Williams 1988). Swaminarayan sects have consciously become globalised by setting up web pages on the Internet and providing up-to-date information for their transnational followers.

Migration and Economic Mobility

The economic and social backgrounds of the followers are varied and their work histories are complex. As migrants, only a small number of businessmen and women and middle-class professionals such as doctors, pharmacists and chartered accountants were successful in recreating their Indian or East African class position in Britain. In their initial entry into the labour market, most had to set aside their white-collar or professional aspirations and accept manual jobs as a temporary stepping stone to self-employment or a profession. This meant going through a short-term process of proletarianization. Members of the family usually pooled their resources enabling the family to maximize its savings over the years. After investing in a residential property, they usually tried to move out of manual work into self-employment, concentrating on small-scale business enterprises to become self-reliant. This transition to self-employment accorded them a different class position and better material prospects. However, such a transition was by no means universally inevitable as large numbers of men and women had to continue with manual or white-collar salaried employment (Modood 1997). It was common for Gujarati families to suffer exclusion and marginality in the labour market.

One example of a successful upward ascent was the Leva Kanbi Patels, who trace their origin to the Kutch part of Gujarat, and the Patels who come from the Charottar district in central Gujarat. These caste groups belong to different sectarian groups within the Swaminarayan movement (Barot 1987). The Leva Kanbi Patels achieved prosperity through cooperation and hard work based on their traditional occupation in building work and carpentry. They transferred these traditional skills to East Africa and entered the construction world as manual labourers. Gradually they were able to run their own construction firms and in time became successful entrepreneurs – a mark of success that was reflected in further consolidation of their sect, Shree Swaminarayan Siddhanta Sajivan Mandal.

Not surprisingly, after their arrival in Britain, they started working on construction sites. Some were enterprising enough to establish small family firms that specialized in repair work in their own neighbourhoods.

A family that I have renamed the Varsani brothers started out as a modest enterprise jointly operated by several brothers. They were highly experienced builders in East Africa before entering the construction industry in Britain in the 1960s. Their poor command of English and their unfamiliarity with construction work in Britain put them at a disadvantage at the outset but they were keen workers and quick to learn new skills. Many were able to use their contacts with the foreman on site to recruit fellow sect members and nurture them until they had acquired the skills and levels of performance that British construction work demanded. Besides their paid work for big companies, the brothers also bought and repaired properties. Once they had accumulated enough capital, they started buying derelict, run-down properties to refurbish and sell in north London's booming property market. They made good profits and established themselves as a large firm by the 1980s. Further success enabled them to move out of the local residential domestic property market and they began to tender for contracts to renovate high-rise apartments and hotels throughout London. When I met the brothers ten years after my initial fieldwork, they confirmed that their business was a multi-million-pound enterprise. The story of their success was a matter of great pride for the entire community, which benefited from their generous donations for various projects of a religious nature. The Varsani brothers are noteworthy but by no means unique. Numerous Gujarati families have become successful in trade, commerce and industry and many are in the Swaminarayan movement.

The Charottar Patels in London also provide a remarkable example of a community that has been able to find a successful niche in shopkeeping, as recently documented by Patel and Rutten (1999) in their study of this community in Gujarat and London. Besides owning retail businesses and corner shops selling newspapers, confectionery, tobacco and groceries, the Patels have also moved into a wide range of well-paid professions. Gujarati Lohana Hindus have also followed a similar pattern throughout north London. Both communities have had close links with Shree Akshar Purshottam Sanstha and their contributions to the temple community have remained a vital part of the prosperity of the transnational sectarian movement.

According to *Sikshapatri*, a text that Sahajanand Swami compiled to regulate the conduct of his followers, each member of the sect should contribute either a tenth or a twentieth (*dasmo-vismobhag*) of his or her income to the sect. The ability to contribute a large amount of cash is both meritorious and prestigious and offers salvation of the highest kind. The above-cited examples and press coverage given to individual entrepreneurs[5] creates the image of Indians as successful and wealthy people. However it needs to be stressed that not everyone is well off. Semi-skilled and unskilled men and women have suffered from long-term unemployment and disadvantage, especially in less prosperous towns in the north-west of England. Donations by wealthy Indians to their sects act as a symbolic leveller in economically divided communities. While perpetuating the value the community places on entrepreneurial success, they ease social tension that is inherent in a process of economic advance in which all do not participate equally. Making money and spending it on religious and social organizations is regarded as a virtue.

With respect to the entry of Indian women in the labour market, the traditional stereotype that Indian women stay at home and bring up children bears little or no relation to reality. Women in all the Indian communities known to the author have some rural or urban work experience. Leva Kanbi Patel women often worked on farms doing arduous manual work in their villages and East African Asian women played a decisive role in running small shops, an experience that they have successfully redeployed in Britain, however unacknowledged it may be. Most importantly, Indian women brought up in the UK have entered a wide range of professional sectors of the labour market. Indian women are still homemakers but they are also active partners in increasing family income, often ensuring that their children receive an education at expensive private schools.

Settlement, Social Conservation and Change

Migration and economic change are key factors in the successful settlement of Swaminarayan sects in Britain. Somewhat paradoxically the dynamic of the movement is lodged in conservation of many Indian social values, which must be shared amongst family and community members for the movement to flourish. This section examines the tensions embedded in a religious movement premised on geographical mobility and economic success, which must retain a core of social values that can be traced back to rural Gujarat.

Members of the sects recognize the positive value of their migration outside India but they continually stress the hard work and group endeavour that allowed them to reach their current economic position. For example the Leva Kanbi Patels trace their origins back to Kutch and their work as *kadiya* builders. To reinforce their awareness of their origins and the long struggle to their current position in British society, most sects organize special visits to the headquarters of their sect and their own towns and villages in Gujarat. These trips are organized like Hindu pilgrimages to sacred places. The visitors are afforded the opportunity to renew their ties with relatives and to establish their own social presence in their local communities of origin in India. In pursuing such interests, members of the Shree Swaminarayan Siddhanta Sajivan Mandal deposit large amounts of money in banks in their villages to buy land and to build modern, comfortable houses. They also send donations for various village projects like the construction of clinics and schools. Continuity and change mark the kind of institutional organizational framework that the followers of the Swaminarayan sects have created in Britain. In establishing their communities and temples, they have achieved their aim to preserve and sustain their identities as Hindus of the Swaminarayan movement. Their keen commitment to religious salvation is not merely a sectarian matter. It is also partly a consequence of their adaptation to life in Britain. Living in Britain has both positive and negative sides. Although they have new economic opportunities and a better life in Britain, it has also exposed them to social tensions. Unavoidably, many British cultural practices clash with their traditional perspectives.

While South Asians in Britain may face personal and institutional racism imposed on them by the wider society, they also have to contend with internal strains within the movement, and even within families. Growing class differences between Swaminarayan sects constitute a focus for strongly held views as to which sect is the most legitimate expression of the divinity of Swaminarayan. Those who are born and brought up in Britain and have been exposed to a more egalitarian cultural ethic may find that they no longer share the norms of hierarchical esteem embodied in the family and the community. Traditional gender inequality in some Indian castes and sects can be a source of deep unease, especially for young Indian women educated to expect equality but having to cope with strict patrilineal codes of behaviour. The pattern of gender segregation that is traditionally prescribed has come under increasing pressure to give way to more egalitarian norms. Intergenerational tensions erupt when youth defy patrilineal decision making over their education and occupational careers. Higher education for the community's youth tends to be guided towards 'respectable professions'. The unwillingness of young men and women to accept their family traditions of business or work may create serious dislocations between generations.

Generational differences also emerge with regard to the clash of traditional non-egalitarian and youth's egalitarian gender norms. The possibility of acute conflict cannot be avoided on vital issues such as who one should or should not marry. The tradition of endogamy is a source of deep anxiety and tension, especially for young women who come under great pressure to preserve the status quo. In extreme circumstances of inter-generational gender conflict not only does violence lurk in the background but in rare cases a family may even murder a disobedient daughter in order to save its honour. Although Gujarati Hindus are less likely to resort to extreme forms of violence, the author recollects one instance in which a brother killed his sister in a Gujarati Hindu family as she was meeting a boy from outside the community. More recently, *The Times*[6] reported the murder of a 19-year-old Muslim girl, Rukhsana. Although she was married, she had a lover who had made her pregnant. The family had suffered such a degree of dishonour in Derby that her brother and her mother killed her and were subsequently jailed for life, clearly illustrating the passion with which some communities regard virginity, sexuality and honour.

Generally, intergenerational conflicts lead to a gradual transformation of traditional norms to accommodate the emergence of less traditional practices or outright rejection of less democratic and authoritarian conventions. In dealing with these intractable issues much is at stake and families and communities feel compelled to minimize alienation that can undermine the family and the community.

The conservation of traditional social values is also challenged by a growing lack of awareness of one's cultural heritage. Pocock (1976) highlighted the problems of sustaining the literary and linguistic inheritance of the movement. The extent to which a knowledge of Gujarati is a necessary precondition for understanding salvation is a moot issue in all Swaminarayan sects. Translating main religious texts into English is an adaptive response to the need of British-born followers and English as the main language of communication among the young is tacitly accepted. However, leaders stress the importance of Gujarati and organize classes that operate with varying degrees of effectiveness (Logan 1989). Looking at sects like the International Society for Krishna Consciousness, leaders believe that transition into English is not necessarily going to result in diminished commitment to the Swaminarayan.

In view of the strong pressures to conform to traditional social values and resulting intergenerational dislocation and alienation, some young men and women may see breaking away from their caste and sectarian communities to lead their own individual lives as an attractive option. During my fieldwork, there was one example of total breakdown in the relationship between a father and his son. The father's violence towards the son eventually brought about intervention by the social services and removal of the child from his home and his eventual unwillingness to associate with his family and the sectarian community. However, it ought to be emphasized that such instances are infrequent. At the same time, it is also equally important to recognize that they occur in circumstances of stress that spark or exacerbate discontinuity between a person, his family and his community.

Youth rebellion and individualist paths are tempered by the external force of racism, and especially the climate of intimidation, harassment and violence that the young face and that causes them to develop a community-based defensive posture. For example, adverse social and political conditions in the East End of London have transformed the youth into a highly militant and political segment of the local Bengali community (Carey and Shukur 1985). Articulated in different ways and to different degrees, the expression of such a political sentiment is increasingly common among the young.

Conclusion

The economic and social history of the Swaminarayan movement and its geographical dispersal over four continents has necessarily been schematic. I have attempted to demonstrate how economic change and social continuity have been accommodated in the movement. The movement has been characterized through time by segmentation on the basis of charismatic patriarchal leadership. It has often thrived in the face of political hostility. Currently the movement faces generational and gender tensions that may challenge the patriarchal leadership of the community and the family. There are still, however, hostile external forces acting on the movement and that provide a counterbalancing need for unity. In this way, the Swaminarayan movement remains intact and flourishes, challenging modernist sociological theory, which conceptualizes social change as a unilineal transition from holistic communities to more particularized communities to self-centred optimizing individuals.

References

Barot, R. (1980), *The Social Organisation of a Swaminarayan Sect in Britain*, London, School of Oriental and African Studies.

Barot, R. (1987), 'Caste and Sect in the Swaminarayan Movement', in R. Burghart, *Hinduism in Great Britain: The Perpetuation of Religion in an Alien Milieu*, London, Tavistock Publications.

Barz, R. (1976), *The Bhakti Sect of Vallabhacharya*, Faridabad, Thomson Press (India) Ltd.

Carey, S. and Shukur, A. (1985), 'A Profile of the Bangladeshi Community in East London', *New Community*, 12(3): 405–17.

Clarke, C., Peach, C. and Vertovec, S. (eds) (1990), *South Asians Overseas: Migration and Ethnicity*, Cambridge, Cambridge University Press.

Dave, H.T. (1974), *Life and Philosophy of Shree Swaminarayan 1781–1830*, London, George Allen & Unwin Ltd.

Dotson, F. and Dotson, L. (1968), *The Indian Minority of Zambia, Rhodesia and Malawi*, New Haven, Yale University Press.

Eisenstadt, S.N. (1968), *Max Weber on Charisma and Institution Building*, Chicago, University of Chicago Press.

Fuchs, S. (1965), *Rebellious Prophets: A Study of Messianic Movements in Indian Religions*, London, Asia Publishing House.

Ghai, D.P. and Ghai, Y.P. (1970), *Portrait of a Minority: Asians in East Africa*, Nairobi, Oxford University Press.

Humphry D. and Ward, M. (1974), *Passports and Politics*, Harmondsworth, Penguin Books.

Knott, K. and Toon, R. (1981–4), *Muslims, Sikhs and the Hindus in the UK: Problems in the Estimation of Religious Statistics*, Leeds, University of Leeds, religious research papers.

Kuepper, W.G., Lackey, T.L. and Swinerton, N.E. (1975), *Ugandan Asians in Great Britain: Forced Migration and Social Absorption*, London, Croom Helm.

Logan, P. (1989), 'Mother-tongue Teaching: A Case Study', *New Community*, 15(2) 241–52.

Mamdani, M. (1973), *From Citizen to Refugee*, London, Francis Pinter.

Migration News, (2000), 'Indian Transnationals', 7(4) 1–2, http://migration.ucdavies.edu, April.

Modood, M., Berthoud, R., Lakey, J., Nazroo, J., Smith, P., Virdee, S. And Beishon, S. (eds) (1997), *Ethnic Minorities in Britain: Diversity and Disadvantage*, London, Policy Studies Institute.

Morris, H.S. (1968), *The Indians in Uganda*, Weidenfeld and Nicolson.

Nandakishoredasji, S.G. (1981*), Shree Swaminarayan Dwishtabaddhi Smriti Granth Samvat 1837–2037*, Ahmedabad, Swaminarayan Mandir, pp. 316–22.

O'Brien, J. (1972), *Brown Britons: The Crisis of Ugandan Asians*, London, The Runnymede Trust.

Patel, P. and Rutten, M. (1999), 'Patels of Central Gujarat in Greater London', *Economic and Political Weekly*, (April 17–24): 952–4.

Pearson, M.N. (1976), *Merchants and Rulers in Gujarat: The Response to the Portuguese in the Sixteenth Century*, Berkeley, University of California Press.

Pocock, D. (1976), 'Preservation of Religious Life: Hindu Immigrants in Britain', *Contributions to Indian Sociology*, New Series, 10(2): 341–65.

Srinivas, M.N. (1966), *Social Change in Modern India*, Berkeley, University of California Press.

Tandon, Y. (1973), *Problems of a Displaced Minority: The New Position of East African Asians,* Report no. 16, London, Minority Rights Group.

Tinker, H. (1974), *A New System of Slavery: The Export of Indian Labour Overseas 1830–1920,* London, Oxford University Press.

Tinker, H. (1976), *Separate and Unequal: India and the Indians in the British Commonwealth 1920–1950,* London, C. Hurst and Co.

Tinker, H. (1977), *The Banyan Tree: Overseas Emigrants from India, Pakistan and Bangladesh,* Oxford, Oxford University.

Twaddle, M. (ed.) (1975), *Expulsion of a Minority: Essays on Ugandan Asians,* London, The Athlone Press, University of London.

Williams, M.M. (1882), 'The Vaishnavite Religion with Special Reference to the Sikshapatri of the Modern Sect called Swaminarayan', *Journal of the Royal Asiatic Society,* 14: 289–316.

Williams, R.B. (1984), *A New Face of Hinduism: The Swaminarayan Religion,* Cambridge, Cambridge University Press.

Williams, R.B. (1988), *Religion of Immigrants from India and Pakistan: New Threads in the American Tapestry,* New York, Cambridge University Press.

Notes

1. This study is based on my long-term association with the Swaminarayan movement in Britain and India (Barot 1980). I am grateful to Professor Michael Banton and to my colleague Dr Kieran Flanagan for their constructive criticism of the first draft.

2. Now also represented among the Gujarati Hindus in Britain.

3. In an extended interview, a follower of the Ahmedabad-based Swaminarayan sect, Shree Nitinbhai Yagnik, expressed this theme, drawing a clear boundary between the primary and schismatic secondary sects. I am grateful to him for bringing this view to my notice.

4. The Ahmedabad and Vadtal-based primary sect has temples in the Streatham, Willesden, Harrow, Woolwich and East Ham areas of London as well as in Bolton, Oldham, Leicester and Cardiff. There are also additional major centres where members assemble every day to pray and meditate. Shree Swaminarayan Siddhanta Sajivan Mandal has its main temple in Golders Green in London and a temple in Bolton. Shree Akshar Purshottam Sanstha has its main temple in Neasden and four additional temples in Leicester, Ashton-under-Lyne, Birmingham, Wellingborough and Preston with many more informal places of worship. The organizers of Gunatit Jyoti and Anoopam Mission are in Denham near Uxbridge.

5. From time to time, the British press has publicised stories of successful Indian businessmen. For instance, on 26 April 1987, *The Sunday Times* published a

profile of Arunbahi Patel and his acquisition of 300 Finlay newsagents under the headline 'Mr Morning Rises Early to Build a British Empire'. In recent years, *The Sunday Times* has also regularly published lists of the richest men and women in Britain. See Beresford and Boyd's twelfth survey of Britain's richest people (*The Sunday Times Rich List 2000*, 19 March 2000, London: Times Newspapers Ltd.). This compilation contains the names of 49 rich Asians (a number of Gujaratis among them) whose wealth is valued at billions of pounds.

6. *The Times* (London), 26 May 1999.

Part V

Economic and Political Networking

11

Hybridization of Religious and Political Practices amongst West African Migrants in Europe

Monika Salzbrunn

Since the 1980s, the political and economic influences of Islamic brotherhoods have been strengthening in West Africa as international networks take over the responsibilities no longer being carried out by African states. These include technically equipping villages, constructing a social security system, marketing agricultural products, and education. In this chapter, I examine to what extent Islamic practices in Senegal and in migrant communities abroad, especially in France, have coalesced as an important solidarity factor. The Senegalese presidential election in 2000 is an example of recent changes demonstrating links between religion and politics. I focus on several individuals acting as interfaces at both the micro and macro level and ask a series of questions. Is the Islamic religion still a basis of solidarity between migrants and their family and/or home village? Are there reference points, idols, and symbols of a new, not necessarily Western, conception of modernity? How can a juxtaposition and/or elevation of religious and non-religious systems of reference that do not exclude each other be explained? Is there a counter-reaction in the form of a purification of religious practices (for example, proselytizing movements which appeal for a return to the only true Islam)?

The first section of this chapter presents an overview of the economic and political situation in Senegal and the origins of migration. Globalization as a well-established phenomenon in Senegal is explained through the activities of religious networks. The next section focuses on the specific case of Senegalese Islam with its Sufi brotherhoods (Tidjâniyya, Murîdiyya) and an analysis of the meaning of Islam for migrants through the eyes of a Wolof Tidjane woman living in France. Interactions between Islamic authorities and the French Republic are considered before presenting the Senegalese presidential elections in 2000 as an example of the success of network politics.

Islamic Networks and the State in West Africa

Relations between Islam and power in Sub-Saharan Africa are contentious. Coulon (1983) talks about an international 'Muslim connection' that is virtually beyond state control in West Africa. However, more recent works on clientelism and development brokers (Blundo 1995, Salzbrunn 1996) underline the connections some individuals entertain between official power structures and Islamic authorities. Official political power has never openly declared itself against the Islamic religion, which has, in turn, accepted the secular conception of the Senegalese state. Only some minor fundamentalist movements influenced by Saudi Arabia might contest this secularism but it has not been a point of conflict for the Senegalese, 90 per cent of whom are Muslim. Senegal's most respected president, the late Leopold Senghor, was Catholic. The previous president, Abdou Diouf, who is a member of the Tidjane brotherhood, enjoyed the support of a number of Mouride *marabouts* (religious authorities) who, in return, received material goods and support in exchange for services.

Members of the Islamic brotherhoods have played a key role in structuring Senegalese society. Some have secured a well-intended control function in the political arena, but others have collaborated with represent-atives of the ruling institutions, like the *marabouts* in colonial times who were used by French governors to maintain the peace in rural regions. Both phenomena can now be observed in Senegal as well as in migrant communities in Europe where their commercial activities and political influence are growing. These links are obvious not only at higher political levels, but also at the level of the individual migrant.

The current importance of international networks of Islamic brother-hoods can only be assessed through an understanding of economic and political changes in post-colonial Senegal. Until the end of the 1980s, the groundnut economy was the major source of income of Senegalese brotherhoods, in particular that of the Murîdiyya (cf. works by Copans 1988, Cruise O'Brien 1979, and Coulon 1983), whereas in the 1990s with the implementation of SAP, trade and petty trade activities became much more important. Senegal became a model for structural adjustment programmes. It was known to be a relatively stable democratic country untroubled by political disturbances, except for those in February 1994, encouraged by the Moustarchidine wa Moustarchidati. This movement is an Islamic branch of the Tidjâniyya led by Moustapha Sy.[1] Their civil uprising took place amidst growing dissatisfaction with government corruption, the devaluation of the Franc CFA, and rising food prices, especially for bread, which contrasted with the removal of taxes on imported goods which favoured higher income Senegalese.[2]

As a consequence of the SAP-prompted disengagement of the state, the brotherhoods and other associative networks started filling the vacuum, taking over social and other functions no longer performed by the state. In Touba, the capital of the Murîdiyya and the second most important city after Dakar, a special brigade, financed by the state but under the command of the Mouride Khalife général, monitors laws considered to be Islamic, like the prohibition of tobacco and alcohol, and the compulsory use of the veil by women. The largest hospital in Senegal is to be constructed in Touba with Mouride migrants' money, earned from the sale of various plastic and decorative objects exported by trade women nicknamed *nanas Benz*.[3] In the eastern part of the country, the electrification of entire villages has been paid for by migrants from Italy living in Naples.

The transformation processes are supported by the growing, but not entirely new influence of the Sufi brotherhoods, organized in networks all over the world, which are leading to important changes in the concept and practice of Islam.

Transnational Social Communities in Europe: An Actor's Perspective

According to Robin (1996), there are roughly 128,000 West Africans living in France, 74,000 in Germany and 63,000 in Italy. However, the real number in France is no doubt higher because of the ease of obtaining French nationality, especially for children born in France. Three types of migration have been pinpointed: long-term migration leading to assimilation; short-term migration with the aim of returning to the migrant's home country; and migration leading to the creation of a diaspora with integrative social relations in the foreign country. However, a fourth type seems to be gaining dominance now, namely the creation of transnational social spaces.

My study focused on the latter. Following a constructivist approach in the tradition of Berger and Luckmann (1966), I adopted an actor's perspective.[4] Pries's (1996) concept of transnational social spaces and the hybridization of migrants' everyday life practices as well as Evers and Schiel's (1988) strategic group theory inform my network focus. Networks change according to the resources that appear or disappear but the common interest of reaching the same goal is not the only factor determining membership in a specific network. Islam seems to be one of several reference points that define the network. Membership in Sufi brotherhoods is not synonymous with being a male Senegalese Muslim.

Nor can it be assumed that Islam is necessarily exerting influence on the social, economic and political activities of Senegalese migrants living in France.

Pries (1996), while studying migration between Mexico and the US, identified the transmigrant, a working migrant who is situated in pluri-local social spaces. Transmigrants interact in highly complex transnational networks that provide information about employment, facilitate the transfer of money to family in the home village, and offer a means of identification with the home country by network members' sharing everyday practices like preparing food and organizing social gatherings according to well-established rites. The networks are structured by mutual obligations and are the result of a complex system of loyalty. The positions and identities created in this way are hybrid because they take into consideration elements of the original and host countries. These trans-national social spaces are the result of new forms of delimitation and are different from geographic or national boundaries, transcending a simple coexistence of the two systems of reference (Pries 1996: 456).

The Islamic Factor in Transnational Networks

Indisputably, networks of Islamic brotherhoods, in particular the Tidjâniyya and the Murîdiyya from Senegal, are creating transnational social spaces, but the role being played by Islam in the establishment and the enter-tainment of these solidarity systems is less clear. What are the points of reference for the organization of migration and how are these changing? To what extent and in what ways do these migrant networks help their reference group at home? What role do French and African organizations, domestic politics and diplomatic relationships between the different countries play, and how do they affect the individual? How are informal networks such as family networks, transnational organizations of people born in the same village and religious circles changing? What are the motivations or the constraints upon such a complex system of solidarity?

The mystic Sufi brotherhoods emerged a long time after the prophet Mohammed so there is no mention of them in the Koran. Although a growing number of Senegalese Muslims claim to not belong to any brotherhood, there are four main Sufi brotherhoods: Quadiriyya, Layène, Mourides and Tidjâniyya. The oldest brotherhood is the Arabic Quadiriyya, founded by Abd-el-Qadir el Jilâni (1077–1166). For a long time, this was considered the most important brotherhood in Sub-Saharan Africa. In Senegal, the order is located in the north-western town of Ndiassane. The relatively insignificant Layène brotherhood is characterised by its refusal to participate in pilgrimages to Mecca, as one of the five pillars of Islam. The Layène accept women during religious ceremonies, but, as I was also invited to religious ceremonies of the Baye Fall branch of the Mourides during my fieldwork in Senegal, I cannot generalize about rules forbidding women's participation in ceremonies. The Mourides are, in contrast to the dominance of brotherhoods of Arab origins, the only brotherhood founded by a black African Muslim, Cheikh Ahmadou Bamba (1850–1927), who was forced into exile in Gabon by the French colonial government because of the powerful influence he had over believers. The capital of the order is in Touba, which boasts one of Africa's biggest mosques and Bamba's grave. The Tidjâniyya, founded by Cheikh Ahmed El-Tidjani (1735–1815), is the biggest but not necessarily the most influential brotherhood in Senegal. Their main centre is located in Tivaouane, but there are rival branches like the Niassène in Kaolack, and the Omariens or the Mustarchidine wa Mustarchidaty guided by Mustapha Sy.

My study consisted of observing networks of Tidjanes in France within workers' homes, within Senegalese opposition parties, and within West African women's groups in and around Paris, and their links with their home countries, Senegal and Mauritania. I was particularly interested in whether migrants' gifts sent to their home areas, ranging from the electrification of a Wolof village financed by Mouride migrants living in Italy to the construction of a mosque paid for by Mauritanian migrants living in France, are based on religious, family, ethnic or other links. Certainly, there are strong ethnic and local village links amongst the Soninke and Pulaar from the Senegal River region as illustrated by Timera (1996, 1997) and Kane (Chapter 13). My research on the Wolof suggests that their links tend to be based more on religious and political ties. In all cases, the migrants' engagement with their home country and growing parallel markets stretching across national boundaries are directly linked to the disengagement of the nation state and globalization. A professionalization of the informal sector has accompanied political and economic developments in the home countries as well as the changing impact of the Muslim religion.

Contrary to the prevailing discourse, which views globalization as a totally new phenomenon, networking in West Africa has a long history. The Islamization of the Wolof Empire in the tenth century can be seen as an early moment of globalization and mobility over long distances. Since the first Hadj (pilgrimage) to Mecca, pilgrims from different countries have crossed borders exchanging goods, knowledge, and practices. Thus there is a history behind current transnational practices. It is also important not to confound what can be seen as appropriation of new technologies with modernization, or to see modernization as inherently contrary to age-old traditions.

New transnational boundaries now transcend the old geographical and political constituencies, replaced by a medley of Senegalese, Muslim and French elements. There is no homogenization of life practices or knowledge. Encounters with different systems of knowledge and culture are in the process of creating something new, whereby the total becomes more than the sum of its components. A juxtaposition of photos of Lady Di and Steffi Graf next to those of the personal *marabout* on the wall of a Mauritanian worker's room in Paris, can be interpreted as an expression of the current processes of hybridization. The Mauritanian Soninke is also proud of the mosque in a village in the valley of the Senegal River constructed with money earned by his fellow migrants in Paris. Adding new elements does not necessarily negate or exclude old traditions.

Islam's Guiding Light? Individuals within Muslim Networks

Globalization and the hybridization of practices are clearly evidenced by the life of Yasmine, a Senegalese Wolof woman living in a Paris suburb. She founded the Association of West African Women, and communicates with her husband via the Internet. A photo showing him reading the intellectual French newspaper *Le Monde* is stuck to her refrigerator. She is Tidjane and associated with the Niassène branch. In contrast to the Mouride brotherhood, whose spiritual leaders are descendants of its founder Cheikh Ahmadou Bamba and considered as almost holy, the Tidjanes claim religious knowledge and culture as a prerequisite to becoming a *marabout* (as a mediator between Allah and the believers). Yasmine likes the discrete modesty of the Tidjanes who have migrated. On her apartment door are photos of the Tidjane *marabout* Ibrahima Niass from Kaolack to whom she is affiliated, and a calendar displaying a photo of El Hadj Aziz Sy, the last Khalif général (the highest representative of the Tidjanes in Senegal). On the cupboard next to the door is a Benetton postcard showing a white child and a black child. On the shelf, an Arabic-French version of the Koran stands next to works by Albert Camus.

When left-wing parties won the regional elections, Yasmine lost her job in the regional assembly. Her thirteen-year-old daughter, who defines herself as a Muslim, plays basketball at a local club and loves the music of the latest girl bands, without seeing any contradictions.

The mosque is located in one of the other buildings near Yasmine's apartment. Only men have access to the prayers, which take place in the small room, but Yasmine says that she prays five times a day at home. With a bit of humour, she says that she should wear a veil, but she does not. Because of her conviction that fashion norms are culturally different, she finds it absurd that some Senegalese women cover their whole bodies. She is strongly opposed to female circumcision, which is still a hidden practice in the name of tradition and Islam amongst Soninke living in France. Since genital mutilation is a punishable offence in France, a lot of young girls are sent back to West Africa for the operation. Some mothers manage to save their daughters from this journey whereas others inflict the violence to which they themselves were earlier victims on their daughters. Mothers who reject these practices can find support from the Association of West African Women or from French-African groups engaged in the fight against female genital mutilation.

For example, on 2 February 1999, legal proceedings were started in Paris against a 52-year-old French-Malian woman who was accused of having sexually mutilated about 50 girls and young women aged between one month and ten years. Also accused were 22 mothers and five fathers. The process was instigated by an 18-year-old Senegalese woman who was only eight years old when the crime against her was committed. During the trial, many West African women challenged, in public, current opinion in migrant circles for the need for female circumcision to ensure a good marriage, ethnic integration, or for Islamic duty.

As President of the Association of West African Women, Yasmine has found herself acting as a mediator between French institutions and families. She also advises in family conflicts – for example, in cases of violence in polygamous families. She has good contacts with the mayor and with institutions of the French state (for example, social workers). At the same time, she actively participated in the Senegalese presidential election campaign as a member of one of the opposition parties. She followed party meetings in and around Paris, and prepared food for voters who had to travel to Paris in order to vote. During the political campaign in April 2000, she played a key role in organizing food at the meetings with other Christian and Muslim women, both with and without veils. The money raised at these activities was an important source of revenue for Senegalese opposition groups in France, which are entirely financed by migrant members.

Yasmine's activities span 'transnational social spaces' transcending the simple concept of a minority or its diaspora. There are new social realities in the form of norms, cultural milieus, local economies and social networks that qualitatively transform the former social contexts of the home region as well as those of the host region, and that become new social spheres between and above them (Pries 1996).

Islam offers moral legitimacy for Yasmine without representing any contradiction in her activities. She has constructed an identity as an African or black woman through discourses in which she distinguishes herself from Afro-Americans. Her identity as a Muslim is only one of various aspects of her personality bringing her in contact with other women in town who trust her. Yasmine does not hide her membership of a special branch of the Tidjâniyya, but she does not proclaim it in public either.

Likewise, Ibrahim, a Mouride petty trader in Bielefeld, Germany, also sees no contrast between his religious practices and his social life in Germany. He maintains regular contact with his Senegalese *marabout* in Thiès and visits other Mouride *marabouts* when they travel to northern Germany (especially to Bremen where a Mouride centre is located). His official professional activities being insufficient, he earns large sums of money from his petty trading activities at weekends at regional flea markets by selling T-shirts, musical instruments and artwork from Senegal. Before deciding to marry a German woman, he consulted his *marabout* in Senegal and his family, who would have preferred him to become a *marabout* following his religious education during his childhood. Ibrahim has no difficulties in practising his religion and does not feel discriminated against because of his identity as a Muslim in Germany.

Growing Islamic Influence in France

While individuals may see no contradiction between their Muslim, African and European identities, European governments deem otherwise. In so doing, the role of European states *vis-à-vis* Islam is coming to the fore, raising the question of Islam's autonomy as a religion and Muslims' rights to practise privately their religion. In many European states, social problems have been linked to practices considered to be Islamic whether they figure in the Koran or not. Polygamy, for example, is becoming highly contentious. The former French Minister of the Interior, Jean-Pierre Chevènement (who worked with a socialist Prime Minister), refused to provide official papers for second and third wives, leading to their exclusion and insecurity in the name of a republic in which everybody should have equal rights. Some North African Muslim organizations are demanding political changes to take account of the growing number of

Muslims in France. What Casanova (1994: 5) calls the 'deprivatization of religion' can be seen here:

By 'deprivatization' I mean the fact that religious traditions throughout the world are refusing to accept the marginal and privatized role, which theories of modernity as well as theories of secularization, reserved for them. Social movements have appeared which either are religious in nature or are challenging in the name of religion the legitimacy and autonomy of the primary secular spheres, the state and the market economy. Similarly, religious institutions and organizations refuse to restrict themselves to the pastoral care of individual souls and continue to raise questions about the interconnections of private and public morality and to challenge the claims of the subsystems, particularly states and markets, to be exempt from extraneous normative considerations. One of the results of this ongoing contestation is a dual, interrelated process of repoliticization of the private religious and moral spheres and renormativization of the public economic and political spheres.

The claim for political representation as religious equals to Catholics, Jews and Protestants in France is one of the demands of French Muslims in the public sphere. However, the majority of the organizations and religious leaders participating in official meetings with the French Minister of the Interior have North African origins rather than representing a spectrum of different Muslim cultures.

While a deprivatization of Islam can be identified, the recent political campaign for the Senegalese presidential elections that spilled over into the lives of Senegalese migrants in France is an example of a reprivatization of Islam because people were generally not given political direction from the *marabouts* and refused to obey the few who gave a direct order to vote for the Socialist Party (PS) candidate.

Marabouts in Senegal traditionally provided the interface between the political authorities and the population, especially in the rural areas. During the colonial period, French governors used these religious authorities to legitimize their presence. However, there were cases of popular revolt led by *marabouts* against the colonial power. After independence, these *marabouts* continued to act as interfaces between the representatives of the country's Socialist Party and the population. They were able to benefit from numerous advantages from land rights in national parks to direct financial support. In exchange, there were systematic appeals for them to vote in favour of the socialist party.

During the 1990s, the Senegalese population began to renounce the political recommendations of the *marabouts* (Sall 1996). These tendencies were strongly in evidence during the 2000 presidential election campaign in Senegal. Furthermore, it was apparent that migrants were having a growing impact on events in addition to members of brotherhoods who were acting as politicians at some distance from their *marabouts*.

Achievements of Networking: The Senegalese Presidential Elections of 2000

The importance of Senegalese migrants in France can be illustrated by the course of Senegal's presidential election campaign during 2000. The campaign was led by the opposition whose candidate, Abdoulaye Wade, had decided to organize his campaign during a year-long stay in Versailles. During the final days of the campaign, political leaders underlined this gesture as proof of solidarity with migrants and not as a lack of interest in the problems of Senegal:

> He has lived with us, he came to the workers' homes in order to ask us about our everyday problems. He has even produced a video especially for the migrants! [a speaker during the closure of the campaign in Paris, 17 March 2000]

This video was reproduced by members of the PDS (Parti Démocratique Sénégalais), an opposition party, and sold in several French cities during the campaign to raise money for the French campaign. 'The campaign is officially closed, but it is not forbidden to phone home. Call your parents, your relatives, and persuade them to vote for the opposition.' In fact, the propaganda was important in the rural areas because the PS maintained its leading position there, whereas the opposition was able to win in the big cities during the parliamentary elections in 1998.

The important role of the migrants in the Senegalese election campaign can be explained by their strong relationship with their families living in the home country. By planning and successfully leading his campaign from France, Wade not only reached migrants living in France, but much more importantly the rural population whose support finally determined his victory. A phone call from Paris or Washington or a visit by friends or family members is much more effective than a direct campaign in the numerous villages that are not easy to reach. It would not have been technically possible to lead a direct campaign or to reach such a large sector of the population during the 10 days that separated the official confirmation of the results of the first ballot and the closure of the campaign for the second round. At this political level, as at the economic level, the consequences of successful strategies to influence voter opinion from outside can be appreciated. Transnational systems of communication in effect directly influenced the results of the election.

Another important observation during the campaign was the distance the *marabouts* maintained regarding their involvement in politics. During the campaign in Paris, one speaker, a deputy for the opposition PDS in the Senate, the second chamber in Senegal, declared that he had convinced his own *marabout* to refrain from influencing voters although the *marabout* had always recommended the PS in public. He was proud of having influenced his *marabout*'s political role – ultimately a wise decision in view of the victory of the opposition.

The Internet pages of Sudonline offer access to the critical daily newspaper *Sud Quotidien* and helped play an important role in discussions and opinion formation within the Senegalese migrant community. As direct access to the Internet is restricted for many, photocopies and faxes of newspaper articles were also in circulation. On election day, independent journalists communicated the results directly from the different offices by mobile phone to limit the possibilities of cheating.

Despite changes to the political propaganda, there has been no radical renouncement of advice from religious authorities. President Wade's first official visit was to Touba, the capital of the Mourides. As he is known to be a member of this brotherhood, it was important to officially and publicly acknowledge his links. This gesture could also be interpreted as a step towards demonstrating changes without excluding the religious aspects of his personality and his politics. There is no question of religion having a prominent position in his political programme and he appears to want to maintain the existing secularism in Senegal. Similar behaviour can be observed in French migrant circles where Islam remains an important factor of personal identity, but the autonomous acceptance of political responsibilities is becoming increasingly important.

Conclusion

Religious practices are changing within new transnational social communities (Pries 1996). An instrumentalisation of religion can be seen, for example, with development brokers using their religious legitimacy as an interface between the population and Western donors (Blundo 1995, Salzbrunn 1996). In addition, a loss of religious-based social control is apparent and is demonstrated by, for example, the new freedom for members of *marabout* families in social contexts where their religious status has a different significance (such as students in Western universities).

However, concurrently there is a hybridization of religious practices with social practices in the new French or other migrant communities, as demonstrated by the Wolof woman living alone with her daughter in a Parisian suburb where different national, ethnic and religious communities co-exist and where religious practices are less visible in the public sphere. As Muslim traditions and practices of Sub-Saharan Africans become less visible in public than those of Turkish or North African migrants, they do not seem to be in contrast to other aspects of their identity. This reprivatization of religion extends to a higher political level, as was demonstrated in the Senegalese presidential elections. The reduced impact of Muslim authorities on voting patterns is contrary to traditional Senegalese Muslim practices and marks part of the hybridization by Senegalese migrants' lives in Europe.

References

Berger, P.L. and Luckmann, T. (1966), *The Social Construction of Reality*, New York, Doubleday Inc.

Blundo, G. (1995), 'Les Courtiers du Développement en Milieu Rural Sénégalais', *Cahiers d'Etudes Africaines*, XXXV, 1 (137): 73–99.

Casanova, J. (1994), *Public Religions in the Modern World*, Chicago, University of Chicago Press.

Copans, J. (1988), *Les Marabouts de l'Arachide: La Confrérie Mouride et les Paysans du Sénégal*, Paris, L'Harmattan.

Coulon, C. (1983), *Les Musulmans et Le Pouvoir en Afrique Noire: Religion et Contre-culture*, Paris, Karthala.

Cruise O'Brien, D.B. (1979), 'Ruling Class and Peasantry in Senegal 1906–1976: The Politics of a Monocrop Economy', in R. Cruise O'Brien (ed.), *The Political Economy of Underdevelopment. Dependence in Senegal*, London, Sage.

Evers, H-D. and Schiel, T. (1988), *Strategische Gruppen*, Berlin, Dietrich Reimer.

Pries, L. (1996), 'Transnationale Soziale Räume. Theoretisch-empirische Skizze am Beispiel der Arbeitswanderungen Mexico-USA', *Zeitschrift für Soziologie*, 25(6): 456–72.

Robin, N. (1996), *Atlas des Migrations Ouest-africaines vers l'Europe 1985-1993*, Paris, ORSTOM/EUROSTAT.

Sall, B. (1996), *'Paysans, Marabouts et Pouvoirs Politiques: Vers un Déclin de la Médiation Confrérique?'*, *Sociétés Africaines et Diaspora*, 2: 57–71.

Salzbrunn, M. (1996), 'Leaders Paysans et Autorités Religieuses Comme Courtiers du Développement en Milieu Rural Sénégalais', Contribution au Colloque de l'APAD à l'Université de Stuttgart-Hohenheim, 5–8 June 1996, 'Le Développement Négocié: Courtiers, Savoirs, Téchnologies', *Bulletin de l'APAD*, 11: 108–28

Timera, M. (1997), 'Sans-Papiers Africains Face aux Communautés d'Origine', in D. Fassin, A. Morice and C. Quiminal, *Les Lois de l'Inhospitalité: Les Politiques d'Immigration à l'Epreuve des Sans-Papiers*, Paris, La Découverte.

Timera, M. (1996), *Les Soninké en France: D'une Histoire à l'Autre*, Paris, Karthala.

Notes

1. Moustapha Sy was arrested with Abdoulaye Wade, a former minister and opposition leader who later won the presidential election in 2000.
2. Rich *marabouts* were afforded the opportunity to import electronic and computer products directly from South-East Asian countries where their disciples were living.
3. These women travel throughout the world. Their goods are sold by young men, who are to be found under the Eiffel Tower in Paris, on the beaches of the Costa Brava, and on Fifth Avenue in New York.
4. My fieldwork encompassed qualitative empirical research methods including formal and informal conversations, semi-guided interviews, group discussions, triangulation, and participatory observation. The research took place from 1994 to 2000, mainly in Senegal and France, and to a lesser extent in Germany and Spain.

12

South of North: European Immigrants' Stakeholdings in Southern Development

Reynald Blion

This chapter explores the links that immigrants and ethnic minorities maintain with their countries of origin, arguing that migration can contribute to development beyond that of the migrants themselves. Development has commonly been perceived as bridging the divide between 'haves' and 'have nots', an economic divide that largely coincides with the physical divide between the continents of the northern and southern hemisphere. Through immigration, migrants are seen to be bridging the physical divide and hoping to overcome the economic divide as well. Nonetheless, in Europe immigration is posited as a social problem, a zero-sum game in which migrants gain while people in the receiving and sending countries stand to lose. Economic underdevelopment is portrayed as the fundamental cause of the immigration of people from the south towards the north, to the exclusion of any other explanatory factor. The solution to the problem then becomes obvious: developing the migrants' countries of origin can curb migration. The first section of this chapter briefly reviews recent migration history in Europe and attitudes towards its control. The following sections discuss migration concepts and legal and political barriers to migration before turning to a consideration of ethnic minorities' and migrants' links with their home areas and their developmental impact.

Migrants to Europe

Of the estimated 17 million immigrants living in the EU, half originally came from countries in the southern hemisphere. These immigrants' everyday lives and social networks encompass development and immigration processes and play a central role in the dynamics of north-south relations. Immigrants are the human link between societies of the North and those of the South.

Most of Europe's immigrants from the South originally came from North Africa or Turkey, although some are from South and South-East Asia. Fewer, but a growing number, come from Sub-Saharan Africa and Latin America. In the 1960s and early 1970s, the main motive for moving to Europe was economic, to find better jobs, which often bolstered the resources of the families who stayed behind in the country of origin. The two main types of links that immigrants maintained with their countries of origin were the financial remittances they sent back to their families and their return visits for holidays.

When European countries tried to close their frontiers in the mid-1970s, the motives for immigration became more diverse. After that, a large part of the migrant stream consisted of wives and children joining their husbands and fathers. Some migrants still came for economic reasons and settled illegally, as is apparent from the regular campaigns to rectify the status of illegal immigrants in France, Italy and Spain during the 1980s and 1990s. This change in the composition of the migratory flow affected the nature of links between the countries. While most still wanted to send financial remittances to their communities, the needs of their families living with them in Europe meant a reduction in the amount sent back to their countries of origin,[1] even when there were strong social obligations on them to maintain the level of financial remittances. This is perhaps why some pool their efforts through associations or informal organizations, initiating collective projects in education and health directed at their community of origin. But this is only one of the ways immigrants are responding to their social obligations.

Rethinking Migration Concepts and Contexts

The current terminology employed when dealing with questions of immigration and development is the focus of considerable debate. The framework in which immigrant stakeholders develop their initiatives, whether individual or collective, often appears restrictive and inappropriate, not giving due recognition to those immigrants' practices that transcend national boundaries.

The plurality of situations and practices that arise from successive waves of migrants with multiple motives cannot be adequately described using one or two concepts. Their globality remains too contingent. Linear and binary frameworks of analysis are inappropriate not only for analysing migrations and all their complexities but also for revealing the dynamics of development. Dichotomous, narrow and overly hermetic divisions between foreigner and national, immigrant and native; and those who belong to the developed world as opposed to the developing world; the rich and poor, do not provide accurate reflections of the contemporary reality of societies in the north and south.

Any conceptual consideration launched at a European level leads almost inevitably to schisms between Anglophone and Francophone analytical frameworks that may be caricatured as pragmatism versus idealism. In fact neither approach adequately reflects the multiplicity of situations and practices that have arisen from migrations in the past.

Border closures in EU countries, whether or not they belong to the Schengen Agreement, mean a dramatic reduction in legal migrant arrivals on the European continent. A migrant is someone who is in the process of migration. In fact, different generations and profiles of migrants have succeeded one another and the generic term 'immigrant' has become obsolete for certain ethnic groups. The qualification, in French, whereby the children born of immigrant parents are referred to as 'second generation' can be interpreted by them as abusive in the sense that they are not part of the second or third wave of *immigration*. They are citizens born of immigrant parents living in a political, geographic and cultural space that is their own, even if their history and its cultural affiliation, is undeniable.

Political and Legal Barriers

A plurality of situations and practices, largely ignored in political debate, has arisen during the course of recent migration to Europe. Immigration was at the core of much political debate during the 1980s and 1990s. The principal opponents in the debate have clung to border control as the Gordian knot of all entry and residence policies with respect to the movements of non-European Union nationals. Residence in one of the EU member countries is thus not necessarily a guarantee of free movement within the Union. Some member countries remain outside the Schengen agreement, resulting in frustrating red tape for any foreigner from the EU who wants to go to another EU country.

The term 'migrant' in political discourse is symptomatic of this. The obsession with absolute control of the borders of the European Union is reflected in the Treaty of Amsterdam; member states have accepted the transfer of immigration policy making to the Union at the end of a transition period. The agreements that the EU is trying to sign with countries bordering the Union, including the setting-up of buffer zones, further demonstrate the efforts being made to control migratory flows.

The political context of the debate is fashioned out of distrust and suspicion rather than security and stability for the populations concerned and is reflected in various legal texts defining the rules of entry and especially of residence in countries of the EU. This is at the price of repeated violations of the most elementary human rights and international law, making a mockery of rules of international law that affirm freedom of movement as a fundamental and inalienable right.

Migrants face three main restrictions on their conditions of settlement and freedom of movement. In most EU countries, migrants without EU nationality do not have the right to vote in local or national elections and therefore only have an indirect influence on decision makers. Second, unlike EU nationals who have the right to live and settle wherever they want within the EU, a non-national does not have the right to settle in any other EU country. This is a handicap for those immigrants and ethnic minority members who have family members living elsewhere in the EU and those who want to develop economic activities elsewhere in the EU. Third, extra-community residents require a visa for travel to EU countries outside the Schengen zone.

These restrictions act as a brake on the actions of immigrants and ethnic minority members in general. The restrictions reveal how political decision makers view extra-community residents. Their view is based on the assumption that immigrants are here only for a short time before they return to their country of origin. In fact, most immigrants in the EU have now settled in Europe. They want to live in Europe and enjoy the rights of European citizenship while maintaining links with their country of origin.

Development Co-operation to Prevent Migration

The anti-migrant discourse reached its peak in France at the end of the 1980s and during the 1990s, although more recently other countries such as Belgium and the Netherlands have also begun to adopt this perspective. These attitudes inform the links some EU members have attempted to create between their policies of development co-operation with southern countries and their immigration policy. By dovetailing the two, the objective of improving the wellbeing of populations in the south becomes subordinate to reducing immigration pressure on Europe's borders and screening the settlement aspirations of migrants. Several European countries have initiated programmes employing levers of development co-operation to encourage the return of migrants to their country of origin. For example, in France, the Programme Développement Local et Migration (PDLM), funded by the French Ministry of Employment, has operated for the last six years to promote the return of immigrants to their country of origin by assisting them to develop micro-enterprises there. Evidence suggests that this programme has failed to achieve its objectives. Between 1995 and 1998, 26 projects were started under this programme in Senegal but only two people were still pursuing their micro-projects in their country of origin in the year 2000. In Belgium, a similar programme has been introduced to fund micro-projects of returned immigrants. Such programmes rest on the assumption that returned migrants' micro-projects can generate development, while ignoring the complex nature of development needs in the countries of origin, be they Senegal, Mali or Morocco. Development is equated with the accumulated sum of micro-projects of unproven social and economic value.

However, initiatives linking migration and development have the potential to generate a win-win situation for all parties if they are democratically formulated and not organized from the top down. The first objective of any programme centred on the relationship between migration and development should be to get to know and make known the investments already initiated by immigrants and ethnic minorities themselves in their countries of origin. By analysing the motives, objectives, contents and impact of development practices initiated by immigrant communities, valuable insights emerge and genuine development disconnected from the political contingencies of societies in the north can be pursued.

Beneficial Directional Flows in Transnational Space: Immigrants in the North Linked to Development in the South

Development-directed activities carried out by immigrant communities reveal the extent to which they operate in a transnational space and with a transnational logic, thus upsetting traditional national references. Their actions have plural objectives and impacts.

Initiatives developed by immigrant populations in favour of the development of their country of origin take many forms, have an array of different motives, and include both material and non-material transfers directed towards the country of origin. Transfer initiators and their beneficiaries can be individuals, families or communities (villages, regions or associations).

Financial flows are the most visible expression of migrants' development-directed efforts. For example, in 1994, remittances by immigrants represented an annual resource of US$5 billion in Morocco (UNDP 1996, World Bank 1996). This is equivalent to about six times the country's balance of payments deficit or more than twice its public development aid budget. In Mexico, migrants' annual transfers are estimated at about US$4 billion or one fifteenth of total income from exports of goods and services, 15 per cent of the balance of payments deficit and 10 times the level of development aid received. In India, the income from overseas migrants is estimated at US$5 billion per year, or one-fifth of total income from exports of goods and services, twice the balance of payments deficit and three times public development aid.

Revealingly, in France, remittances sent by immigrants are estimated at US$5 billion, while the country's public development aid is about US$7 billion. Eighty per cent of Malian and Senegalese immigrants living in France send an estimated US$36m per year to each country (Blion and Verriere 1998). Annual transfers per person are estimated at US$1,300. A third of Malian and Senegalese immigrants living in France are also involved with an association or informal organization representing their village in France (see Kane in this volume). Another 10 per cent belong to an organization representing several villages. This involvement includes financial contributions estimated at around US$200 per person annually in addition to the remittances they send to their families.

The impact of immigrants' money transfers has been widely debated (Tapinos and Garson 1981, Chaney 1986, Ma Munge 1990, Sinon 1990, UNDP 1992, Russels 1992, Blion and Verriere 1998). It is commonly agreed that the bulk of transfers are destined for families' daily expenses.

Migrant Projects and Organizations Facilitating Flows

The development projects initiated by immigrant associations have been largely overlooked until recently. The material, financial and cultural exchanges between the North and the South, in which immigrants have long been intermediaries, argue in favour of recognizing their special status. Some of the immigrant and ethnic minority organizations (IEMOs) in Europe are now running professional and efficient global development programmes and projects in their countries of origin, based on their continuing links there. This is why they have come to be referred to as development stakeholders. Yet most IEMOs do not stand much chance of being awarded funds from bilateral or multilateral development agencies. This is true not only in France, but also in the UK, Belgium and the Netherlands. Various studies (AFFORD 1998, Sacre 1999, Allal and Ponsignon 1999) have observed discrimination between national development non-government organizations (NGOs) and IEMOs in terms of access to official funds related to lack of information and training and the perceived lower professional capacity of IEMOs.

Nonetheless IEMOs carrying out development projects are beginning to become more numerous in Europe, exemplified by the Alternative for Indian Development,[2] Abantu for Development or Kushandira Pamwe[3] in Britain, Réseau des Associations pour le Développement de la Vallée du Fleuve Sénégal (RADVFS)[4] and Migrations et Développement in France, and Le Centre Euro-Méditerranéen pour les Migrations et Le Développement (EMCEMO) in the Netherlands.[5] The objectives of the programmes initiated by immigrants seem to have strong social and political dimensions and less salient economic goals. This sets them apart from local NGOs.

The origin of this difference in objectives is probably to be found in the migration history of the promoters of these associations. The example of AID in Britain, created by militant students and volunteers originally from India, illustrates the translation of political activism into community approaches. More recently established IEMOs have given a new impetus to questions of development and north-south relations because they do not necessarily share a history of student political activism. Some derive from fraternal workers' organizations (see Kane Chapter 13) or share religious beliefs. Immigrant and ethnic minority organizations espouse a social conscience and are usually oriented towards welfare in terms of education, health, community mobilization, or women's rights. Channelled into these areas, community investment of immigrant funds is generally not perceived as being productive. Immigrant and ethnic minority organizations tend to leave economic activities to individual initiatives. This may be a way of averting conflicts of interest between the various promoters and beneficiaries in societies.

In fact, EMCEMO, AID and Abantu have no direct form of involvement in their countries of origin. They see themselves as relay organizations in the sense that their first role is networking. They put NGOs in their country of origin in touch with NGOs in their host country, facilitating a more egalitarian and comprehensive dialogue by changing the power relationship between NGOs of the North and those of the South. It is not always easy. This approach is also a deliberate attempt to avoid the corporatism of many northern development agencies. On the other hand, northern agencies complain that IEMOs generally initiate projects in a very restricted area – the village of origin – without any links with other actions of local organizations or local development projects.

Although IEMOs' development projects are directed at benefiting the country of origin, in fact many generate advantages for migrants in their countries of residence as well. Immigrant associations that initiate such development projects help sensitize particular groups to the realities in the country of origin, notably children born of immigrant parents. Immigrant youth are exposed to European media images of their parents' countries which often deprecate or even denigrate their cultural identity. Thus, development projects can become a means of helping young people construct their own sense of identity, serving as vehicles for new forms of citizenship, both for the beneficiaries of these programmes, and also for their promoters.

Private Initiatives as a Way of Contributing to Development

Examples of private initiatives include the extension to the country of origin of an economic activity previously developed, or an investment in a new or existing activity developed by a third party. These individual initiatives contribute to economic and social dynamism. Several commercial networks have been set up between countries of the North and South. Similarly, it is becoming increasingly common to meet businessmen developing activities in various countries, notably in their country of origin, while maintaining a significant activity in their host country.

Economic success depends on choosing profitable sectors for investment and having technical and/or business experience in that sector. However, studies in Portugal involving Cape Verdean immigrants to Portugal and Portuguese immigrants to France and in Cape Verde show clearly that when immigrants invest in the host country, they invest in sectors where they have some professional experience. However, when they start activities in their country of origin, they generally enter sectors where they have had no previous experience. The search for profit is their foremost selection criterion. Lack of judicious decision making leads to high rates of failure in this latter area compared to those observed in the first case (Panos/Ciemi 2000).

Transfer of Skills and Know-how at the Core of these Links

Transfers of money are far from being the primary advantages of actions initiated by immigrant associations or private initiatives. The observation of initiatives developed or supported by organizations like Abantu for Development, AID or EMCEMO reveals a plurality of areas of involvement (for example environment, education, health, women's rights) that nevertheless share the common feature of imparting new skills.

In other cases, IEMOs centre their approach on uniting to claim rights, access to education or healthcare, or initiating community projects for specific disadvantaged groups. They often grow out of a struggle for rights in their host country. For example, EMCEMO supports associations of immigrant Moroccan women in the Netherlands, which are in contact with groups of women in Morocco. The same holds for Abantu for Development, an organization created by immigrant African women in the UK, whose projects are concerned with women's issues.

Transfers of skills and know-how, in the widest sense, underpin many community-oriented initiatives. Associations often promote or support projects initiated in areas where their members have acquired certain skills and social or cultural techniques as migrants. One of the essential dimensions of skill transfers based on social mobilization is the dynamizing force they release in the original home community.

A Plural Impact

It is difficult to evaluate the impact of initiatives started by immigrants in favour of the development of their countries of origin. Unlike the economic assessment of development projects, there are few recognized analytical methods for impact assessment. Perhaps the most important impact of actions initiated by immigrant associations is to be seen in the new forms of citizenship that they generate, both in the North and the South.

Questioning the power relationships between various social groups may dissolve some ossified social structures. Internal resistance to change can be reduced if innovations are introduced by migrants. This can be illustrated in Mali with the activities of RADVFS in the field of education. In a region resistant to colonization, literacy has often justifiably been seen as a tool for assimilation to the forms of social organization of the colonizer, and has consequently been opposed. Resistance has been overcome by associations within RADVFS, who have promoted an alternative approach which emphasizes literacy in the traditional languages. They have advanced education as an indispensable tool for any form of citizenship thereby facilitating local people's claims for rights in a region largely overlooked by the Malian state and international agents of development co-operation.

Whatever the type and content of actions initiated by the immigrant populations, the heart of these practices consists of intercultural relations. By acting either collectively or individually, initiators carry out projects that directly or indirectly put two societies, two cultures, sometimes two radically different worlds, in contact with one another thereby forming a link between societies of the North and South.

There are many examples of associations whose projects deal with exchange visits of young people between societies of the North and the

South. Immigrant associations aim to encourage youth to adopt a positive outlook towards their parents' country to facilitate the process of constructing a blended identity. But this may have beneficial effects on the social dynamics of the host country, bringing out a mixed cultural heritage that is not divided in time, space or between societies.

While the actions of IEMOS favour the emergence of a strong civic society in the south, they also mobilize immigrant populations in the host societies and giving them *in situ* civic recognition. By negotiating a grant or premises at the town hall or some other local government office, or by drawing the attention of national or community authorities to their work, these associations create new forms of citizenship in the towns of the North.

Possible Pitfalls and the Role of Northern Development NGOs

These new multiform practices, logics and strategies operate in transnational space, dislodging the classic dichotomy between 'here' and 'over there'. The vicinity of these activities needs to be taken into account by authorities and private organizations in both North and South. Currently few northern development NGOs either support or even understand the role that IEMOs can play in international development policy. Northern NGOs and donors in general criticize the various limitations and pitfalls of immigrants' development initiatives in their countries of origin. Some limitations are real but do not justify the generally suspicious attitude that may be observed in relations between IEMOs and DNGOs. The main limitation of IEMO projects is that many are focused on a restricted space – the village of origin. According to a recent study (Daum 2000) over a third of IEMOs in France develop projects solely for their own village of origin.

Another criticism refers to the size of the projects that IEMOs initiate. In France, the average annual financial resources of IEMOs are around US$15,000 per organisation (Daum 2000). Public or private donors make additional contributions of around US$8,000 per year and per organisation. Compared to the resources available to northern development NGOs (DNGOs), the financial capacities of IEMOs are extremely limited. Comparing scale of operation is not the point, however. IEMOs are proliferating and cumulatively have the potential to make a positive difference to the lives of countless people.

Lack of training and experience in international development projects are recurrent criticisms levelled at IEMOs. In most cases, these criticisms reveal just how difficult it is for IEMOs, especially the smaller ones, to gain access to information and funds. In France, 80 DNGOs carry out 90 per cent of all non-governmental projects supported by the French Ministry of Foreign Affairs (Allal and Ponsignon 1999). If there is no diversification in this official support, most of the IEMOs will remain small and with few projects. One of the main challenges in the coming years will be to find the proper mechanisms to support training and access to information for IEMOs so that they can overcome these basic limitations.

It is also important to avoid an attitude of competition between IEMOs and DNGOs. They must become partners, not competitors. But, if development co-operation becomes a market, as it appears it might, in the sense that increasing numbers of stakeholders are competing for access to decreasing public subsidies, the temptation will be for the traditional stakeholders (DNGOs) in this market to try to prevent the entry of new ones. Some analysts share this pessimistic but partially realistic conception of development co-operation. The challenge is to show IEMOs and DNGOs that they both stand to gain from collaboration rather than competition, taking into account their respective strengths and weaknesses.

An Uncertain but Potentially Promising Future

For societies in both the North and the South, it is vital to recognize the importance of initiatives by immigrant populations directed at development in their countries of origin. An understanding of the objectives, practices, and impact of these initiatives could fertilize the seeds of a dynamic relationship between societies in the North and South to mutual benefit. Increased understanding is also a means to avoid any political use of these practices for ends other than development, and to avoid seeing them as a way of stemming migrant flows to Europe.

The time seems ripe to publicize these initiatives by immigrant populations. They are a promising vehicle for rethinking our traditional approach to questions of development. Above all, Northern NGOs must avoid reproducing the errors and patterns of the past, which served to marginalize Europe's immigrant societies, especially when they came from the countries of the south.

References

AFFORD (1998), *A Survey of African Organisations in London – An Agenda for AFFORD's Action*, London, AFFORD.

Allal, M. and Ponsignon, J. (1999), *Etude d'Opportunité de la Création d'un Programme d'Appui à l'Accès aux Financements Publics pour les Organisations de Solidarité Internationale*, Paris, Coordination SUD.

Blion, R. and Verriere, V. (1998), *Epargne des Migrants et Outils Financiers Adaptés*, Paris, Ministère de l'Emploi et de la Solidarité.

Bredeloup, S. (1995), 'Sénégalais en Côte d'Ivoire, Sénégalais de Côte d'Ivoire', *Mondes en Développement*, 23(91): 13–30.

Chaney, R. (1986), *Regional Emigration and Remittances in Developing Countries: The Portuguese Experience*, New York, Praeger Publishers.

Daum, C. (2000), 'Typologie des Organisations de Solidarité Internationale Issues de l'Immigration', Paris, GREM, Institut Panos, Ministère des Affaires Etrangères.

Ma Mung, E. (1990), 'Les Immigrés et l'Argent: Contes, Légendes et Realités', *Immigration Business*, (September) 20: 7–20.

Panos/Ciemi, (2000), 'Les Immigrés, Acteurs du Développement: Actes du Séminaire', *Migrations Société*, (January/February): 62–7.

Russels, S. (1992), *Les Rapatriements des Salaires des Migrants et le Développement*, Geneva, OIM.

Sacre, C. (1999), *Les Communautés de Migrants, Actrices de Développement*, Bruxelles, CNCD.

Schmidt di Friedberg, O. (1996), *The Mouride Brotherhood: An Alternative to the State?*, Rhode Island, Providence.

Schmidt di Friedberg, O. (1997), 'La Cohabitation dans le Nord de l'Italie. Marocains et Sénégalais à Turin et à Brescia', *Migrations et Sociétés*, 55: 87–106.

Sinon, G. (1990), *Les Effets des Migrations Internationales sur les Pays dÓrigine: Le Cas du Maghreb. Les Transferts de Revenus de Travailleurs Maghrébins vers Leur Pays dÓrigine*, Paris, SEDES.

Tapinos, G. and Garson, J.P. (1981), *L'Argent des Immigrés*, Paris, INEO.

UNDP, (1992/1996), *Human Development Report*, New York, UNDP.

World Bank, (1996), *World Development Report*, Washington, World Bank.

Notes

1. A recent study on the savings and remittances of the Malian and Senegalese immigrants in France (Blion and Verriere 1998) shows that the amount of money they send home is correlated with the length of their migration. The longer it is since an immigrant and his family settled in the host country, the less they send to the country of origin. Furthermore, with the arrival of their wives and children, immigrants are faced with higher costs and education, health and needs that they did not have before.

2. AID is an organization created by Indian citizens living in the UK. It develops projects in India, mainly in Punjab but also in the UK and Europe, to raise awareness of the problems of child labour in the carpet industry in India.
3. Abantu for Development and Kushandira Pamwe are organizations created by African immigrant women living in the UK. They have initiated several programmes in Africa, mainly in East and Southern Africa. Abantu for Development focuses on gender issues in development processes and projects.
4. The Réseau des Associations pour le Développement de la Vallée du Fleuve Sénégal (RADVES) is a network of organizations created by immigrants from the Senegal River Valley and is made up of around 300 different organizations initiating projects to improve water, health, education, and so forth.
5. Migrations et Développement and EMCEMO are both organizations set up by Moroccan immigrants living in France and in the Netherlands to initiate programmes in the North (EMCEMO) or in the South (Migrations et Développement). Their projects are mainly concerned with the basic needs of the population, but are also involved in new information and communication technologies.

13

Senegal's Village Diaspora and the People Left Ahead

Abdoulaye Kane[1]

For more than 15 years, immigrants from the three West African countries bordering the Senegal River Valley have pursued innovative community-directed strategies, refusing to be cut off from their country of origin while striving to integrate in France (Daum 1994). This chapter focuses on the organization of Senegalese village-based migrant communities in France. The transnational character of these migrant social networks is paradoxical because they arise in the context of globalization but are fundamentally rooted in highly localised West African village associational ties. How do village mutual-help societies extend their organizational capacity through transnational space? What is the nature of their relationship to their villages of origin? What are their achievements and limitations? What challenges do these social networks face at present?

These questions are explored through a detailed case study of the Thilogne Association Développement (TAD). The first section describes TAD's organization at village level and its achievements since its founding. The development of TAD in France is traced, relating developments to the Senegalese state's policy of disengagement and structural adjustment policies during the 1980s. Finally, the conflicts, limits and challenges facing TAD-France due to the ageing of its membership are considered.[2]

The Village and Its Transnational Associations

'Village associations', otherwise referred to as village mutual-help societies, gather individuals belonging to the same village at a local and national level. Finance originating from periodical contributions of members or from partners' financial assistance is used to sustain nationals in difficulty in the host country, and to implement community projects linked to the local development of the village of origin. Village associations have become a pronounced organizational feature of Senegal River Valley villages, an area of heavy male out-migration over the past four decades. Men migrate to African, European and American cities, and every village mutual-help society has sections in the different migration destinations where nationals from the village converge. This branching-out of village mutual-help societies gives the associations their transnational character.

Thilogne is a village that had a population of nearly 5,000 in 1988.[3] Located in the middle valley of the Senegal River, it is an ethnically homogenous community solely inhabited by *Haal pulaars*[4] who have a rigid hierarchical caste social system. Extensive male out-migration has resulted in the majority of the population consisting of women, old people and children under 15.

The migration pattern has unfolded in response to the pulsation of local and international push and pull factors. Repeated droughts in West Africa during the 1970s and the dislocation of local production systems spurred out-migration. Initially, migration was seasonal and covered short distances but as drought conditions worsened, longer absences and more distant destinations became the trend. Migration was originally cyclical, with men migrating out and then returning to the village, where their families resided. As distance and periods away lengthened, it was difficult for the migrant to maintain ties with his village. He endeavoured to transfer money home in order to build a house in Thilogne as well as in Dakar or elsewhere where he was working. Concurrently, he was expected to remit regular sums of money to support his family.

Immigration policies in foreign countries, notably France, allowed legal migrants to proceed to family regrouping, bringing about the integration and settlement of whole families. But contrary to what one might expect, the possibility of family unification and permanent settlement abroad does not necessarily imply a loosening of ties between the migrants and their communities of origin. Solidarity between migrants in different countries with their villages of origin persists alongside the migrant's integration into his host society. Thus it is possible to talk about the village diaspora dynamizing local development of Senegalese River Valley villages like Thilogne.

TAD's Village Outreach

The men who have migrated from Thilogne have retained a material presence in their village by virtue of the resource flow they channel to it. The Thilogne Association Development (TAD), founded in the late 1970s, links all people originating from the village throughout the world and is composed of several geographically-based sections. The most dynamic are in Thilogne itself, in Dakar, France, Libreville, the US and Italy. All sections, except that in Thilogne, are required to collect regular, usually monthly, membership dues.

Table 13.1: Thilogne Association Development Membership and Subscription Dues

Location	Number of members	Amount of subscription[*]
Thilogne	All residents	0
Dakar	309	Membership cards (500 F CFA/year)
Libreville	60	2,500 F CFA/month
USA	94	US$20/month
Italy	35	75 FF/month
Paris	228	100 FF/month

Source: author's fieldwork, 1997–8

[*] Subscription rates vary from section to section. Each section sets its monthly subscription autonomously.

The various sections of TAD were not established simultaneously. The Thilogne and Dakar sections were created in 1978. Bural of Thilogne, the organizational predecessor to TAD, represented a merger of youth associations at the end of the 1960s. The French TAD section originated from a village mutual help society dating back to 1966. The Libreville, US and Italy sections are more recent, only emerging in the early 1990s. The dates of sectional creation reflect the history of foreign out-migration from Thilogne.

The different organizational sections of TAD all display the common objective of contributing to community projects that enhance the social welfare of the local village population, specifically in the fields of education, health and water supplies. This has spontaneously grown out of TAD's original mutual-help objectives and the protection of migrant members in their host areas (Diop 1965). Today, this continues to be a concern but the mutual-help dimension is much more widely defined and embraces the welfare of people in the home village, Thilogne.

The following table chronologically summarizes TAD's achievements in education and health. It reveals two stages of Thilogne migrants' contributions. Initially, contributions were directed towards meeting the social welfare needs of migrant members in their respective host localities. Contributions to the village were relatively small and had a religious theme, notably funding for religious buildings. During the 1980s, this pattern was superseded by village-oriented contributions intended to compensate for the vacuum left by the Senegalese state in its policy of disengagement from rural social welfare. Contributions were made to provide for villagers' basic needs with respect to education, healthcare and water supplies.

Table 13.2: TAD's Village Development Achievements

Year	Achievement	Total cost (FF)	Externally generated funds (%)
1977	Erecting graveyard wall	50,000	
1978	Renovating maternity hospital	10,000	
1980	Building three primary school classrooms	20,000	
1982	Building primary school classrooms in connection with Id celebrations	25,000	
1984	Purchase of desks, benches for classroom	16,000	
1986	Equipment for maternity hospital	6,750	
1987	Equipment for maternity hospital	6,173	
1988	Erecting primary school enclosure	61,079	
	Four classrooms for senior high school	104,510	86
1989	Remittances of financial help to migrants repatriated from Mauritania	10,000	
	Equipment for schools and dispensary	50,000	80
1991	Library for high school	27,000	
	Primary school renovation	12,000	81
1993	Gift of medicines for the dispensary	n.a.	100
1994	Bore hole equipment	120,000	
	Repair to village water system	11,000	
	Three classrooms for primary school	30,000	66
1995	Extension of village water system	700,000	71

Source: author's fieldwork 1997–8, archives of TAD-France

Until 1987, TAD relied entirely on its own resources and did not approach any French agencies for support. During the mid-1980s, young Thilognois, some of whom had a university education, took the lead in the association. Their first initiative was to have TAD officially registered as an organization in France, making it possible to seek contact and partnership with NGOs and French municipalities. This brought a burst of new funding for village projects.[5]

Currently, coordination of the efforts of different TAD sections to establish a transnational network of the Thilogne diaspora throughout Africa, Europe and the US are being coordinated to allow for more concerted and efficient intervention. Its goal is the mobilisation of funds for village community development projects.

TAD's Transnational Character

The Thilogne Association Development demonstrates three major transnational characteristics. First, it is a village organization found in several different countries namely Senegal, Gabon, France, and the USA, to mention only the most dynamic branches (Quiminal 1991, Daum 1994, Delville 1991). The association is officially registered in each of these countries. Second, different sections in different countries share one objective: to implement community projects in their village of origin. Third, there is an effort to coordinate activities in the domain of local development. Sections of the TAD maintain regular contacts by post, telephone, fax or e-mail. They organize cultural meetings in Thilogne village, where section leaders meet to discuss actions and their financial modalities. These cultural meetings are organized every three years and aim to reaffirm members' attachments to their native land and their ancestral traditions. They are also an opportunity for villagers to honour the migrants as heroes. The local population expresses their thanks and gratitude towards the diaspora for all the contributions in the field of local development. On 23 January 1998, the leaders of the TAD sections of Thilogne, Libreville and the US were invited to attend the annual General Assembly of TAD-France. An umbrella organizational committee of the different sections was set up at this meeting.

A pragmatic division of labour operates between the sections. Those in Paris, New York and Libreville constitute the sponsors who make the financing of projects possible. The Dakar section is more oriented towards smoothing relations with government officials and facilitating the selection of personnel for TAD's development projects, notably teachers and health workers. They negotiate with customs officials when equipment sent by TAD sections arrives at the harbour or airport. The local village section supplies manual labour for building projects, and manages and maintains project equipment.

The TAD rests on several major poles around which the village diaspora gravitates. There are two poles in Senegal, one in the village itself and another in Dakar, with sections in other African countries according to the number of Thilognois there. Libreville and Ouagadougou are most prominent. According to the same logic of demographic concentration, there is one pole in Paris and another in New York.

The arrows in Figure 13.1 show three types of movement. First, flows of migrants leave the village heading for the poles of attraction. The most frequently travelled routes during the 1960–90 period were Thilogne–Dakar–Paris and Thilogne–Dakar–Libreville–Paris. At the beginning of the 1990s, the Thilogne–Dakar–Ouagadougou–New York path began to

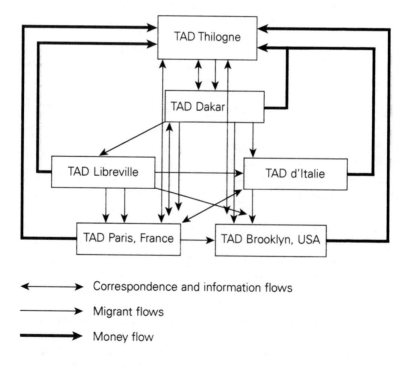

Figure 13.1 Structure and Inter-relationship between Thilogne Association Development Sections

dominate. The second type of movement shown is flows of monetary transfers, medicine and equipment going from migration areas to the village. The TAD section in France accounts for the largest number of transfers of this kind. Third, information flows between the different sections by letter, telephone, fax and e-mail. In 1999, the local section was connected to the Internet to facilitate communication with the different TAD sections abroad.

The transnational network surrounding Thilogne is common for Senegalese villages.[6] It is easy to explain mutual help between migrants, but it is more difficult to understand the persistence of village community links in a transnational space. Two possible answers can be advanced to solve this enigma. First, it is the moral duty of migrants to pay the social debt that they incurred towards their community of origin along the path of migration. As migrants, they relied on a certain number of mechanisms of community solidarity to reach their destinations and succeed in their new surroundings. Some received regular financial support from their families, and others enjoyed free accommodation from relatives, neighbours or friends whose origins can be traced back to the village. Migrants thus owe something, in one way or other, to their village community.

The second explanation is socio-psychological and stresses the prestige that migrants gain from assisting local development in their village of origin. The gratitude offered by their community of origin confirms their 'success'. It contrasts with and helps to compensate for feelings of marginality experienced in their host society. Moreover, the villagers' gratitude can lead to decision-making power being conferred on the migrants in their land of origin. A recent striking example is the case of a returned retired migrant who was chosen as the first deputy mayor of Thilogne.

The History and Logic of Senegalese River Valley Migrant Associations

Migrants from Thilogne in Dakar originally clustered together on the basis of kinship and neighbourhood connections. Persons originating from the same village or the same ward were expected to help each other in surroundings perceived as foreign and uncertain. According to the same logic, persons from the same enlarged family or the same caste joined together as well. These associational ties played a major role in the adjustment process of Thilognois to urban life in Dakar and Paris. The practice has been continually renewed such that present-day migrants to

Dakar and in other African, European or American cities can count on well-organized associations of fellow countrymen as soon as they arrive.

However, before TADs were set up at a local level, solidarity mechanisms existed at a village level in the rural community itself. The struggle against certain scourges, such as the destruction of crops by birds or locusts, requires the participation of all village inhabitants. Sowing and harvesting efforts are often pooled. Making quickset hedges around fields and herding cattle to prevent crop damage is often a collective village task.

The origin of village associations formed in different cities is not simply a reaction to adverse circumstances linked to the difficulties faced by people with a rural background in an urban environment. Mutual-help structures at the village and neighbourhood level long preceded migrant mutual-help associations. Migrants from Thilogne did not have to innovate in order to meet their needs for social welfare in a strange urban environment (Dia and Colin-Noguès 1982). Mutual support was an age-old village tradition that involved families taking care of the sick, the physically or mentally disabled, youth and old people, the poor or victims of disaster. In cities abroad, the reduced presence of family representatives made collective forms of social support more problematic.

Following the Thilognois migrants, different social welfare units reproduced themselves. Extended family, caste, ward or village associations formed the principal social units. The dynamism of these units depended essentially on the actual representation of families, castes, wards and of the village members amongst the migrants. A certain widening of the basis of cooperation is perceptible as the distance between the village and migration destination lengthens. Somewhat schematically, at the village level, the fundamental unit of social protection is the extended family. Cooperation rests on kinship rather than on neighbourhood relationships. In Dakar, castes and ward associations are the most important level of mutual support, taking the place of the extended family for migrants. Ward associations, established around religious preoccupations and exclusively gathering men of 40 years or older, are less dynamic than sport and cultural associations that welcome youth of both sexes and different castes.

In Paris, ward,[7] caste[8] and village[9] associations are found. Groupings are primarily based on village of origin, as in the case of Thilogne, which is a large village, or a grouping of smaller ones like Agnam. It is at the level of village association that the heaviest social costs are shouldered, notably the repatriation of remains of deceased members, financial help to widows and orphans following the death of a migrant, or help for victims of an accident, fire or any other calamity.

One can draw a parallel between village mutual-help societies like TAD and nineteenth-century European workers' friendly societies. They both fill an explicit security function for their members and face similar pitfalls, notably clientage and favouritism in relation to the granting of assistance (De Swaan 1995). However, there are also many differences. In nineteenth-century workers' friendly societies, individuals with the same social background but originating from different regions or localities joined together in order to help each other, whereas in village community mutual help associations, members come from the same village and share the same social conditions in the host locality. Participants identify with their village of origin, whatever their status or social position The tendency in nineteenth-century workers' friendly societies was 'cooperation between equals' that excluded individuals from lower social strata. Participation was voluntary, whereas Senegalese village associations of nationals are based on obligation. Furthermore, European societies limited their mandate to the welfare of their members and their immediate families whereas Senegalese village associations embrace the welfare concerns of their home villages to reinforce their identity, and also because their home villages are currently facing a welfare crisis connected with government implementation of structural adjustment policies.

De Swaan (1995) explains how nineteenth-century workers mutual help societies constituted a stage in the general process of collectivization of social security that spurred the formation of national social security systems in the West. It is clear that village associations cannot be considered as building blocks for the transition to regional or national social welfare systems. Paradoxically, in nineteenth-century Europe, the existence of workers' societies signalled a weakness in national welfare, which prompted the establishment of robust formal institutions under the shield of the state and private insurance companies.

Senegalese village associations appear to be undergoing a different evolution on a much-reduced time scale. Rather than being replaced by the state, they are taking over welfare functions from the Senegalese state in terms of providing physical and social service infrastructure for the rural populations in their home areas. Under World Bank-enforced structural adjustment policies, the Senegalese state has disengaged from a wide range of rural welfare measures. All kinds of resources and goodwill are mobilized through transnational networks, and West African village diasporas throughout the world are at the service of their communities of origin. Thilogne Association Development TAD is simply one example of many transnational Senegal River Valley village associations that are filling the welfare gap left by the Senegalese state. The following section traces the history of TAD-France to illustrate how cooperation ties have unfolded over time and have been entwined with worsening material conditions in Senegalese rural areas.

Origin and History of the TAD Section in France

In 1966, the first seven migrants from Thilogne settled in France and immediately set up a mutual-help society to assist members in difficulty. One of its founding members explained their original objectives:

> As we were all from Thilogne, it was necessary to have solidarity towards one other. The only way to organize mutual responsibility efficiently was to create an association. The idea was well received by everybody. We met at the end of each month in Paris and everyone subscribed 30FF. A number of dispositions were taken with regard to the misfortunes one could run into as a migrant, such as arrest by the police, sickness in all its forms, and death. It was decided that in case of mental illness or death the members of the association had to take responsibility for expenses linked to the victim's repatriation back to the village, whatever the price. [Author's interview with 59-year-old Demba Thiam][10]

After the devastating 1972–3 drought, several Thilognois chose France as their destination. Membership of the village association shot up from less than 10 to over 60. At the time, it comprised only bachelors or married men who had left their families in the village or in Dakar. In spite of French attempts to halt immigration in 1974, Thilogne citizens continued arriving in large numbers until the late 1970s. It was at this point that the village mutual-help society began to consider the need for improving village living conditions back in Thilogne. Young, recently emigrated Thilognois, who had witnessed the difficulties of local populations in the face of successive droughts, proposed that the village association buy and stock cereals thereby creating a cereal bank to prevent grain speculation and alleviate hunger in the village. The idea was rejected by the founding members who felt that it was each migrant's responsibility to remit enough money to his family to prevent famine. At the same time, they proposed the construction of a fence around the large village cemetery. Membership fees went up from 30FF to 50FF a month. To cope with the costs of the erection of the graveyard enclosure, each member was asked to contribute a sum of 500FF. Many young people refused to pay fees amounting to 500FF as required by the association's founding members, angry at the sum demanded and its use for mosque and graveyard improvements rather than for preventing starvation and death.

The graveyard issue deeply divided the association, offending many older members whose relatives were buried in the cemetery in question. The crisis was rendered all the more acute because the older members were convinced that the young people's objections to the extension of the cemetery walls were motivated by a superiority complex related to their membership in more socially dominant village castes. Frustration was evident, with some declaring that: 'The dead, whatever their social origin, deserve respect. It is unthinkable that social inequality be reproduced even after death.' Hailing from lower castes in the social hierarchy, their dead were buried in the second village cemetery. To them, refusing to build a wall around this area was nothing short of a discriminatory measure, especially in view of the membership fee, which was equal for all.

Some of the young members resigned from the association, claiming that it was monopolized by conservative old men only preoccupied with increasing their social prestige in the eyes of village religious authorities. But the young leaders of the mutual help society, convinced that the priority was to assist the living, refused to give in. Simultaneously, they worked on a project to build a borehole and a canal to provide the village with safe drinking water.

This first serious crisis did not paralyse the association. Gradually, the youth, under pressure exerted by their relatives in France or in the village, rejoined the association. They were accorded more and more decision-making power within the society, even though the elders continued their domination, manifested by the elders' insistence on a financial gift of 2,000FF for the *griots*, sheriffs and *marabouts* who came from the village to visit Thilognois migrants.

With Mitterand's accession to power in 1981 and the new French government's measures to encourage migrants' integration in French society, a second wave of Thilognois arrived between 1982 and 1985. The policy of family reunion allowed Thilognois citizens to reside legally in France and be joined by their wives and children.

The TAD was strengthened thanks to the recruitment of new migrants, essentially young people under 30 years of age, many of whom had studied at university level. The membership went up from 110 to more than 198. In 1985, the TAD was legally registered in France with nearly 200 members. Its direction passed from the original emigrants to the younger generation. This change was not simply one of leadership but of opposing philosophies. The first migrants were relatively uneducated, which limited their capacity for innovation and their ability to recognize and seize external opportunities.

Their leadership emphasized on outward-directed village development rather than merely the social welfare of its members. One of the leading figures of this generation, who had earlier been excluded from the association, explained that a revolution in thinking occurred. The monthly membership fee per member was raised from 50FF to 100FF to finance development projects. The youthful leaders developed partnerships with a number of organizations and municipalities in France that helped them to realize their ambitious goals.[11]

The growing number of members, as shown in Table 13.3, affords a base for considerable fund-raising. Nonetheless, currently TAD-France relies primarily on its own financial resources. Working members are under obligation to contribute 100FF a month. Students with scholarships have to contribute 50FF. Those officially declared unemployed, the sick and those on leave do not have to pay monthly dues. Traders are given a reprieve during the winter when their open-air trading activities are restricted. The money collected is divided into two equal portions and deposited in separate accounts: the social welfare account to support members in difficulty, and a project account for the execution of community projects in Thilogne village.

Table 13.3:   TAD Membership by Employment Status and Subscription Payment

Employment status	Number	Membership costs (FF)
Employees, traders, craftsmen	167	100
Declared unemployed	30	0
Students	16	50
Sick	5	0
On leave	10	0
Total	228	

Source: author's fieldwork interviews 1997–8

The 228 members of TAD-France are all men. Women do not take an active part in the association, but in their capacity as wives and daughters of members be they in France or in Thilogne, they can claim social welfare support when in need.[12]

The TAD-France section has internal statutes comprising 17 articles defining the rights and responsibilities of membership, sanctions and stipulations regarding the awarding of financial help to members. According to the terms of Article One, participation in the TAD-France section is voluntary for village citizens, but migrants from Thilogne usually feel compelled to join. The ones who decide not to participate are socially scorned. Members who visit them or take part in birth or marriage celebrations at their homes do so on pain of a fine of 500FF.

Articles Two to Eleven deal with subscriptions, disciplinary measures, and the rules of the general assembly. On the second Saturday of each month, the TAD-France section meets at its registered office at the Foyer d'Hautpool in Paris. Members who reside in Paris or its suburbs are expected to attend. Those living outside Paris or in other European countries have to send their subscriptions to the general assembly. Because of the considerable numbers of Thilogne citizens in Orléans and in the Vosges, the general assembly is held in these locations every six months.

Articles Twelve to Seventeen concern collections taken by TAD-France in case of the death either of a member or of a member's relative.[13] There have been nearly ten deaths of TAD members since TAD's creation. Repatriating a member who died in France costs the association between 20,000FF and 25,000FF. Nonetheless, TAD's social welfare account has yet to experience a deficit because the funds are bolstered by an additional contribution of 200 FF that is required from all members in case of the death of a member of his family.[14]

Conflicts and Challenges: Charting TAD's Future

Despite TAD's democratic founding principles and its strong sense of common origins and mutual support, the association's existence is rocked by conflicts linked to generational, caste and individual rivalries. The history of generational conflict has already been outlined. The first group of migrants who came to France in the 1960s and 1970s are now mostly over 55 years of age. Their lack of education ordained that they held low-paid jobs as factory workers or in catering. They faced discrimination in French society and held on to a conservative outlook that gave primacy to tradition, religion, and social prestige. By contrast, the second wave of migrants, now aged between 25 and 45 years of age, have usually had secondary school or even university education. They are open to French society and have a pragmatic attitude towards their village of origin.

Conflicts between these two groups manifest themselves frequently during General Assembly meetings. Clearly the tensions between the groups are not restricted to differing points of view about village association priorities. Instead, differences in their behavioural conduct especially with respect to social hierarchies based on age and caste are at issue. It is shocking to elders to hear a junior member strongly assert his disagreement regarding an idea upheld by one of them. It is common to hear an elder reprimanding a younger member for not knowing how to talk to his seniors.

So too, elderly people from castes at the apex of Thilonge's social ladder have difficulties accepting opposing views of members belonging to lower castes. The most conservative do not hesitate to tell these members that they are defying the community's accepted social hierarchy because they are in France, and that everyone knows his place in the village.

The general assembly, which decides on the composition of the governing council, is always electric with discord. The TAD-France general assembly held on 23 January 1999 is illustrative. It started at 2:30 p.m. and carried on late into the night finally breaking up acrimoniously at 3:30 a.m. At the outset and in defiance of the scheduled agenda, an elder, supported by a small group of youth displeased at not having been requested to take part in certain decisions, vociferously demanded a detailed financial balance sheet from the outgoing council. Chaos reigned for nearly two hours. The elder took the floor without the permission of the chairman. Some were shouting, others were uttering insults. A young member stood up to stress the elder's indiscipline, and called them to order: 'You should be ashamed of behaving in such a way in front of your children. You are forgetting that we have among us guests from other sections of the TAD in Africa and in the United States. You had better collect yourselves and behave in a more responsible way.' The elders reacted emotionally to these words and went on thrashing the youth for his impoliteness even after the meeting.

Favouritism on the part of certain leaders on the council towards their relatives or persons belonging to their own caste is equally a source of tension. Members of the rank and file in a few cases cheat the association by falsely claiming to be unemployed and thereby not liable to membership dues. The testimony of one board member is sufficient to obtain an exemption from subscription in case of unemployment. Certain members of the board try to protect relatives in a precarious situation by helping them obtain such a dispensation and sometimes members exaggerate a sick relative's plight and demand unjustifiable financial aid from TAD.

If these schemes are uncovered, it creates grounds for dispute between castes. The irresponsible attitude of any member of the board is assigned to his caste. In this type of situation, remarks in an ironic tone are often overheard, for example: 'Such are the Sebbe [or the Torobbe or Jawambe] they are always like that, they are thieves.' The strain can drive the protagonists beyond simple quarrels to fist fights. In an attempt to thwart such attitudes of favouritism and cheating, the TAD General Assembly has fixed fines against board or regular members who attempt to give false information.

Having reviewed sources of tensions within TAD, it remains to stress the incredible capacity of village associations like TAD to deflect tensions and cope with internal crises. So far, TAD has always managed to defuse conflicts between generations or between castes in a community framework. Conflicts never escalate to the point of necessitating the judgement of a French court. In some cases, respected elders of Thilogne village have been called upon to arbitrate and reconcile the protagonists. These mechanisms for managing conflict have been known to save the TAD in times of serious crisis. However, beyond these internal conflicts, TAD faces external challenges that may well jeopardize its future.

Village associations like TAD are clearly limited in their operational scope. It operates only in the social sector with its accomplishments essentially related to education, public health, water supply and the domains of religion and custom. There have been no community-based economic achievements. In the long term, only development of the local economy in terms of enterprises and employment generation can have a lasting welfare impact and eliminate reliance on external assistance. In so doing, migrants' voluntary actions to fill the social welfare gap left by the Senegalese state's retreat from rural social service delivery would no longer be necessary.

One of the main challenges facing social transnational networks like TAD is their need to continually renew and maintain close contact with their village of origin. As French immigration policy has become more stringent, enlisting new members in the TAD section of France is becoming problematic. Strict border checks and policies discriminating against the granting of entry visas for economic migrants prevent many new arrivals from Thilogne village.

Between 1993 and 1999, TAD had only six new members, four of whom were Thilognois students who came to study in Europe, against more than 100 respectively for the periods 1966–80 and 1981–93. This means that the ageing of members will sooner or later have a considerable negative influence on the organisation. Nearly half the members will be retired 10 years from now. New members are vital to the association because they are more economically active and those who are well educated are likely to have permanent salaried jobs. They are needed to balance the young people with precarious employment, and the sick and retired members whose contributions are smaller and less reliable.

In the face of the organization's greying membership, there are two counter tendencies offering fragile hope. The first is that the politicians in the host country are beginning to acknowledge the vital role of migrants' organizations *vis-à-vis* Africa, and French authorities are demonstrating a willingness to support village development associations in their efforts to improve living conditions in their regions of origin (see Blion, Chapter 12). The logic sustaining this somewhat late assistance is that, by contributing to the economic and social development of their respective villages of origin, the immigrants from the valley indirectly tackle the causes of the outward migration of this area's inhabitants. Accordingly, they serve the interests of France by acting to lessen the migratory flow from this region. Critics, however, charge that co-development rests on illusory hope.[15]

The co-development policy was proposed by Sami Naïr (1998), the inter-ministry delegate for co-development and international migrations. He defined the major axis of this policy in a report handed to Lionel Jospin on 10 December 1997. It can be summed up as the French government's will to change the orientation of its cooperation with migration areas, including Africa, and to succeed in better checking migratory flows originating from those countries. Naïr describes the originality of the co-development policy by comparing it to the classical cooperation policy in the following terms:

> The cooperation policy is a bilateral, state-to-state policy, wherein exchange relations partake of the well-understood interest of each. The policy of co-development has its place within this frame, but gives it a deeper dimension by adding compelling solidarity to interest. It means going beyond cooperation to set up common objectives. It is in the interest of France and of the countries of origin to turn immigration into a radius vector of development. (Naïr 1998: 49)

The co-development policy rests on the hinge-like position of immigrants between the host country and their country of origin. According to Naïr, individual and collective actors in migration should be stimulated to invest more in creating enterprises in their respective areas of origin. In this perspective, village associations are without doubt peculiarly suitable interlocutors in view of the important achievements for which they are responsible in developing their community of origin. The assistance they will eventually receive from the French authorities may perhaps help to deflect the problem lying in wait for them with the ageing of their membership in France.

The second hope for the survival of social networks like TAD is the coming of age of a new generation made up of the sons and daughters of first-generation migrants, most of whom were born and raised in France. Members of TAD, conscious of the problems of membership replacement, designed a strategy to interest the second-generation youth in the village association. In 1998, they created TAD Jeunes, which encourages the participation of young migrants and migrants' children who have attained the age of 18. It is intended to be the channel leading towards the integration of second-generation young people in the TAD-France section. Meetings, discussions and caravan visits to the village are organized to make youth more sensitive to the need to continue the work begun by their parents. This attempt does not seem very successful to date because several young people older than 18 years of age have yet to join the association. It is often the father who enrols his children when they are of age and pays their membership fees.

Second-generation youth do not feel obliged to take part in the village association. Unlike their parents, who incurred a social debt towards their families based in Thilogne village, the migrants' children do not feel they owe anything to the village. The strong emotional ties between the migrant and his native land – made all the more manifest by the desire for repatriation after death – is not replicated in the second generation of young people. Thilonge village is not their village. The future of TAD may be jeopardized if the association has no other option but to count on the commitment of French-born youth for its perpetuation.

Conclusion

Thilogne Association Développement illustrates the significance of village diaspora to the welfare enhancement of villagers' lives in migrants' localities of origin. Does this suggest that rural Africa is adapting to or even better gaining from the current globalization process?

Whatever the answer to this question, one should not forget that the benefits depend to a great measure on emigration. The current tightening of emigration policies in host countries and the rise of a second generation that owes almost nothing to the village will certainly have a long-term effect on the dynamism of associations like TAD. As migrants integrate into European society, the question looms as to how long the umbilical cord to their home villages can be naturally, as opposed to officially, maintained?

References

Ba, A.H. (1998), 'Incidence des Réseaux Migratoires sur les Pays de Départ: Le Cas de la Migration Sénégalaise', in I. Simon-Barouh (ed.), *Dynamiques Migratoires et Rencontres Ethniques*, Paris, l'Harmattan.

Daum, C. (1998), 'Développement des Pays d'Origine et Flux Migratoire: La Nécessaire Déconnexion', *Migrants et Solidarité Nord-Sud*, 1214: 58–72.

Daum, C. (1994), 'Ici et Là-bas, Immigration et Développement: Les Associations des Immigrés Ouest-Africains en France', *Migrations et Société CIEMS dans Migrations et Développement*, 6(32): 99–110.

Delville, P.L. (1991), *La Rizière et la Valise: Irrigation, Migration et Stratégies Paysannes dans la Moyenne Vallée du Fleuve Sénégal*, Paris, Syros-Alternatives.

Dia, O. and Colin-Noguès, R. (1982), *Yâkâre, l'Autobiographie d'Oumar*, Paris, François Maspero.

Diop, A.B. (1965), *Société Toucouleur et Migration*, Dakar, IFAN.

Jaussaud, E. (1998), 'Les Associations d'Immigrés et l'Emergence d'une Economie de Développement Local', *Economie Solidaire et Migrations*, 10(56): 77–85.

Naïr, S. (1998), 'La Politique de Codéveloppement Liée aux Flux Migratoires', *Migrants et Solidarité Nord-Sud*, 1214: 47–57.

Quiminal, C. (1991), *Gens d'Ici, Gens d'Ailleurs*, Paris, Christian Bourgeois.

Swaan, A. de (1995), *Sous l'Aile Protectrice de l'Etat*, PUF, Paris, (French translation of *In the Care of the State*, Polity Press with Basil Blackwell, 1988.)

Notes

1. I would like to thank Michelle Boin for her translation of this article from French and Deborah Bryceson for her editorial work to distil this chapter from a longer text.

2. The information presented in this chapter has been drawn from interviews I held with the founding members of TAD, and the successive leaders of TAD sections in Thilogne, Dakar and Paris. My participation as a member in Thilogne, Dakar and Paris allowed me access to general assemblies, board meetings and TAD archives. I collected information on other TAD sections at the annual general assembly of the TAD section of France, on 23 January 1999, to which the New York, Libreville and Thilogne sections were invited. I used the opportunity to ask the leaders about the history of their respective sections. As an active member of TAD, I was able to contrast my own knowledge of the organization with that of informants.

3. Direction de la Prévision et de la Statistique (DPS): Répertoire des Villages, Région de Saint-Louis, RGPH 1988: 38.

4. Previously referred to by the French colonialists as the Tukulor or Wolof people.

5. In Nancy, the establishment of an association called Friends of Thilogne made it possible for French people interested in village development to participate in TAD projects.

6. The Association pour le Développement d'Ourosogui (ADO) and the Association Liaison pour le Développement des Agnam (ALDA) show the same characteristics in transnational space (Daum 1994; Ba 1998: 99).

7. Goléra, Diabe Sala, Ndioufnabe and Gamgou are amongst the most important wards of the village of Thilogne. Persons from these wards gather in Dakar as well as in foreign countries, notably France.

8. Torobbe, Sebbe, Maccube and Burnaabe are the most important castes in France. In Dakar, only the castes of the Diawanbe, the Macube and the Sebbe are organized in the form of mutual help associations.

9. For example, Thilogne Association Développement and Association des Ressortissants d'Agnam Thiodaye (Association of Agnam Thiodaye Nationals).

10. Some of the collection is used for the repatriation of the bodies of deceased members. From this point of view, TAD can be considered as a burial society. Moreover, the collections provide members with financial allowances when they face situations of adversity.

11. Notably, Ingénieurs sans Frontières, Comité Laïque pour l'Education et le Développement des Ardennes, l'Association Club Prévention de Sedan Ouest, l'Association Orléans Tiers-Monde and l'Hôpital de Nancy.

12. Not all 228 male members live in France. There are 12 members in Belgium, five in Germany, two in the Netherlands, eight in Italy and three in Great Britain. They send their subscriptions every month to relatives in France, who in turn remit them to the society on meeting days.

13. The amount of financial support offered to members or the bereaved depends on the place of death, the age, the degree of kinship of the deceased in relation to the members, and so forth. Generally, the association transfers 3,000FF to the family of members who die in Africa. For those who die in France, the costs of sending the deceased back to Senegal accompanied by a relative over 18 years of age and 1,000FF for the burial costs are paid. If the deceased was resident in France with his family, the association provides all members of the family with one-way plane tickets if they wish to return permanently to Senegal. However, the spouses of deceased members often choose to stay in France. This saves the association from large expenses because some families can comprise more than 10 people.

14. The most frequent payments are related to cases of death of one of a member's parents. During 1997, four members each received a sum of 1,500FF when one of their parents died. There were only two other deaths: a member died in the village and his family received 3,000FF from the association and a member who lost his young son was allocated a sum of 6,853FF to cover the burial costs in France.

15. Daum (1998) adopts a critical stance regarding the so-called policy of co-development, questioning the validity of the causal link drawn between development cooperation for countries of heavy out-migration and checks on their migration flows.

Epilogue

Deborah Bryceson

As this book was being prepared for press the events of September 11 and their aftermath unfolded. The US and other OECD nation states that see themselves as targets of terrorism are now enacting measures that will impact on immigration policy. President George Bush in his state-of-the-union address of 28 January 2002 referred to the defence of 'our homeland'. The narrative being embroidered is one of two opposing worlds, one 'civilized', the other 'barbarian', a so-called 'axis of evil'. This trajectory of events, interpretations, and policies has a direct bearing on the subject matter of this book.

Those involved in the bombing of the World Trade Centre were young men who shared a common religious cause. Furthermore, they were mostly members of transnational families, families with the financial wherewithal to travel and to send their sons abroad. Whereas attention is now being focused on terrorists and their threat to the current world political order, there is indeed another more home-bound struggle with far-reaching significance. These young men were members of families that were generally unaware of their activities or even their whereabouts. The men constructed purposeful associational networks that largely displaced their long-distance familial ties. Their networks were based on the rejection of the values of their home areas and their host countries. They became a law unto themselves, frontiering in a vacuous no-man's land where human life was weighed against absolute principles.

Juxtaposing the stories of transnational families and networks contained in this collection with the experience of the suicidal bombers of September 11 may provide solace as well as perplexing thoughts. The case studies suggest that the fractured transnational families of these young men were aberrations from a mainstream of highly interactive transnational family life. The varied contexts and forms of transnational families found in Europe and beyond are often internally contentious, but also integrative and laden with the human emotions that bind people to one another.

The many permutations that families and networks take as people relativize their familial and associational ties in new cultural surroundings and material circumstances testify to the impossibility of identifying any simple categorizations or tendencies. The motivation for the spatial movement of transnational family members in the first instance tends to be welfare-enhancement, but the actual form and dynamics of transnational families are part of a creative social process that is impossible to predict. The unknown frontier is a mixture of cultural, social, economic and political horizons that are constantly being mapped, then remapped. Overall, this experimentation results in creative, welfare enhancement to the benefit of the individuals, the families and the societies involved. Families are buffers against the outside world, mediating the inequities of the world with more humane and caring attitudes for one another within the confines of the family through the successive life-cycle stages of individual members. Transnational families simply deal with life-cycle change over a broader geographical space, addressing family members' emotional and material needs as families do everywhere.

While 11 September did happen and it was a truly transnational event involving transnational people with transnational conceptions of place and personal identity, it represents only one of millions of transnational stories, albeit a dramatic one. Young men fighting international causes are hardly new, but the fervour with which these young men pursued their cause is remarkable. Youth and their generational conflicts accentuate change and societal contradictions. Youth's desire for change, for mobility, and for excitement and even heroics may be especially flammable in this age of transnational movement.

Transnational movement creates a kaleidoscope of impressions. The stark contrasts between the world's rich and poor and the powerful and weak become all too readily apparent revealing a seemingly unbridgeable gap. The jolting experience of this uneven world is likely to affect youth more than others. Unburdened by responsibilities for family provisioning, they have the time to think and act on the basis of their assessment of the world's moral order. These are tensions that every family faces, but particularly transnational families who personally confront the world's yawning material welfare gaps.

Transnationalism offers great promise of welfare enhancement and personal fulfilment, but it also harbours the disappointment of failed expectations and the discomfort of living in unmeaningful circumstances. Al-Ali (Chapter 4) writes of the feelings of deprivation of living like 'a piece of wood'. Poor language skills, lack of understanding of the host culture, or the economic need to live on welfare can seriously erode one's self-esteem. There are many personal and societal failures in the panoply of transnational family experiences.

Transnational families are a response to difference and are generated by members moving away from the sameness of a predictable *in situ* family life. Transnational families can be expected to proliferate in our 'globalized world' of widening material differences. They bridge these differences – they provide international welfare systems at the same time as they propagate brain drains to the already educationally endowed West. At the micro-level, transnational families are generated by rational welfare decision making, but at the macro-scale their geographic placement can exacerbate world economic divisions.

Transnational capital and labour flows are an integral part of the 'globalized world' advanced by the WTO and other international financial institutions. The proliferation of transnational families is directly related to the existence of international agencies. Transnational families are part and parcel of a wider global process. They and their diversity, complexity and unpredictability are inherent in a world of glaring welfare differentiation. Above all, the cultural diversity that transnational families offer nation states is an enormous strength rather than a danger. One need only look at various countries of in-migration, such as the US, Cananda and Australia, to verify this. Europe, hitherto a continent primarily of out-migration connected with 300 years of colonial and settler history, is beginning to confront the significance of in-migration for national economic and social development.

These fluid global processes and the contradictory position of transnational families within these processes point to the need to avoid rigid dichotomies and absolute dictums. The international search for terrorists will be futile if it is based on the assumption that there are civilized and barbarian worlds that can be starkly contrasted. Family life everywhere, transnational and non-transnational, has to confront the moral dilemmas of living in the twenty-first century. The search for human meaning amidst this chaos will produce saints and sinners, pacifists and terrorists. Joseph Conrad's 'heart of darkness' has moved from the barbarous world of 'out there' to the cozy sitting rooms of families watching the television news at night.

Index